D0765760

Deploying License-Free Wireless Wide-Area Networks

Jack Unger

Cisco Press

Cisco Press
201 West 103rd Street
Indianapolis, IN 46290 USA

Deploying License-Free Wireless Wide-Area Networks

Copyright© 2003 Cisco Systems, Inc.

Published by:
Cisco Press
201 West 103rd Street
Indianapolis, IN 46290 USA

Printed in the United States of America 1 2 3 4 5 6 7 8 9 0

First Printing March 2003

Library of Congress Cataloging-in-Publication Number: 2001098196

ISBN: 1-58705-069-2

Warning and Disclaimer

This book is designed to provide information about license-free wireless wide-area networks. Every effort has been made to make this book as complete and as accurate as possible, but no warranty or fitness is implied.

The information is provided on an "as is" basis. The author, Cisco Press, and Cisco Systems, Inc. shall have neither liability nor responsibility to any person or entity with respect to any loss or damages arising from the information contained in this book or from the use of the discs or programs that may accompany it.

The opinions expressed in this book belong to the author and are not necessarily those of Cisco Systems, Inc.

Trademark Acknowledgments

All terms mentioned in this book that are known to be trademarks or service marks have been appropriately capitalized. Cisco Press or Cisco Systems, Inc. cannot attest to the accuracy of this information. Use of a term in this book should not be regarded as affecting the validity of any trademark or service mark.

Feedback Information

At Cisco Press, our goal is to create in-depth technical books of the highest quality and value. Each book is crafted with care and precision, undergoing rigorous development that involves the unique expertise of members from the professional technical community.

Readers' feedback is a natural continuation of this process. If you have any comments regarding how we could improve the quality of this book, or otherwise alter it to better suit your needs, you can contact us through e-mail at feedback@ciscopress.com. Please make sure to include the book title and ISBN in your message.

We greatly appreciate your assistance.

Publisher	John Wait
Editor-in-Chief	John Kane
Executive Editor	Brett Bartow
Cisco Representative	Anthony Wolfenden
Cisco Press Program Manager	Sonia Torres Chavez
Cisco Marketing Communications Manager	Tom Geitner
Cisco Marketing Program Manager	Edie Quiroz
Production Manager	Patrick Kanouse
Acquisitions Editor	Michelle Grandin
Senior Development Editor	Christopher Cleveland
Project Editor	San Dee Phillips
Copy Editor	Karen A. Gill
Technical Editor(s)	Greg DesBrisay, Jim Geier, Dr. H. Paul Shuch, Ph.D.
Team Coordinator	Tammi Ross
Book Designer	Gina Rexrode
Cover Designer	Louisa Adair
Compositor	Mark Shirar
Indexer	Tim Wright

CISCO SYSTEMS

Corporate Headquarters
Cisco Systems, Inc.
170 West Tasman Drive
San Jose, CA 95134-1706
USA
http://www.cisco.com
Tel: 408 526-4000
      800 553-NETS (6387)
Fax: 408 526-4100

European Headquarters
Cisco Systems Europe
11 Rue Camille Desmoulins
92782 Issy-les-Moulineaux
Cedex 9
France
http://www-europe.cisco.com
Tel: 33 1 58 04 60 00
Fax: 33 1 58 04 61 00

Americas Headquarters
Cisco Systems, Inc.
170 West Tasman Drive
San Jose, CA 95134-1706
USA
http://www.cisco.com
Tel: 408 526-7660
Fax: 408 527-0883

Asia Pacific Headquarters
Cisco Systems Australia,
Pty., Ltd
Level 17, 99 Walker Street
North Sydney
NSW 2059 Australia
http://www.cisco.com
Tel: +61 2 8448 7100
Fax: +61 2 9957 4350

Cisco Systems has more than 200 offices in the following countries. Addresses, phone numbers, and fax numbers are listed on the Cisco Web site at www.cisco.com/go/offices

Argentina • Australia • Austria • Belgium • Brazil • Bulgaria • Canada • Chile • China • Colombia • Costa Rica • Croatia • Czech Republic • Denmark • Dubai, UAE • Finland • France • Germany • Greece • Hong Kong Hungary • India • Indonesia • Ireland • Israel • Italy • Japan • Korea • Luxembourg • Malaysia • Mexico The Netherlands • New Zealand • Norway • Peru • Philippines • Poland • Portugal • Puerto Rico • Romania Russia • Saudi Arabia • Scotland • Singapore • Slovakia • Slovenia • South Africa • Spain • Sweden Switzerland • Taiwan • Thailand • Turkey • Ukraine • United Kingdom • United States • Venezuela • Vietnam Zimbabwe

About the Author

Jack Unger, the founder and president of Wireless InfoNet, Inc., is a pioneer in the broadband fixed-wireless industry. Since founding Wireless InfoNet in 1993, he has personally designed and installed hundreds of license-free outdoor broadband wireless network sites and consulted on countless others. In 1995, he designed and deployed one of the world's first public outdoor wireless Internet access points-of-presence. This wireless POP is still in service today in Palo Alto, California. In 2001, based on his wireless ISP experiences, Jack created the world's first vendor-neutral wireless ISP training seminar. To date, in this seminar, he has personally trained more than 800 ISP personnel across the United States.

Prior to founding Wireless InfoNet, Jack worked for 14 years in the Silicon Valley telecommunications industry for ROLM, IBM, Siemens, and NEC. Prior to that, Jack worked for 7 years selling wireless communications equipment, including television and radio station broadcast equipment. He has a total of 45 years of wireless experience since his "initiation" into the wireless world as an amateur radio operator at the age of 11. Jack has received A.A., A.S., and B.A. degrees and has completed extensive work in the U.C. Berkeley Extension Telecommunications Engineering Program. He holds FCC Amateur Extra and General Radiotelephone licenses as well as an FAA Private Pilot license. He also served as a volunteer firefighter for 11 years in the mountains of Santa Cruz County, California.

Jack is an experienced technical writer who has written numerous telecommunications hardware and software manuals and close to 100 Cisco IOS Release Notes for the Cisco 2600, 3600, 3810, 4000, and IAD2420 router product lines. *Deploying License-Free Wireless Wide-Area Networks* is the industry's first book written specifically to help wireless ISPs and corporate IT department personnel successfully deploy outdoor, license-free, wireless WANs and broadband wireless Internet access. Jack welcomes your comments, suggestions, corrections, and questions via e-mail. You are invited to contact him at suggestions@ask-wi.com.

About the Technical Reviewers

Jim Geier is the founder and principal consultant of Wireless-Nets, Ltd., a consulting firm that assists companies with the development and deployment of wireless LAN products and systems. His 20 years of experience includes the analysis, design, software development, installation, and support of numerous client/server and wireless network-based systems for retail, manufacturing, warehousing, healthcare, and airline industries throughout the world. Jim is the author of several books: *802.11 Unleashed*, *Wireless LANs*, *Wireless Networking Handbook*, and *Network Reengineering*, as well as numerous articles. He is a voting member within the Wireless Ethernet Compatibility Alliance (WECA), responsible for certifying interoperability of 802.11 (Wi-Fi) wireless LANs. He served as chairman of the Institute of Electrical and Electronic Engineers (IEEE) Computer Society, Dayton Section, and chairman of the IEEE International Conference on Wireless LAN Implementation. He has been an active member of the IEEE 802.11 Working Group, responsible for developing international standards for wireless LANs. Jim's education includes B.A. and M.A. degrees in electrical engineering and an M.A. degree in business administration. You can contact Jim at jimgeier@wireless-nets.com or visit his website at www.wireless-nets.com.

H. Paul Shuch, Ph.D. is the aerospace engineer who is credited with designing the world's first commercial home satellite TV receiver. Paul has served as executive director of the grassroots, nonprofit SETI League, Inc. since its inception eight years ago.

The author of more than 300 publications, Paul holds a Ph.D. degree in engineering from the University of California, Berkeley and has taught on various campuses for 30 years. His teaching and research have won several international awards. Paul is a Fellow of the Radio Club of America and a Fellow of the British Interplanetary Society; he has served on the boards of directors of several nonprofit organizations.

A licensed commercial pilot and instrument flight instructor, Paul serves as an accident prevention counselor for the FAA, as a military program evaluator for the American Council on Education, and as a lecturer for the Air Safety Foundation. He is listed in *Who's Who in Aviation and Aerospace*, *Who's Who in California*, *Who's Who of American Inventors*, *Who's Who in Science and Engineering*, *American Men and Women of Science*, *Who's Who in American Education*, and the *International Directory of Distinguished Leadership*.

Paul lives on a radio-quiet hilltop in central Pennsylvania with his biologist wife, five of their seven recombinant DNA experiments, three motorcycles, two radio telescopes, and an antique MG-TD. He can be found on the web at http://drseti.com.

Jack Unger, the author of this book, is Paul's former student, former employee, fellow radio amateur, and lifelong friend.

Dedications

I dedicate this book to my mother, Virginia Blossom Kaufman-Unger-London and to my father, Milton Unger. Thank you both for loving me unconditionally.

Acknowledgments

Literally thousands of people have made indirect contributions to this book.

First, thanks to all of my public school teachers (from kindergarten through college) who patiently helped me, encouraged me, and taught me how to learn. Next, thanks to the many members of the amateur radio community who showed me how to actually make wireless equipment work. Further, I extend my thanks to the many members of the wireless ISP community who shared their experiences and their ideas with me. Next, thanks to my colleagues, J.V. Rudnick, Bob Fike, and Phil Marcelis, who many times showed me a better way to erect an antenna, route a cable, or configure a wireless router. Last but certainly not least, I'd like to thank my Cisco Press editors, Michelle Grandin and Christopher Cleveland, and my technical reviewers, Dr. Paul Shuch, Jim Geier, and Greg DesBrisay, for graciously contributing their energy, their experience, and their knowledge to this book.

Finally, allow me to make a gentle request of you, the reader. If you find this book helps you to learn more about and to experience the magic of wireless, please feel free to generously pass your new learning along to others who share your interest in wireless.

Contents at a Glance

Contents

Introduction

Thank you for choosing to read this book. I wrote it for the following reasons:

- Wireless is both fun and satisfying. I want to share that fun and that satisfaction with you.

- Wireless allows you to be creative. Using the techniques in this book, you can be both creative and successful with your wireless wide-area network.

- Wireless networks save money. You can be a hero by delivering broadband bandwidth at a lower cost than traditional wired bandwidth. The more people who save money, the better it is for everyone.

- I wanted to fill the need for a practical, license-free outdoor wireless WAN book. The book needed to be based on real-world WAN deployments. The book also needed to be unbiased and vendor-independent—that is, to be free of all marketing and sales material.

Who This Book Is For

This book is for you, if you

- Find yourself intrigued by the magic of wireless

- Want to advance your knowledge and want to learn practical wireless networking skills

- Want to advance in your career and in the wireless field

- Are interested in providing broadband wireless service to others in their community

- Want to save money, have fun, and be creative

How to Use This Book

The chapters in the book are arranged in a logical order. If you have never been exposed to wireless ("exposed to wireless"… "radio-active"——you get it?), you can start reading at Chapter 1 and read right through to Chapter 9. On the other hand, if you just want to look up one particular topic, use the index or the table of contents, locate the topic, and go directly to that page or chapter. Here are the topics covered by each chapter:

- Chapter 1, "An Introduction to Broadband License-Free Wireless Wide-Area Networking," presents basic broadband wireless terminology and history. It outlines the advantages and the challenges of working with outdoor networks. Finally, it discusses the safety issues that you need to address.

- Chapter 2, "Understanding Wireless Fundamentals," helps you understand wireless fundamentals. Even if you have never worked with wireless before, you can be successful if you take the time to learn these fundamentals.

- Chapter 3, "Choosing Your Network Architecture," describes the four basic wireless network architectures, including the advantages and disadvantages of each architecture.

- Chapter 4, "Performing Site Surveys," discusses physical site surveys and wireless site surveys. Site surveys are an important step in building a reliable wireless network.

- Chapter 5, "Selecting Antenna Systems," describes how antennas work and how to use them. Proper antenna selection and use is vital to successful wireless WAN operation.

- Chapter 6, "Evaluating and Selecting Wireless Equipment," helps you to understand the range of features available in wireless equipment. When you understand the features and how they determine your network capabilities, you can select the best equipment for your network.

- Chapter 7, "Installing Outdoor Wireless Systems," explains the techniques to safely install, ground, and test your outdoor wireless systems.

- Chapter 8, "Solving Noise and Interference Problems," discusses the causes of noise and interference and explains the techniques that you can use to minimize noise and interference problems. This chapter also provides some suggestions about how you can cooperate and coordinate with other wireless network operators to reduce interference between your networks.

- Chapter 9, "Providing Broadband Wireless Internet Access," provides extra tips and techniques for those of you who want to be wireless Internet Service Providers (WISPs) and provide wireless Internet access service to your communities.

- Appendix A, "Wireless Standards Summary," provides a summary table of the 802.11 standards. It also includes related standards, such as 802.1x and 802.16.

- Appendix B, "Wireless Hardware, Software, and Service Provider Organizations," contains a listing of organizations that provide wireless hardware, software, peripherals, and services.

- Appendix C, "Answers to Chapter Review Questions," provides answers to the review questions that appear at the end of Chapters 1 through 9.

CHAPTER 1

An Introduction to Broadband License-Free Wireless Wide-Area Networking

This chapter introduces broadband wireless networking terms, summarizes license-free wireless history, and describes both the advantages and the challenges of deploying license-free wireless wide-area networks (WANs).

Differences Between Wired Networks and Wireless Networks

Most of the time, users of a broadband wireless network do not experience a difference between using a wireless network and using a wired network. Your experiences as you design and build a wireless network, however, will be quite different compared to your experiences when you design and install a wired network. Table 1-1 summarizes the differences that you need to be aware of.

Table 1-1 *Differences Between Wired and Wireless Networks*

Network Characteristic	Wired Network	Wireless Network
Visual determination of network connectivity	If you can see the network cable going to a location, that location can be connected to the network.	Wireless networks sometimes connect locations that you *cannot* visibly see. Additionally, wireless networks *might not* connect locations that you *can* see visibly.
Visibility node-to-node on the same network	All of the nodes on a wired network can hear all other nodes.	Many nodes on a wireless network cannot hear all of the other wireless nodes on the same network.
Visibility network-to-network	Wired networks are invisible to other wired networks. The presence of one wired network has no effect on the performance of another wired network.	Wireless networks are often visible to other wireless networks. One wireless network *can affect* the performance of other wireless networks.

continues

Table 1-1   *Differences Between Wired and Wireless Networks (Continued)*

Network Characteristic	Wired Network	Wireless Network
Atmospheric properties	Wired network performance is not affected by the properties of the atmosphere.	Wireless network performance *can be* affected by the properties of the atmosphere.
Terrain properties	Wired network performance is not affected by the properties of the earth's terrain.	Wireless network performance is *strongly affected* by the properties of the earth's terrain.
User connectivity and mobility	Connectivity is possible only to or from those physical locations where the network cabling extends.	Connectivity is possible *beyond* the bounds of physical network cabling.

Wireless Terminology and Evolution

Today, you can design and build wireless networks that possess three characteristics that were not available in the past. These characteristics are broadband capability, wide-area coverage, and license-free operation. The definition of these terms is somewhat vague; therefore, it is important to define the terms clearly. The following sections provide these definitions as well as some wireless history.

Broadband

Broadband is a subjective term that has been used in various ways throughout the communications industry. Broadband is used when new communications technologies are developed that provide enough additional bandwidth for the user experience to feel substantially faster than it felt before.

Most Internet users today have experienced dialing into the Internet at bandwidths ranging from 28,800 bits per second (28.8 kbps) up to 56,000 bits per second (56 kbps). They perceive a faster Internet connection, such as a 1.5 million bit per second (1.5 Mbps) connection, as a broadband connection.

Some users have access to the Internet using a web browser on a cell phone. Their connection bandwidth ranges from 9.6 kbps to 14.4 kbps. Comparing the cell phone connection speed to a dialup 28.8-kbps connection, the cell phone connection feels slow. It certainly doesn't feel like broadband; in fact, it feels like "narrowband."

For the remainder of this book, any wireless connection that has a bandwidth of 128,000 bits per second (128 kbps) will be defined as broadband. Given the Internet experiences of users who have either browsed the Internet using a cell phone or dialed into the Internet, a 128-kbps connection is perceived as broadband.

Wide-Area Network

There is no absolute line between the definition of a local-area network (LAN) and the definition of a wide-area network (WAN). Both terms have been used somewhat loosely. Here's how this book defines them:

- **LAN**—A network that connects stations contained within a single building
- **WAN**—A network that connects stations located in different buildings or in different parts of a city

---

NOTE   Some books use the term *MAN* to indicate a metropolitan-area network or, in other words, a citywide network. This book refers to a citywide network as a WAN.

History of License-Free Wireless Networking

The purpose of this book is to help you deploy broadband wireless WANs without needing to apply to the Federal Communications Commission (FCC) for a license. The following sections provide a historical overview of some of the events that led to the present privilege of using some broadband wireless equipment without needing to obtain a license.

History of Wireless Licensing

Wireless technology has passed through several regulatory phases during its history. In the late 1800s and early 1900s, there were many wireless scientists, experimenters, and hobbyists. In these early days, transmitting distances were limited and population density was low; it was unnecessary to require a license for transmitting. As more wireless stations came on the air, interference between stations became a serious problem. In 1921, the United States government began requiring licenses for all transmitters, including commercial broadcast transmitters, experimental transmitters, and amateur radio transmitters.

Radio system usage continued to grow rapidly during the remainder of the 20th century. The U.S. government continued to regulate radio transmissions and to license radio transmitters. These licensing regulations played a useful role because they allowed many different radio systems to share the available radio frequencies without interfering with each other.

The downside to governmental regulation was that it took both time and money to obtain a license to transmit on a specific frequency. This limited the use of broadband wireless equipment to those companies or individuals who could afford the cost of obtaining the FCC license and purchasing the rather expensive wireless equipment.

In 1985, the U.S. Federal Communications Commission (FCC) issued regulations that, for the first time, allowed the use of broadband wireless transmitting equipment without the need to apply for, pay for, and wait for a license. To operate license free, the wireless equipment had to do the following:

- Operate at low power levels
- Use spread spectrum modulation
- Transmit within three specified frequency bands

Broadband license-free wireless equipment began to be manufactured and sold at a much lower cost than the licensed broadband wireless equipment.

Table 1-2 provides an outline of the wireless events that led full-circle from the days when licensing was not required, to the days when licensing was required, to today, when broadband wireless equipment can be deployed license free.

Table 1-2 *Brief History of Wireless Development*

Year	Event
1600	Dr. William Gilbert detects electromagnetic activity in the human body and describes it as "electricity."
1837	Samuel F.B. Morse invents the Morse telegraph and sends messages over wires by using Morse code.
1865	Scientists, inventors, and hobbyists begin performing experiments with wireless.
1867	Scottish mathematician and physicist James Clerk Maxwell develops the theory that predicts the existence of electro-magnetic waves.
1886	German physicist Heinrich Hertz is the first person to demonstrate the existence of electromagnetic waves as predicted by James Clerk Maxwell.
1896	Italian Guglielmo Marconi demonstrates electric-wave telegraphy.
1901	Marconi transmits the letter "s" in Morse code across the Atlantic Ocean from England to Canada.
1906	Professor Reginald Fessenden broadcasts voice and music in Massachusetts.
1910	The U.S. government requires all ships to be equipped with a wireless telegraph.
1912	The "unsinkable" Titanic ocean liner sinks after striking an iceberg in the North Atlantic. The wireless telegraph is used to summon help from other ships in the area.
1912	The regulation of radio broadcasting is started by the U.S. Department of Commerce, Bureau of Navigation. Transmitting stations simply had to supply the government with a description of their transmitting equipment.
1912	Radio station KQW makes frequent broadcasts from San Jose, California.
1920	Radio station KDKA begins regular commercial broadcasting from Pittsburgh, Pennsylvania.

Table 1-2   *Brief History of Wireless Development (Continued)*

Year	Event
1921	The U.S. government requires all broadcasting stations to apply for a broadcasting license.
1927	The responsibility for regulating radio transmission is transferred to the Federal Radio Commission.
1934	The Communications Act of 1934 establishes the FCC. The responsibility for regulating radio transmission is transferred to the FCC.
1985	The FCC authorizes license-free spread spectrum transmission in three industrial, scientific, and medical (ISM) bands at 900 megahertz (MHz), 2.4 gigahertz (GHz), and 5.8 GHz. Maximum legal transmitter output power is 1 watt (1W).
1994	The FCC begins using spectrum auctions. Corporations bid hundreds of thousands to millions of dollars to buy the right to use specific wireless frequency bands.
1997	The FCC authorizes license-free transmission in three 5.1 to 5.8 GHz Unlicensed-National Information Infrastructure (U-NII) subbands. Maximum legal transmitter output power ranges from 50 milliwatts (50 mW) to 1 W.

History of Spread Spectrum

Modulation is the process of adding information or intelligence to a wireless signal.

NOTE   In the wireless world, the term *intelligence* sometimes has no discernable relationship to the process of using one's brain to make a wise decision.

A modulated wireless signal carries intelligence to the receiver where the intelligence is removed and used. The intelligence might be voice, music, data, or video. For example, the process of *amplitude modulation* adds voice and music to AM broadcast station signals. The process of *frequency modulation* adds voice and music to FM broadcast station signals. The process of *spread spectrum modulation* adds data to broadband license-free wireless signals.

The development of spread spectrum modulation began during World War II. Hedy Lamar (the actress) is credited for inventing spread spectrum modulation. The story goes that she was opposed to the actions of the German military during the war and decided to find a way to transmit and receive messages that would remain undetected by the German military. She devised the spread-spectrum principle of frequency hopping. Frequency hopping changes the transmitter frequency rapidly to prevent the transmitted messages from being detected by anyone except the person intended to receive the messages. The spread spectrum receiver knows the proper sequence of frequency changes and follows them to decode (demodulate) the transmitted message.

Two different types of spread spectrum modulation are in general use today, both of which spread the signal out over a broad band of frequencies:

- **Frequency hopping spread spectrum (FHSS)**—Changes frequency from 8 to 32 times each second

- **Direct sequence spread spectrum (DSSS)**—Stays on one center frequency but spreads out the signal at low power over a wide frequency band

The resulting transmitted signal simply looks like weak noise. Only a receiver that knows how to despread the signal can demodulate it and recover the original intelligence.

Development of License-Free Spread Spectrum

Prior to 1985, the FCC permitted low power, short-range devices such as baby monitors and garage door openers to operate license free. These devices operated indoors or with short-range transmitters and did not cause interference problems with other wireless systems. In 1985, the FCC considered the following points and then decided to allow the operation of license-free spread spectrum systems:

- Spread spectrum signals spread their wireless energy over the frequency spectrum rather than concentrating it all on one frequency. By spreading out the energy, the signals are *less likely to cause interference* to other spread spectrum and non-spread spectrum systems.

- Spread spectrum signals are *less susceptible to being interfered with* than non-spread spectrum signals.

- Low power spread spectrum transmitters operating in the ISM bands will be limited to line-of-sight operation. The *signals will not carry very far*; therefore, many spread spectrum systems can operate in the same general area without causing significant interference to each other.

- Many spread spectrum systems will be used indoors. *The building walls will absorb much of the wireless energy* before it can go very far and cause interference problems.

The first license-free spread spectrum wireless systems were short-range, indoor LANs. These systems were used for applications such as retail price marking and inventory management. Next, wireless equipment manufacturers began to offer spread spectrum equipment with improved antenna systems that could be used for longer-distance outdoor point-to-point links between buildings. These outdoor links offered a low-cost alternative to the expensive leased-line connections offered by the local telephone companies. Soon, cities, school districts, and corporations began to use this outdoor equipment in point-to-multipoint network configurations. By 1995, the first few Internet service providers (ISPs) began to use the technology to provide license-free broadband wireless Internet access to the public. The era of the license-free broadband wireless WAN had begun.

NOTE   Although spread spectrum systems are unlicensed, it does not mean that they are unregulated. The FCC specifies the rules and regulations that govern the manufacture of spread spectrum systems. Equipment manufacturers are responsible for manufacturing equipment that complies with the FCC regulations. Equipment installers are responsible for installing the wireless equipment properly so that it does not violate FCC regulations.

License-Free Wireless Frequencies

In 1985, the FCC authorized the use of license-free spread spectrum wireless equipment in the following three ISM bands in the United States:

- 900 to 928 MHz (900 MHz range)
- 2.4 to 2.483 GHz (2.4 GHz range)
- 5.725 to 5.850 GHz (5 GHz range)

Further, in 1997, the FCC authorized the use of license-free low-power *non-spread-spectrum* wireless equipment in the following three U-NII bands:

- 5.15 to 5.25 GHz
- 5.25 to 5.35 GHz
- 5.725 to 5.825 GHz

Advantages of License-Free Wireless Networks

Following are the advantages of deploying a license-free broadband wireless WAN:

- Cost savings
- Fast deployment speed
- Network architecture flexibility
- Network independence

Cost Savings

Saving money is perhaps the largest benefit of deploying a license-free wireless WAN. After the costs to design and install a wireless WAN are paid, there are no ongoing monthly rental, leasing, or service charges. Contrast this with the charges to lease a broadband line from the telephone company, which can range from $250 to $1000 or more each month. Wireless WANs also have no right-of-way costs. This is the monthly cost to place cable or fiber on telephone poles.

Compared to the cost of leased lines, the monthly costs for broadband digital subscriber line (DSL) and broadband cable Internet access service are more moderate. These costs range from $39 to $300 per month, depending on bandwidth. In many areas, however, neither DSL nor cable Internet access is available. In a few areas, two-way Internet access service is starting to be available via satellite. Costs for this service range upward from $80 per month.

In areas where DSL, cable, or satellite Internet access is available, there is frequently only one provider; many times it's the telephone company offering DSL service. Because of this lack of competition, the telephone companies are now raising their DSL prices. This trend is likely to continue indefinitely into the future.

Fast Deployment Speed

After a broadband wireless network has been designed and the access points deployed, the installation of new wireless end users can take place quickly. Typically, the time needed to install a new end user is a few days. Contrast this with the typical installment time for a new DSL or leased-line end user. The installation time is often weeks or months.

Network Architecture Flexibility

The architectural flexibility of a wireless network is unmatched by any other broadband medium. As long as a line-of-sight wireless path exists to one or more new locations, a wireless link can be deployed or redeployed in as little as one day. Redeployment consists of removing the antenna system and wireless equipment from the old location and reinstalling it in the new location. After antenna aiming is complete, the link should be ready to use.

Network Independence

A wireless WAN is the only network that can be built without relying on infrastructure that another carrier owns. Traditional broadband leased-line circuits rely on using a local loop (copper wire) circuit owned by the local telephone company; the same is true for DSL service. Providing Internet access over cable requires obtaining approval to access cable lines that the cable company owns. Cable companies routinely deny this access to competing ISPs.

In all of these cases, providing broadband service depends on using infrastructure that another company owns. Wireless WANs do not rely on obtaining permission from (and making payment to) any other company or carrier. The choice to use a wireless WAN is a choice to build, own, and operate your own broadband network.

ISPs that want to offer broadband Internet access while maintaining control of their cost structure might decide that deploying a license-free broadband wireless WAN is the only way to proceed profitably.

Challenges of License-Free Wireless Networks

To obtain the most benefit from wireless WANs, you need to understand the challenges to their successful deployment. These challenges are as follows:

- Understanding wireless fundamentals
- Overcoming real-world obstacles
- Maximizing available bandwidth
- Working safely

Challenge of Understanding Wireless Fundamentals

Wireless signals are invisible to the human eye. Making this invisible phenomenon become visible requires some learning and practice.

NOTE   What does it mean to say you can make invisible wireless signals visible? It means that you can make wireless signals predictable, controllable, and usable. You can become so familiar with their behavior that it is almost as if you could physically see them.

Successful wireless deployment requires an understanding of wireless principles. These principles determine the behavior of wireless signals, such as how they do the following:

- Spread out and get weaker as they leave an antenna and travel from point to point
- Lose strength when they hit a tree, hill, or other obstruction
- Reflect off of a building, the ground, and bodies of water

Chapter 2, "Understanding Wireless Fundamentals," contains an explanation of these and other basic wireless principles. The deployment of wireless WANs that provide *reliable* service at anything beyond short distances requires that these fundamental physical laws governing the behavior of wireless signals be understood and followed.

Challenge of Overcoming Real-World Obstacles

The previous section emphasized that it is important to understand wireless principles. After you understand these principles, the next step is to apply that understanding in the real world. Every wireless WAN deployment takes place in a unique and different real-world environment.

NOTE   The previous sentence might sound like a contradiction. How can the real world be real if every wireless WAN is deployed in a unique and different real-world environment? How many real worlds are really out there? Please continue reading for an explanation.

To understand the real world faced by a 2.4-GHz wireless signal, try to imagine that you are a wireless signal. You are five inches long, and you are about to start on a 20-mile journey. Your journey will take you from an antenna on the roof of a ski lodge at the top of a 10,000-foot mountain down to an antenna on the roof of an office building. The office building is located 35 miles away, in the middle of a city in the desert at sea level. Your mission is to carry and to deliver a big (and important) data packet to a computer inside the office building.

You are handed the data packet; then some powerful but invisible force roughly pushes you up to the antenna on the roof. As you reach the roof, the antenna suddenly spins your body around toward the city. The giant unseen force slams you out of the antenna and into the air. You feel strong, but you can't see the city and you have no way of steering yourself. Snow is falling, and you're freezing; the trees below you are covered in white. You hug the data packet tightly against your body. You know you are only five-inches long, but you can feel your chest slowly puffing out; you are expanding. You're getting wider and your skin is getting thinner. You feel yourself brush against the icy snow-covered treetops and some of your strength leaves you. You hug your data packet tighter as you fall. Down, down, down—your body keeps expanding, but now, as you expand, you feel the moisture in the icy air start to bend and warp you. You don't remember ever feeling this cold and swollen. You're weaker. Your chest is so big that you feel like you're about to burst. You suck in a breath but this time you don't feel that familiar icy pain in your nose. Have you gone numb? Then you realize that the air may be getting warmer. The foothills are below you. The snow is gone, but your body is now so big and so thin that it bumps against some of the foothills. You don't have much strength left and now it's getting hot. You grip the data packet as the hot, dry air starts to bend your body and wave you around. You see the city buildings ahead getting closer, taller. The end of your journey is there, somewhere, in that huge mass of steel, concrete, and glass. Closer, closer, your data packet is starting to slip away. You're so thin, so weak. The buildings are hitting you, bouncing you around. There's a roaring in your ears; hundreds of other signals are surrounding you, bumping, shoving, pushing. Your antenna is just ahead, but all of your energy is gone. The packet... the packet.... The antenna is reaching for you.... Almost there.... Almost... there.... In the rooftop cafeteria, a worker suddenly zaps a microwave oven on. Aaaaaaaaaaahhhhh!

In the world of broadband wireless, every journey between two antennas is a unique one. The terrain, the trees, the buildings, the weather, the packet size, and the other wireless signals combine to make the real world different for every wireless signal on every journey at every moment. Understanding the effects that these real-world influences have on wireless signals allows the design and the construction of broadband wireless networks that deliver reliable performance in the presence of all the real-world influences.

Challenge of Maximizing Available Bandwidth

The two preceding sections described the importance of understanding wireless fundamentals and overcoming real-world obstacles. The next challenge to deploying broadband wireless networks is maximizing the available throughput.

During broadband wireless network design, installation, and operation, one consequence always occurs when a mistake is made at any point in the process: the throughput of the network goes down. The throughput of a network going down is a sure sign that one or more problem areas exist that need to be identified and corrected. The goal of this book is to help you design and build a reliable, money-saving, high-bandwidth network and to avoid the common and the sometimes not-so-common mistakes that reduce network throughput.

Challenge of Working Safely with Wireless

A fast, reliable, low-cost broadband wireless network is not beneficial if an employee or a bystander is hurt or killed by a falling tool or a falling antenna. Safety must be the top priority of each person involved in designing, building, and maintaining a wireless network. It is crucial to promote and emphasize safety by conducting and documenting safety meetings that cover the following topics:

- Working with heights
- Working with microwave energy
- Watching the weather
- Using lightning protection
- Using personal safety equipment
- Climbing safely
- Other safety procedures

Working with Heights

Wireless antennas are usually mounted high above the ground on masts, rooftops, and towers. During design and installation, the following safety issues must be addressed:

- **Falls**—A fall from as little as 18 inches can be enough to cripple a person for life. A fall from a roof or a tower is often fatal. Only properly trained personnel should be assigned to install towers and rooftop antenna systems.
- **Falling objects**—The installation process must be safe for the installation personnel as well as for other people passing by who are below the antenna. An object as small as a screwdriver falling from a roof can cause serious injury if it hits somebody below. Imagine the injury that a larger object such as an antenna mast could cause!

Working with Microwave Energy

Wireless networks transmit microwave energy. High levels of microwave energy or the cumulative effects of low levels of microwave energy are known to have adverse effects on the human body. To minimize the chance of injury, network installation personnel must observe the following safety procedures:

- Always turn off the wireless equipment when working around or in front of a microwave antenna. Never point a microwave antenna toward another nearby person.

- Mount all antenna systems high enough so that they do not focus and radiate energy toward a nearby area where people could be present.

- If there is a high-power transmitter located on the same tower as the broadband wireless antenna system, ask that the transmitter be turned off temporarily so that work on the wireless antenna system can be performed safely.

Watching the Weather

Always consider the following weather conditions when deciding if it is safe to work on outdoor antenna systems:

- **Wet conditions**—Water makes surfaces slippery. It is dangerous to work on roofs or towers when it has been raining or when it is about to rain. Make it a rule to direct installation supervisors to stop outdoor antenna work when it is raining or when rain is expected within a short period.

- **Icy conditions**—Like water, ice makes surfaces slippery. Prohibit your installation crews from working outside near towers when it is icy. Remember: Ice that falls from a radio tower can be heavy and sharp. It can damage equipment or smash a skull.

- **Lightning strikes**—When lightning strikes a person, it is not always fatal. Occasionally, the person survives the lightning strike with only burns or scars. It is, however, not wise to run the risk of having an installation crew struck by lightning. When lightning threatens, installation crews should stop work and take shelter inside the nearest building.

Using Lightning Protection

The previous section discussed protecting installation crews from lightning. Wireless equipment, customer property, and customer personnel also need protection from lighting. Last, your company or agency needs legal protection from the possibility of performing negligent work. If lightning hits a wireless antenna and then destroys the wireless users' building or business, you could be sued for damages. Even worse, if lightning hits an antenna system and travels inside the building where people are working, someone could be hurt or killed.

Every responsible adult must realize that each outdoor wireless antenna system installation must include lightning protection. The cost of including a lightning arrestor and a proper ground connection is approximately $50 for the parts and one hour or more of extra installation labor. Following are the benefits of installing lightning protection on each outdoor antenna installation:

- Protecting your customers from serious injury or death

- Protecting your customers' building and equipment from being destroyed by lightning

- Protecting your customers' businesses from stopping while they move their entire business to a new location, replace their network equipment, restore their software, recover their databases, and recover from the revenue losses that occurred because of the lightning strike

- Protecting yourself and your business from being sued for negligence because an antenna system you installed did not contain lightning protection

- Allowing yourself to relax and avoid worry when a lightning storm passes through the area

- Feeling the satisfaction that comes from spending a few dollars more but knowing that you chose to do installations the right way, the safe way, the legal way, and the ethical way

Using Personal Safety Equipment

Every person involved in wireless antenna system installation should be provided with the following personal safety equipment:

- A hard hat to protect his head from falling objects

- Gloves to protect hands from punctures and abrasions

- Safety glasses to protect eyes from injury

- Sunscreen to protect skin from sunburn

Climbing Safely

In addition to the personal safety equipment listed in the previous section, each person who must climb a tower to perform antenna installation or service work should be provided with the following:

- Proper, professional training on safe tower climbing and installation practices. If no one in your organization has received tower safety training, it is necessary to hire an experienced tower or antenna erection company to perform this work.

NOTE   See Appendix B, "Wireless Hardware, Software, and Service Provider Organizations," for information about organizations that provide tower safety training.

- A safety belt.
- A body harness.
- Boots with a steel shank inside the soles.

Other Safety Procedures

It is beyond the scope of this book to address any or all the other safety challenges that you and your company or organization might face. As you receive additional safety ideas, suggestions, and thoughts, it is wise to follow up and include these issues in your safety policy, your safety meetings, and your safety procedures.

Review Questions

1 This book defines a broadband wireless connection as any wireless connection with a bandwidth of ____.

2 What year did the U.S. government first require licenses for all transmitters?

3 What year did the FCC first allow broadband wireless equipment to be used without applying for a license?

4 What does the process of modulation do?

5 Name one way that a license-free broadband wireless WAN saves money.

6 Why is the real world different for every wireless link?

7 During antenna system installation, what safety practice helps protect workers on the ground from being injured by falling objects?

8 A fall from 18 inches can cripple a person for life. True or false?

9 If you need to work in front of a wireless antenna, what should you do first?

10 Every outdoor wireless antenna system should include a lightning arrestor. True or false?

Understanding Wireless Fundamentals

This chapter describes the wireless fundamentals that underlie the successful design, deployment, operation, support, and expansion of wireless wide-area networks (WANs). This book focuses on the application of these fundamentals in license-free wireless networks; however, these same wireless principles apply to licensed wireless networks and to all wireless signals.

Wireless Propagation

Wireless propagation is the total of everything that happens to a wireless signal as the signal travels from Point A to Point B. Although invisible to your eyes, the wireless signal interacts with everything that it comes near or passes through, including trees, hills, buildings, bodies of water, the earth's atmosphere, people, vehicles, and so on. The better you understand these interactions, the more easily and more successfully you will be able to deploy wireless WANs. First, it is important for you to understand how wireless signals are created.

Wireless communication is possible because changes in the electron flow within a wire cause changes in the magnetic fields and in the electric fields that surround the wire. Magnetic fields and electric fields are invisible, but you can see the results of their presence. If you have ever used a magnet to attract a piece of iron or steel, you have seen the result of a magnetic field. If you have ever seen a bolt of lightning, you have seen the effect of an electric (or electrostatic) field.

When electron streams change direction rapidly within a wire or antenna, the electrostatic and magnetic fields around the wire or antenna change at the same rapid rate. These rapidly changing fields are called electromagnetic waves. The electromagnetic waves do not simply stay near the antenna; they travel away at nearly the speed of light—186,000 miles per second (300,000,000 meters per second). The changing electron flow within the antenna has been transformed into electromagnetic (wireless) waves traveling away from the antenna.

TIP   Keep a mental picture of a moving wave in your mind; it is not a spot or a line; it is a wave. If you drop a rock into a pond, the waves spread out from the point where the rock hit the water. If you place an antenna in free space, the wireless waves spread out from the antenna. Wireless waves pass through air, space, people, and objects. If you can visualize electromagnetic waves traveling away from an antenna and radiating outward, you will be off to an excellent start toward successfully deploying wireless WANs.

Wireless Frequency

As an ocean wave travels, its height changes; as the front of the wave approaches you, the height increases. When the crest passes you, the height of the wave decreases. The height decreases further as the trough passes you. Finally, the height of the sea is back to the level where it was before the wave appeared. You have just experienced one complete up-down-up wave cycle. Without changes in the wave height, there would be no wave cycle or wave.

Changes in the electron flow in an antenna cause the same changes in the electromagnetic fields around the antenna. Another word for electron flow in a wire is *current*. Without changes in the antenna current, there would be no change in the electromagnetic fields around the antenna; therefore, there would be no useable wireless signal moving outward, away from the antenna. The number of times each second that the current in the antenna goes through one complete positive-negative-positive change-cycle is the same as the *frequency* of the wireless waves that radiate outward from the antenna. If you drew a graph of the current flow in the antenna, the resulting graph would be a sine wave. The positive distance (above the centerline) and the negative distance (below the centerline) represent the *amplitude,* or strength, of the current. The greater the amplitude of the current, the stronger the radiated electromagnetic waves.

Figure 2-1 shows two complete cycles of positive-negative-positive current flow in an antenna. If there are 100 complete cycles in one second, the frequency of the current flow (and the frequency of the resulting wireless wave) is 100 cycles per second. Around 1960, the term *cycles per second* was replaced with the term *Hertz* (abbreviated Hz). The frequency of this wireless wave is 100 Hz.

Wireless signals cycle back and forth so quickly—millions of times each second—that the following abbreviations are used to specify their frequency:

- Kilohertz (kHz): Thousands of cycles per second
- Megahertz (MHz): Millions of cycles per second
- Gigahertz (GHz): Billions of cycles per second

Figure 2-1   *Antenna Current Alternating Between Positive and Negative*

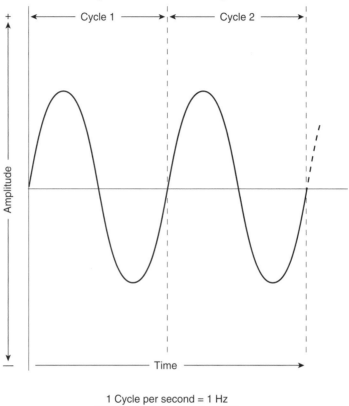

1 Cycle per second = 1 Hz
1000 Cycles per second = 1 kHz
1,000,000 Cycles per second = 1 MHz
1,000,000,000 Cycles per second = 1 GHz

Wireless Wavelength

It is important to be able to visualize the physical size of a wireless signal because the physical size of each signal determines how that signal interacts with its environment and how well it is propagated from antenna to antenna within the wireless network. The signal's physical size also determines how large or how small the antennas that transmit and receive the signal must be; the smaller the signal size, the smaller the antenna.

Figure 2-2 shows two wireless signals on two different frequencies—2.45 GHz and 5.775 GHz. All wireless signals travel through the air at the same speed. That speed is the speed of light, which is 186,000 miles per second (300,000,000 meters per second). The distance that a radio signal travels during a single cycle is called the *wavelength* of that signal. Higher-frequency waves have less time to travel during a single cycle than lower-frequency waves, so the wavelength for higher-frequency waves is shorter than for lower-frequency waves.

Figure 2-2   *Physical Size (Wavelength) of Wireless Waves*

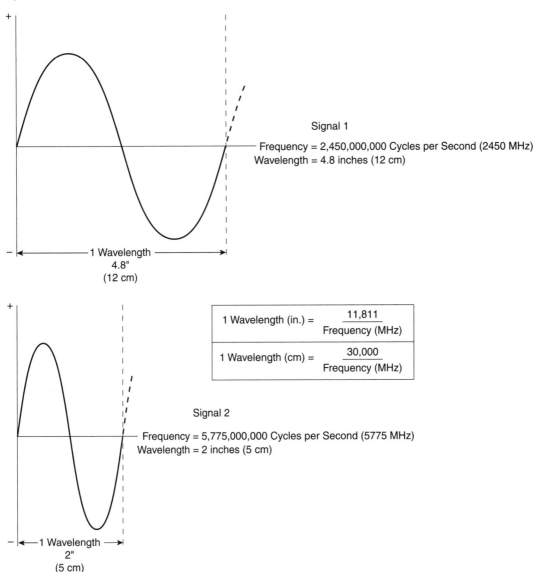

In Figure 2-2, each cycle of Signal 1 (2.45 GHz) has time to travel 4.8 inches (12 cm). Therefore, Signal 1's wavelength is 4.8 inches (12 cm). Signal 2 is changing more rapidly; each cycle of Signal 2 has time to travel only 2 inches (5 cm). Therefore, the wavelength of Signal 2 is only 2 inches (5 cm). There is a corresponding physical wavelength for every wireless frequency. The lower the frequency, the longer the wavelength; the higher the frequency, the shorter the wavelength.

Attenuation

Attenuation is the loss in amplitude that occurs whenever a signal travels through a wire, through free space, or through an obstruction. Figure 2-3 shows a 2.45-GHz (2450 MHz) signal as it encounters a tree. The signal is attenuated; that is, its amplitude is reduced. The amount of signal that emerges on the other side of the tree is much less than the amount of signal that entered the tree. Often, after colliding with an object, the signal strength remaining is too small to make a reliable wireless link.

Figure 2-3   *Attenuation of a 4.8-inch (5-cm) Signal by a Tree*

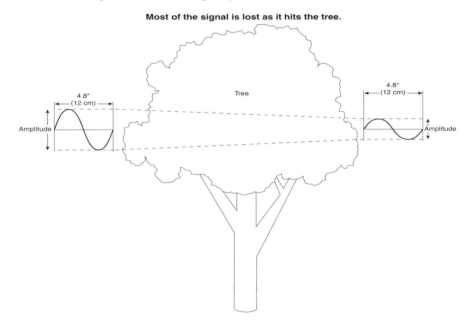

In addition, the shorter the wavelength of a wireless signal, the more it is attenuated when it encounters an object. The longer the wavelength of a wireless signal, the less it is attenuated when it encounters an object. Figure 2-4 shows a signal in the AM radio broadcast band at a frequency of 1000 kHz (1 MHz).

Figure 2-4 *Attenuation of a 984-ft (300-m) Signal by a Tree*

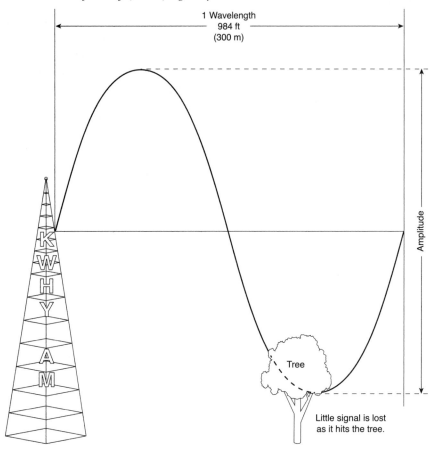

When this signal encounters a tree, the wavelength of the signal (984 ft/300 m) is so much greater than the size of the tree that the amplitude of the signal remains almost unchanged.

NOTE   A sharp-eyed reader will look at Figure 2-4 and says "Sure, the amplitude is still large after the collision. The amplitude of the AM broadcast signal was a lot larger than the amplitude of the 2.4-GHz signal to begin with." Well, sharp-eyed reader, you are correct. Yes, the AM broadcast signal had higher amplitude (more power) to begin with—perhaps 50,000W compared to the 2.4-GHz signal that started out with 4W, but here's the point. Even if the AM broadcast signal started out with 4W, a lot more of it would *still* be left over after encountering the tree, compared to the remaining 2.4-GHz signal. This would be true because the tree is many times larger than the physical wavelength of the 2.4-GHz signal, and the tree is many times smaller than the physical wavelength of the 1000-kHz KWHY-AM signal.

Free-Space Waves

A free-space wave is a signal that propagates from Point A to Point B without encountering or coming near an obstruction, as in Figure 2-5.

Figure 2-5   *Free-Space Wave*

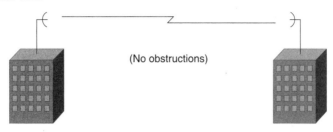

(No obstructions)

The signal arrives at its destination with as much amplitude as possible because the amplitude is not reduced by attenuation from objects. The only amplitude reduction that occurs is the normal reduction due to the signal being propagated through free space. A signal path like this, with no obstructions, is an ideal wireless scenario.

Reflected Waves

When a wireless signal encounters an obstruction while traveling from Point A to Point B, two things normally happen:

- **Attenuation**—In general, the shorter the wavelength of a signal, relative to the size of the obstruction, the more the signal is attenuated.

- **Reflection**—The shorter the wavelength of the signal relative to the size of the obstruction, the more likely it is that some of the signal will be reflected off the obstruction.

The following sections describe two types of reflected waves. One of these two types occurs at microwave frequencies and is important to your understanding of microwave propagation. You might already be familiar with the first type of reflected waves: sky waves.

Sky Waves

The first type of reflected waves is sky waves. Sky waves generally occur at short wave frequencies, where wavelengths range from 328 to 33 feet (100 to 10 m). Sky waves often reflect off the ionosphere—layers of ionized particles that exist from 30 to 300 miles (48 to 482 km) above the Earth, as shown in Figure 2-6.

Figure 2-6   *Sky Wave: Reflected Signal at Non-Microwave Frequencies*

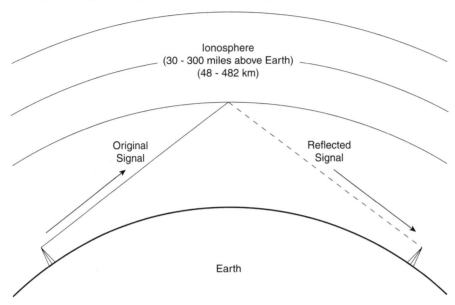

Sky waves arriving via ionospheric reflection make it possible to receive short wave broadcasts from stations located in other countries, thousands of miles away. Sky waves sometimes also make it possible for you to receive AM broadcast stations at night that are hundreds or thousands of miles away. Ionospheric reflection, however, seldom occurs at microwave frequencies.

Microwave Reflections

Microwave signals have frequencies between 1000 MHz (1 GHz) and 30 GHz and a physical wavelength from approximately 12 in. (30 cm) down to less than 1 in. (2.5 cm). Microwave signals reflect off of objects that are larger than their wavelength, such as buildings, cars, flat stretches of ground, and bodies of water. Figure 2-7 illustrates microwave reflection off of a building.

Each time a microwave signal is reflected, its amplitude is reduced. Microwave reflection can be an advantage or a disadvantage. The advantage is that sometimes the reflection (or *bounce*) off of a building or water tank allows a microwave link to work even though obstructions, such as the trees in Figure 2-7, block the direct wave. The disadvantage of microwave reflection is that a phenomenon called multipath can occur.

Multipath occurs when reflections cause more than one copy of the same microwave signal to arrive at the receiver at slightly different times, as shown in Figure 2-8.

Figure 2-7 *Microwave Signal Reflection*

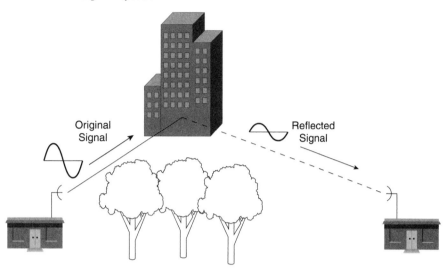

Figure 2-8 *Microwave Signal with Multiple Reflections*

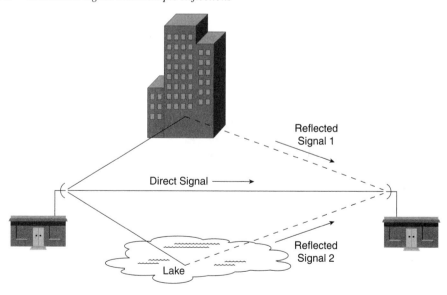

Reflected Signals 1 and 2 follow slightly longer paths than the direct signal; therefore, they arrive slightly later than the direct signal. These reflected echoes sometimes cause problems at the receiver by partially canceling the direct signal, effectively reducing its amplitude.

The link throughput slows down because the receiver needs more time to either separate the real signal from the reflected echoes or to wait for missed packets to be retransmitted. Multipath is a significant problem for designers of microwave networks. Methods that you can use to minimize the effects of multipath are discussed later in the book.

Diffraction

Diffraction of a wireless signal occurs when the signal is partially blocked or obstructed by a large object in the signal's path, as shown in Figure 2-9.

Figure 2-9   *Signal Diffraction Around an Obstruction*

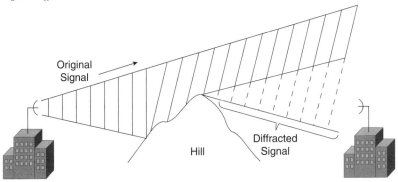

The edge of the hill partially blocks the microwave signal. As the bottom part of the signal intercepts the hilltop, the signal is diffracted, causing part of the signal energy to bend slightly around the hilltop.

The diffracted signal energy is usually attenuated so much that it is too weak to provide a reliable microwave connection. In a few cases, however, the diffracted signal, although weakened, might still be strong enough to allow a connection to be made to a nearby location that would otherwise be blocked.

TIP   Always try to obtain an unobstructed path between the microwave antennas that you set up. Do not plan to use a diffracted signal in place of a direct signal because most of the time, the diffracted signal is too weak to provide a reliable link.

Weather and Other Atmospheric Effects

Microwave signals must pass through the earth's atmosphere (unless you are communicating from spacecraft to spacecraft, which is a not-too-distant possibility). The earth's atmosphere is a dynamic environment consisting of regions of constantly changing temperatures, pressures, water vapor, and weather. These changes affect the passage and the propagation of microwave signals. Understanding these propagation changes helps you design reliable wireless WANs.

Precipitation

Rain, snow, hail, fog, and sleet are all forms of precipitation—water or water vapor—that is present in the air. As you evaluate the effect that each form of precipitation has on your wireless WAN, keep in mind that the physical size of a wireless signal plays a big role in determining how that signal interacts with the precipitation that it encounters.

Rain, Snow, and Hail

One cycle of a wireless signal at 2.45 GHz has a wavelength of 4.8 in. (12 cm); one cycle at 5.7 GHz has a wavelength of 2 in. (5 cm). Compared to the size of a raindrop—even a big raindrop in a heavy downpour—these wireless signals are quite a bit larger than the raindrops. As a result, the raindrops do not significantly attenuate these signals. At higher wireless frequencies (at or above 10 GHz), where the signal wavelength decreases to less than 1 inch (3 cm), rain, partially melted snow, and partially melted hail *do* start to cause significant attenuation.

Rain can, however, have other effects on the operation of a wireless system. Wherever a tiny hole exists anywhere in an antenna system, rain usually finds it and gets inside the system. After the rain is inside, the water degrades the performance of the system. Eventually, the system fails completely and the antenna cabling must be replaced. Rain can also make surfaces (such as buildings and leaves) more reflective, increasing multipath fading.

TIP   This is another reason to use nonobstructed paths between your antennas. If you try to "blast through" trees, you are just setting yourself up to have problems.

Ice

Ice buildup on antenna systems impacts the operation of wireless WANs in two different ways:

- Reducing system performance
- Physically damaging the antenna system

A thick buildup of ice on a microwave antenna changes the performance of the antenna and the performance of the wireless link degrades.

Ice buildup also adds substantial extra weight, which increases the chance of antenna system failure, especially under windy conditions. A heavier than normal antenna might bend under the extra weight or might even fall from the antenna tower. Ice can also fall from a higher antenna onto a lower one, damaging the lower antenna or antenna cable.

NOTE   To minimize problems in snow and ice-prone areas, many commercial microwave antennas are protected with radomes that are designed to cover the antenna. Some radomes also have heaters to melt ice buildups. If you are located in an area that has heavy winter icing conditions, you might want to consult with a local two-way radio shop to see what methods it uses to reduce icing problems on its antenna systems.

Wind

Wind can have a significant impact on the reliable operation of wireless WAN systems. The force from a moderate or heavy wind pushes against both the antenna and the tower or mast that holds the antenna in position. Under this force, several things could happen:

- The antenna could turn on the mast or tower, causing signal levels to decrease as the aim of the antenna changes.
- The tower or mast could sway or twist, changing the aim of the antenna and causing signal levels to decrease or to vary.
- An antenna or tower that has not been properly designed, installed, guyed, or maintained could fail in a strong wind—potentially causing physical injury or property damage.

NOTE   *Safety is priority one* in the design, installation, and operation of a wireless WAN systems. Please pay special attention to the safety sections and notes throughout this book. Give them special attention as you design and install your wireless systems.

Refraction

The changes in temperature, pressure, and water vapor content in the atmosphere play a significant role in the propagation of microwave signals—refracting (or bending) the signals. The refractivity of the atmosphere changes depending on the height above ground. The refractivity is usually largest at low elevations, closest to the surface of the earth. The refractivity is usually smallest the higher you go above the earth. This refractivity change (called the refractivity gradient or *k-factor*) usually causes microwave signals to curve downward slightly toward the earth, as shown in Figure 2-10.

Figure 2-10 *Signal Refraction in the Atmosphere*

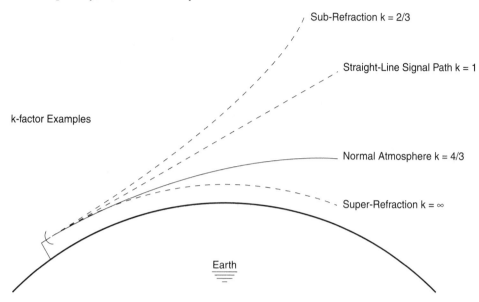

The k-factor can change frequently, such as from hour to hour, from day to night, from weather pattern to weather pattern, or from season to season. Different regions of the earth have slightly different average k-factors. A k-factor of 1 indicates no bending; a signal radiated under this condition travels in a straight line.

A k-factor higher than 1 means that microwave signals bend slightly downward, toward the earth. In most regions, *the median k-factor is 4/3*. A k-factor of 4/3 has the effect of making the radio horizon farther away than the visual horizon. In other words, the length of the microwave path is increased by approximately 15 percent. At times, weather conditions can temporarily cause the k-factor to become infinite. When this occurs, the amount of signal bending equals the curvature of the earth. This effect is called *super-refraction*, or *ducting*. Ducting causes a microwave signal to be propagated for hundreds of miles or until the atmospheric conditions change enough for the ducting to stop.

Changes in the k-factor are a common cause of fading on microwave paths. Sometimes, due to atmospheric conditions, the k-factor is less than 1; for example, the k-factor could be 2/3. This condition, called *subrefraction*, has the effect of bending the microwave signal path upward, away from the earth. Subrefraction reduces signal levels, causing fading at the distant receiver. Over longer microwave paths, the k-factor might be different at different points along the path.

Working with Wireless Power

- Working with wireless WANs requires knowing how to work with wireless power. Following are facts about wireless power:

- Power can be either increased (a power gain) or decreased (a power loss).

- Power can be relative, for example, twice as much power or 1/2 as much power
  or
  Power can be absolute, for example, 1 watt or 4 watts.

- Both absolute and relative power are always referenced to initial power level, either to a relative power level or to an absolute power level.

- Wireless WAN power levels become very small, very quickly after leaving a transmitting antenna.

- Wireless WAN power does not decrease linearly with distance; it decreases inversely as the square of the distance increases. Here are some examples:

  — If we double the distance of a wireless link, we don't have 1/2 of the original power reaching the end of the new link; we receive only 1/4 of the original power.

  — If we triple the distance of a link, we receive only 1/9th of the original power.

  — If a new link is 5 times longer than an existing link, we receive only 1/25th of the power that arrived at the receiver of the original link.

- Wireless power calculations are done in dB, for the following reasons:

  — dB values are logs—that is, they increase and decrease not linearly but logarithmically, just like the way that wireless power increases or decreases.

  — dB values can be used to conveniently represent very small power levels, like the levels of wireless power that arrive at a receiver.

  — Although they are logarithmic, dB values can be added and subtracted together (with each other) using just regular (linear) math. For example: 3 dB plus 3 dB equals 6 dB.

The following sections help you become comfortable using dB to calculate relative power levels and dBm to calculate absolute power levels. Later, you will also use dBi to calculate and compare antenna gains relative to the reference level of an isotropic antenna.

Ratios

Every db value is a *ratio*. This section explains ratios. A ratio is a comparison between two quantities. Ratios use a colon (:) to divide the two quantities. Figure 2-11 uses pennies to show two examples of ratios.

The first example is a ratio of two-to-one (2:1), and the second example is a ratio of 100:1. The first example shows a pile with two pennies next to a pile with one penny—a ratio between the piles of two pennies to one penny, or 2:1. The second example shows a pile with 100 pennies next to a pile with one penny—a ratio of 100:1.

Figure 2-11 *Penny Ratios*

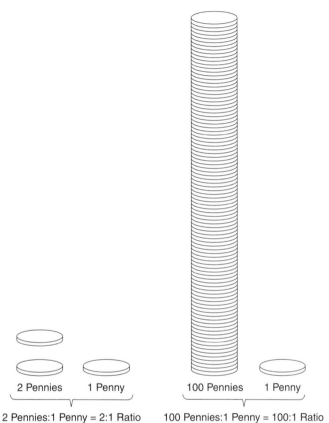

2 Pennies   1 Penny   100 Pennies   1 Penny

2 Pennies:1 Penny = 2:1 Ratio   100 Pennies:1 Penny = 100:1 Ratio

Power Ratios

Figure 2-12 uses two flashlights to show an example of a power ratio.

The flashlight on the left has a power of 40 candlepower (as bright as 40 candles). The flashlight on the right is 10 candlepower. The power ratio, 40 candlepower to 10 candlepower, is 4:1.

NOTE   If you look closely, you'll also notice that the 40 candlepower flashlight beam travels only twice as far as the 10 candlepower beam. Hmmm… four times the power travels only twice the distance? Yes, that is correct. The reason for this will be discussed more at the end of this chapter. You will also see how to quickly and easily determine if you can double the distance of a wireless link. (HINT: Do you have four times the power?)

All power ratios use some quantity as their initial reference point. The flashlight example in Figure 2-12 uses the 10-candlepower level (the smaller flashlight) as the reference point. This 10-candlepower level is abbreviated "FL". + 6 dBFL now means 6 dB (or 4 times) larger than the 10 candlepower reference level, or 40 candlepower (the larger flashlight). As long as the abbreviation (FL) and the power level (10 candlepower) are defined and communicated, then FL can be used indefinitely as a reference level.

Figure 2-12 *Flashlight Power Ratios*

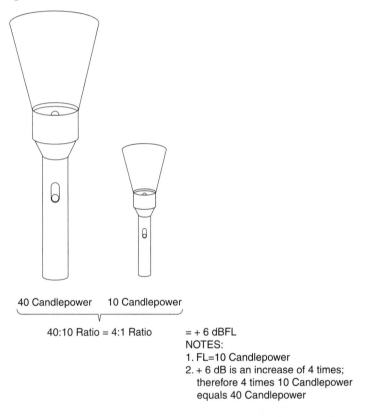

40 Candlepower   10 Candlepower

40:10 Ratio = 4:1 Ratio   = + 6 dBFL
NOTES:
1. FL=10 Candlepower
2. + 6 dB is an increase of 4 times;
   therefore 4 times 10 Candlepower
   equals 40 Candlepower

Wireless Power Ratios

Figure 2-13 shows examples of three wireless power ratios; each uses 1 Watt (1 W) of power as their reference point. The 1-Watt reference point is abbreviated by the "W," the third letter in "dBW." If, for example, you were told that a transmitter had an output of +3 dBW, you would know that the output power was twice (3 dB means two times) greater than (the + sign indicates a power gain) 1 Watt (indicated by the "W") or a total of 2 Watts output.

Figure 2-13   *Power Ratios in dBW (Relative to 1W)*

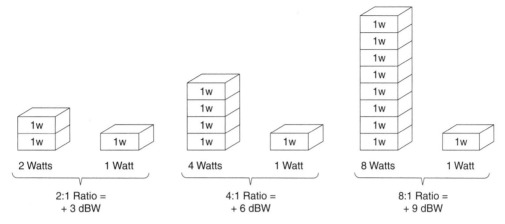

dBm

The most common dB power reference level when working with wireless WANs is dBm. The "m" in dBm stands for 1 milliwatt. A milliwatt is 1/1000 of a watt. There are 1000 mW in 1Watt. 1 milliwatt is 0 dBm. Positive dBm values (such as +30 dBm) indicate power levels greater than 1 mW. Negative dBm values (such as –20 dBm) indicate power levels less than 1 mW.

This is a good place to reaffirm that all absolute-power decibel values contain three things:

- A sign (+ or –) to indicate whether the value is above or below the absolute reference level
- The logarithmic value that represents the ratio of the two powers, in decibels
- The reference-power level, such as the "m" meaning 1 mW

Table 2-1 shows some of the most common wireless power levels (above and below 1 mW).

Table 2-1   *Power Ratios in dBm (Relative to 1 mW)*

Power Level Relative to 1 mW (0 dBm)	Level (+ or – dBm)	Power (Watts)	Power Abbreviation
4000 times more than 0 dBm	+36 dBm	4Watts	4W (4000 mW)
1000 times more than 0 dBm	+30 dBm	1Watt	1W (1000 mW)
Two times more than 0 dBm	+3 dBm	2 milliwatts	2 mW
0 dBm Reference Level	**0 dBm**	**1 milliwatt**	**1 mW**
1/2 of 0 dBm	–3 dBm	1/2 milliwatt	0.5 mW
1/1000 of 0 dBm	–30 dBm	1/1000 milliwatt	0.001 mW
1/4000 of 0 dBm	–36 dBm	1/4000 milliwatt	0.00025 mW

dBm Calculations and Reference Chart

It is possible to calculate a power gain or a power loss in decibels by using the following formula:

dB = 10log(P2/P1)

This says that the power ratio (in decibels) between any two power levels is equal to 10 times the log of the ratio of the two power levels. For example, if you have a transmitter with a power output of 100 mW and you add an amplifier with a power output of 400 mW, the increase in power level (in decibels) is calculated as follows:

The initial power level (P1) is 100 mW.
The new power level (P2) is 400 mW.
The ratio P2/P1 is 400/100, or 4.
The log of 4 (use a calculator here) is .602.
Ten times .602 is 6.02 or, rounding this off, 6 dB.

The power has increased (P2 was greater than P1), so the final decibel value has a + sign (+6 dB) to indicate that there is a four-times relative power gain.

Going the other way, here is an example of a power loss:

The power output of the same 100-mW transmitter suddenly drops down to 25 mW.
P1 is 100 mW and P2 is 25 mW.
The ratio P2/P1 is 25/100 (1/4, or .25).
The log of .25 is –0.602.
Ten times (–0.602) is –6.02, or, rounding off, –6 dB.

The power has decreased (P2 was less than P1), so the final dB value has a – sign (–6 dB) to indicate a power reduction down to 1/4 of the original value.

When you need to convert a power in watts to an absolute power in dBm, use the following formula:

dBm = 10log (Power in watts) + 30

This says that the power ratio in dBm equals 10 times the log of the power in watts plus 30. For example, if you have a transmitter with 1W of output power, the output power in dBm is as follows:

The log of 1 is 0. (Check it on your calculator.)
Ten times 0 is also 0.
Add 30 and the answer is +30 dBm.
1W of power is equal to +30 dBm.

It is usually easier and quicker to use the following reference table (Table 2-2) to find dBm levels; however, from time to time, you should practice using the formulas to keep sharp on how dBm ratios work.

Table 2-2   *Decibel (dB) Reference Chart*

Power Level (dBm) (Relative to 0 dBm or 1 mW)	Power Loss (Relative to 0 dBm or 1 mW)	Power Gain (Relative to 0 dBm or 1 mW)	Comments
–104	40 percent of 1 ten-billionth of 1 mW		
–100	1 ten-billionth of 1 mW		
–85	3 billionths of 1 mW		Threshold where most receivers start working
–40	1/10,000 of 1 mW		
–30	1/1000 of 1 mW		
–20	1/100 of 1 mW		
–13	1/20 of 1 mW		
–10	1/10 of 1 mW		
–9	1/8 of 1 mW		
–6	1/4 of 1 mW		
–3	1/2 of 1 mW		
0 dBm	**No Power Loss**	**No Power Gain**	**0 dBm Reference Level (1 mW)**
+ 3		2 times 1 mW	
+ 6		4 times 1 mW	
+ 9		8 times 1 mW	8 mW
+ 10		10 times 1 mW	10 mW
+ 13		20 times 1 mW	20 mW
+ 16		40 times 1 mW	40 mW
+ 20		100 times 1 mW	100 mW
+ 30		1000 times 1 mW	1W
+ 40		10,000 times 1 mW	10W
+ 85		316,000,000 times 1 mW	316 kW (316 kilowatts)
+ 100		10 billion times 1 mW	10 MW (10 megawatts)

Antenna Characteristics

Antennas are the most important part of every wireless WAN. Every WAN covers a wide area. Without an antenna, wireless power travels only a short distance, perhaps a few dozen feet. To successfully deploy license-free wireless WANs, you need to understand the key concepts of antenna directivity and antenna gain.

Antenna Directivity

Antennas radiate wireless power—that is, antennas accept wireless signal energy from the transmission line connected to a transmitter and launch that wireless energy into free space. Antennas focus the wireless energy like a flashlight reflector focuses the light from the flashlight bulb. Figure 2-14 compares the energy radiated from a bare, unfocused flashlight bulb to the focused energy radiated from a flashlight bulb with a reflector behind it.

Notice that in Figure 2-14, the flashlight bulb on the left radiates light energy in all directions. There is no focusing element, and no direction receives more light than any other direction. The light energy radiated from the unfocused flashlight bulb is similar to the wireless energy radiated from a theoretical isotropic antenna. An isotropic antenna radiates wireless energy equally in all directions and does not focus the energy in any single direction.

Figure 2-14   *Focused Versus Unfocused Energy*

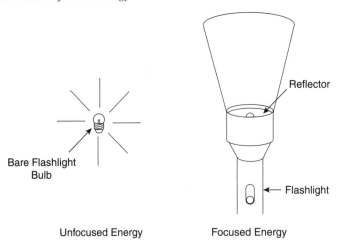

In contrast to the bare flashlight bulb, the flashlight on the right has a reflector behind the bulb. The reflector focuses the light into a beam that comes out the front of the flashlight. The flashlight does not amplify the power or the total amount of light from the flashlight bulb. The flashlight simply focuses the light so that all of it travels in the same direction. By focusing the light, the flashlight provides more *directivity* (beam-focusing power) for the light energy. Similarly, an antenna provides directivity for the wireless energy that it focuses. Depending on their design, construction, and orientation, antennas focus and radiate their energy more strongly in one favored direction. When they are receiving, antennas focus and gather energy from their favored direction and ignore most of the energy arriving from all other directions.

Antenna Radiation Patterns

Antennas exhibit directivity by radiating most of their power in one direction—the direction of their major (or main) lobe. They radiate only a small amount of power in other directions—the directions of their minor (or side) lobes. Figure 2-15 shows a top view of a directional antenna.

Figure 2-15   *Horizontal Radiation Pattern of a Directional Antenna*

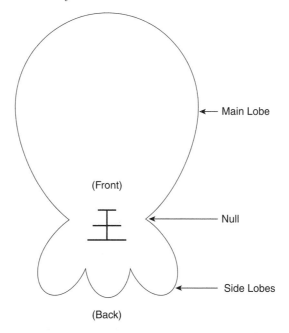

Figure 2-15 illustrates the horizontal radiation pattern of the antenna. It shows both the main and the side lobes. A main lobe exists toward the front of the antenna and several side lobes exist toward the back of the antenna. *Nulls*—areas where no power is radiated—exist to the sides of the antenna.

All antennas provide the same directivity on both transmit and receive. An antenna radiates transmitter power in the favored direction(s) when transmitting. The antenna gathers signals coming in from the favored direction(s) when receiving.

NOTE   When receiving, antenna directivity not only gathers incoming signals from the favored direction, but it also reduces noise, interference, and unwanted signals coming in from other directions. Keep this important point in mind as you select antennas for your networks; use antenna directivity to reduce noise coming from unwanted directions.

Figure 2-16 shows another view of antenna directivity: the vertical radiation pattern, when you look at an antenna from the side.

Figure 2-16   *Vertical Radiation Pattern of an Omnidirectional Antenna*

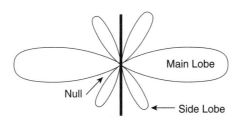

SIDE VIEW

This view shows an omnidirectional antenna with main and side lobes in the vertical direction. An omnidirectional antenna radiates equally well in all horizontal directions around the antenna but has a main lobe in the vertical direction. This main lobe surrounds the antenna like a doughnut.

Antenna Gain

Measuring the power in the main lobe of an antenna and comparing that power to the power in the main lobe of a reference antenna determines the *gain* of an antenna. Antenna gain is measured in decibels, either in dBi or in dBd.

If the reference antenna is a dipole, the measured antenna gain is in dBd. The "d" in dBd means that the gain is measured relative to the gain of a dipole reference antenna.

If the reference antenna is an isotropic antenna, the antenna gain is measured in dBi. The "i" in dBi means that the gain is measured relative to an isotropic reference antenna.

NOTE   Chapter 5, "Selecting Antenna Systems," defines and discusses isotropic antennas and dipole antennas in more detail. For now, the important point to remember is that your wireless WAN uses antennas that have more directivity (and therefore more gain) than either a simple dipole or an isotropic antenna.

Antenna Spillover

Now that you are familiar with the horizontal and vertical directivity of antennas, there is one more point to keep in mind. Wireless power never stops exactly on a sharp line like the main and the side lobe drawings show. Wireless power tapers off—it declines gradually rather than suddenly. In other words, some transmitter power and some receive capability exist outside of the main and side lobes of each antenna.

Antenna Beamwidth

Beamwidth—the width of the main beam (main lobe) of an antenna—measures the directivity of the antenna. The smaller the beamwidth in degrees, the more the antenna focuses power into its main lobe. The more power in the main lobe, the further the antenna can communicate. Beamwidth is specified in two dimensions:

- Horizontal beamwidth around the antenna
- Vertical beamwidth above and below the antenna

Figure 2-17 shows an example of the horizontal pattern of a directional antenna. This antenna has one main lobe that extends outward from the front of the antenna.

Figure 2-17   *Horizontal Beamwidth Showing Half-Power Points*

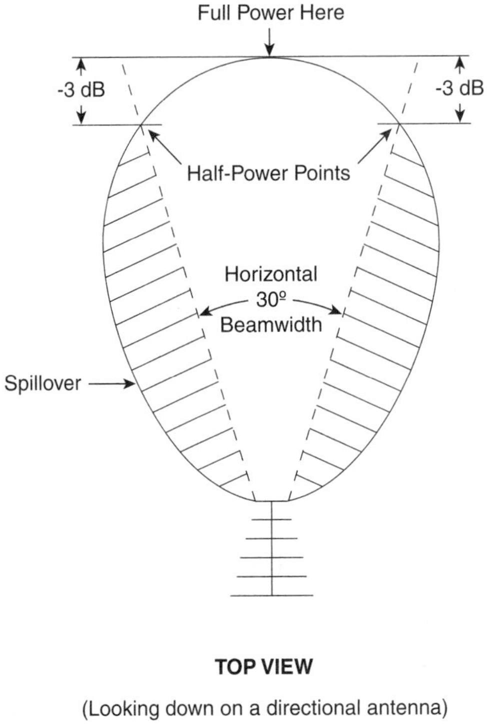

Full Power Here

-3 dB   -3 dB

Half-Power Points

Horizontal
30º
Beamwidth

Spillover

TOP VIEW

(Looking down on a directional antenna)

Figure 2-18 shows an example of the vertical pattern of an omnidirectional antenna. This antenna has one main lobe extending outward in all directions (like a doughnut) from the antenna. The antenna sticks up like a pencil through the center of the doughnut.

Remember from the discussion of wireless spillover that wireless power does not stop and start exactly along a straight line but declines gradually with distance; therefore, a consistent method is needed to define the width of the main lobe. This method is visible in Figures 2-17 and 2-18. The smooth outlines of the main lobes show the approximate intensity of the wireless power at various distances away from the antenna, but the dotted lines inside the smooth lines enclose most of the power of the main lobe. These dotted lines pass through the *half-power points*—the points on each side of the center of the main lobe where the wireless power is one-half as strong as it is at the center of the lobe. The angle between the two dotted lines defines the horizontal or vertical beamwidth of the antenna.

Figure 2-18 *Vertical Beamwidth Showing Half-Power Points*

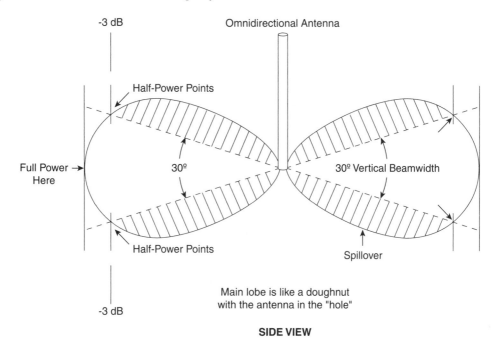

SIDE VIEW

Obtaining Wireless Line-of-Sight Paths

When a wireless signal encounters an obstruction, the signal is always attenuated and often reflected or diffracted. With outdoor wireless WANs, the attenuation from these encounters is usually so great that not enough signal remains to be detected at the other end of the link. When you design a wireless WAN link, it is important to work to achieve a wireless *line-of-sight (LOS)* path. This is a path that has no obstructions to significantly block, diffract, absorb, or attenuate the wireless signal. A wireless LOS path typically requires a visual LOS path plus additional path clearance to account for the spreading of the wireless signal. The following paragraphs describe visual and wireless LOS paths and help you understand how a wireless LOS path is different from a visual LOS path.

Visual LOS Path

If you can see from one antenna to the other, you have a visual LOS path, as shown in Figure 2-19. You might or might not have an unobstructed wireless LOS path.

Figure 2-19 *Visual LOS Path*

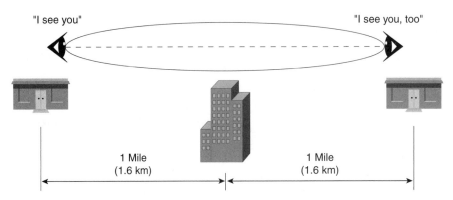

"I see you" "I see you, too"

1 Mile
(1.6 km)

1 Mile
(1.6 km)

Difference Between Visual and Wireless LOS Paths

How can there be a difference between the visual and the wireless LOS paths? There is a difference because of the vast difference between the wavelength of a wireless wave and the wavelength of a visible light wave. Figure 2-20 shows this physical wavelength difference.

Figure 2-20 *Difference Between Wireless Wavelength and Visible Wavelength*

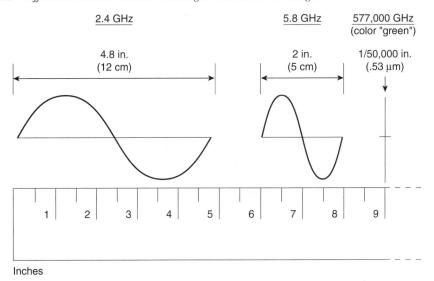

2.4 GHz

5.8 GHz

577,000 GHz
(color "green")

4.8 in.
(12 cm)

2 in.
(5 cm)

1/50,000 in.
(.53 µm)

1   2   3   4   5   6   7   8   9

Inches

The 2.4-GHz signal has a wavelength of 4.8 in. (12.5 cm). The 5.8-GHz wireless signal has a wavelength of 2 in. (5.3 cm). The light wave, which is green, has a wavelength of 1/50,000 of an inch (.53 micrometers), which is much shorter than either of the wireless signals. The wavelength of the green light wave is only approximately 1/100,000 as long as the wavelength of the 5.8-GHz wireless signal.

NOTE   A lightwave is similar to a wireless wave. Both lightwaves and wireless waves are forms of electromagnetic radiation. Although there is a substantial size difference between the wavelength of light and the wavelength of wireless, they both obey the same laws of physics as they propagate. You might want to think of wireless signals as lightwaves that the eye cannot see.

The shorter the wavelength of an electromagnetic wave, the less clearance it needs from the objects that it passes as it travels from Point A to Point B. The less clearance a wave needs, the closer the wave can pass to an obstruction without experiencing an additional loss in signal strength. The next section shows you how to calculate how close a wave can come to an obstruction without experiencing additional attenuation. This clearance distance is called the *Fresnel zone*. For now, look at the waves in Figure 2-21. Both a green lightwave and a 2.4-GHz wireless wave are traveling the same path and passing by the same building.

Figure 2-21   *Visual and Wireless LOS Paths*

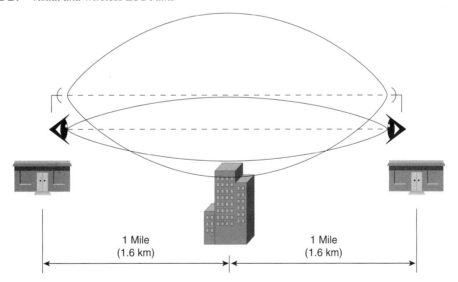

The short wavelength of the green light wave needs to clear the building only by a fraction of an inch to avoid being attenuated. All of the green light wave easily clears the building. The longer-wavelength 2.4-GHz wireless wave has a larger Fresnel zone and needs to clear the building by quite a few feet to avoid being attenuated. The next section provides more information about calculating the necessary Fresnel zone clearance.

Fresnel Zone

The concept of the Fresnel zone (pronounced "frA-nel"; the "s" is silent) provides a method of calculating the amount of clearance that a wireless wave (or a light wave) needs from an obstacle to ensure that the obstacle does not attenuate the signal. Figure 2-22 shows two ways to calculate the Fresnel zone clearance.

Figure 2-22 *Fresnel Zone Calculation*

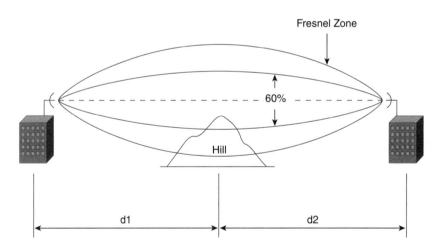

To calculate Fresnel Zone diameter in either
English or Metric units:

$$\text{diam} = \sqrt{\frac{\lambda(d1)(d2)}{(d1+d2)}} \qquad \lambda = \text{wavelength}$$

To calculate Fresnel Zone diameter in English units:

$$\text{diam (ft.)} = 72.1 \sqrt{\frac{(d1)(d2)}{f(d1+d2)}} \qquad \begin{array}{l} d1, d2 = \text{miles} \\ f = \text{GHz} \end{array}$$

The amount of Fresnel zone clearance is determined by the wavelength of the signal, the total path length, and the distance to the obstacle. The Fresnel zone is always widest in the middle of the path, between the two antennas. At least 60 percent of the calculated Fresnel zone must be clear to avoid significant signal attenuation. In Figure 2-22, the top of the hill extends so far into the Fresnel zone that 60 percent of the Fresnel zone is not clear; therefore, part of the signal will be attenuated. Figure 2-23 shows the calculation of Fresnel zone clearance for a green light wave over a two-mile path with a hill located at the middle of the path.

Figure 2-23   *Fresnel Zone Clearance for a Green Light*

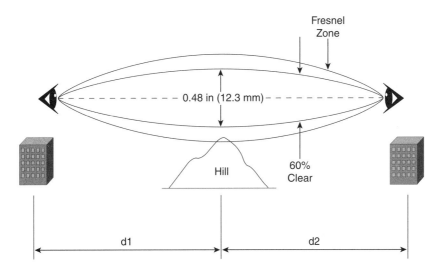

Fresnel Zone Diameter in Feet
d1, d2 = 1 mile
f = 577,000 GHz (Green Light)

$$\text{diam} = 72.1 \sqrt{\frac{(d1)(d2)}{f(d1+d2)}}$$

$$= 72.1 \sqrt{\frac{(1)(1)}{577,000\ (1+1)}} \quad = 72.1 \sqrt{\frac{1}{1,154,000}}$$

$$= 72.1 \sqrt{.0000008666} \quad = 72.1 \ (.000931)$$

$$= 0.0671 \text{ ft.} = 0.8 \text{ in.}$$

$$60\% \text{ of FZ} = 0.6\ (0.8) \text{ in.} = 0.48 \text{ in. (12.3 mm)}$$

Fresnel
Zone

— — — — — — — — 0.48 in (12.3 mm) — — — — — — — —

Hill

60%
Clear

d1   d2

Figure 2-24 shows the calculation of Fresnel zone clearance for a 2.4-GHz signal over the same two-mile path.

Figure 2-24 *Fresnel Zone Clearance for 2.4 GHz*

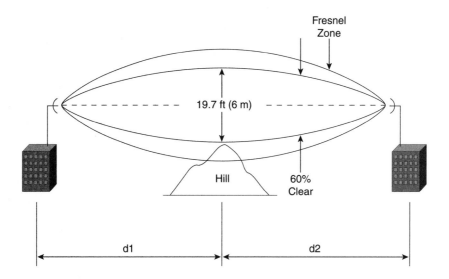

Fresnel Zone Diameter in Feet
d1, d2 = 1 mile
f = 2.4 GHz

$$\text{diam.} = 72.1 \sqrt{\frac{(d1)(d2)}{f(d1+d2)}}$$

$$= 72.1 \sqrt{\frac{(1)(1)}{2.4\,(1+1)}} \qquad = 72.1 \sqrt{\frac{1}{4.8}}$$

$$= 72.1 \sqrt{.208} \qquad = 72.1\,(.456)$$

$$= 32.9 \text{ ft.}$$

60% of FZ = 0.6 (32.9) ft. = 19.7 ft. (6m)

The green light wave in Figure 2-23 must have a clear Fresnel zone diameter that is at least 0.48 in. (1.22 cm), or 60 percent of the calculated Fresnel zone diameter, to avoid being partially attenuated. The required clearance above the hill (the radius of the calculated 60 percent Fresnel zone diameter) is one-half of the diameter, so the green light wave must clear the hill by one-half of 0.48 in., or by 0.24 in. (0.61 cm).

The 2.4-GHz wireless wave in Figure 2-24 must have a clear Fresnel zone diameter that is at least by 19.7 ft (6 m), or 60 percent of the calculated Fresnel zone diameter, to avoid being partially attenuated. The required clearance above the hill (the radius of the calculated 60 percent Fresnel zone diameter) is one-half of the diameter, so the wireless wave must clear the hill by one-half of 19.7 ft, or by 9.85 ft (3 m).

You can see from Figures 2-23 and 2-24 how a visual LOS path can exist that allows you to see from Point A to Point B with no attenuation, whereas a wireless wave traveling the same path *will* experience significant additional attenuation. Many times in your life, you have heard the expression, "Seeing is believing." Figures 2-23 and 2-24 provide a graphic example that, when you are working with wireless, "Seeing is *not* believing." In other words, just because you can see to the other end of a wireless path, do not believe that you have a clear LOS wireless path. The clear, visual LOS path does *not* mean that you have an attenuation-free wireless path. You must calculate the size of the Fresnel zone and confirm that the clearance above any obstacle(s) is at least equal to one-half of 60 percent of the Fresnel zone diameter.

Wireless Link Budget

A wireless link budget calculation totals the signal gains, subtracts the signal losses over the length of a wireless link, and predicts whether the signal level that arrives at the receiver will be high enough for the link to work reliably. If the link budget predicts that the link will *not* work reliably, you can examine the gain of each link budget element to see which elements to change and by how much to get the link to work.

NOTE   The following link budget discussion explains the link budget elements as if the signal path went only one way: from Transmitter A to Receiver B. Wireless WAN links in the real world operate in both directions—with a transmitter and a receiver at each end of every link. Therefore, your two-way wireless links have two link budgets—one in each direction. Due to differences in transmitter power or receiver sensitivity, the link budgets in each direction can be different.

The individual link budget elements are as follows:

- Transmitter power output
- Transmitter antenna system coaxial cable (transmission line) loss
- Transmitting antenna gain
- Free-space path loss
- Receiving antenna gain
- Receiver antenna system transmission line loss
- Receiver sensitivity threshold

Transmitter Output Power

The transmitter generates power and delivers it to the transmitter output connector. This power level is specified in dBm—decibels referenced to 1 mW. Typical transmitter output powers range from 10 mW (+10 dBm) to 1W (+30 dBm). Transmitter output power adds to the link budget.

Transmitter Antenna System Transmission Line Loss

The transmitter antenna system coaxial cable or transmission line carries power from the transmitter output connector to the transmitting antenna. Some power is lost in the cable (and in the cable connectors and lightning arrestor) during this process. The smaller the diameter of the cable and the shorter the wireless wavelength (the higher the frequency), the more power that is lost. Typical power losses at 2.4 GHz are 7 dB for each 100-ft length of 3/8-in. diameter cable. The total transmission line loss is subtracted from the link budget.

TIP   Always design your wireless links to minimize the length of the antenna cables. Place the transmitter and the receiver as close as possible to the antenna. By doing this, you maximize the distance and the reliability of your wireless links.

Transmitting Antenna Gain

The transmitting antenna receives power from the transmission line. The antenna focuses and concentrates this power and radiates it toward the distant receiver. This focusing ability results in an effective power gain in the direction of the antenna's main lobe. For 2.4-GHz antennas, gains typically range from +6 dBi to +24 dBi. The transmitting antenna gain adds to the link budget.

Free-Space Path Loss

You must pay a price to use the magic of wireless. That price is that most of the wireless energy that leaves your transmitting antenna is lost—gone forever. Only a tiny fraction of the transmitted energy ever arrives at the receiving antenna. How much of the energy actually arrives? If you have a 2.4-GHz signal that travels 1 mile, your receiving antenna catches less than 1 ten billionth of the energy that you radiated from your transmitting antenna. All the energy that is lost (remember that there is no wire present) is called the *free-space path loss*. The longer the wireless path and the shorter the wavelength of the wireless signal, the higher the free-space path loss. The free-space path loss can be calculated using the following formula:

$$PL = 96.6 + 10 \log(d^2) + 10 \log(f^2) \ \text{dB}$$

where f is the frequency in GHz and d is the distance in miles.

If you prefer to use metric units to compute the free-space path loss, here is the formula:

PL = 92.4 + 20 log(f) + 20 log(d) dB

where f is the frequency in GHz and d is the distance in km.

Table 2-3 shows several examples of free-space path loss for the 2.4-GHz and 5.7-GHz frequency bands.

Table 2-3   *Examples of Free-Space Path Loss*

	Free-Space Path Loss at 1 Mile (1.6 km)	Free-Space Path Loss at 2 Miles (3.2 km)
2.4 GHz	104 dB	110 dB
5.7 GHz	112 dB	118 dB

Wireless Is Magic!

If you stop and think about wireless signals for a minute, you will probably agree with the statement, *"Wireless is magic."* You know — invisible energy waves that carry voices, pictures, and information almost instantly through the air, through you, and even through interplanetary space at distances of thousands, and sometimes millions of miles. Only a tiny fraction of the transmitted energy ever arrives at the receiving end, and yet wireless works! Wireless has seemed like magic to me since I was 10 years old.

Receiving Antenna Gain

The receiving antenna works like the transmitting antenna to concentrate energy, but in reverse. The receiving antenna gathers and concentrates the small amount of power that reaches it at the far end of a wireless link. Think for a moment about the catcher in a game of baseball. The receiving antenna works a lot like the catcher's glove. The larger the glove, the easier it is for the catcher to grab the ball that the pitcher throws. The larger your receiving antenna, the easier it is for the antenna to grab the incoming signal — and the more signal that the antenna grabs. The more signal the antenna receives, the more gain that is added to the link budget.

Receiver Antenna System Transmission Line Loss

The receiving antenna system transmission line carries power from the receiving antenna to the receiver input. Just like with the transmitter antenna system transmission line, some power is lost in the cable during this process. This cable loss subtracts from the link budget.

Receiver Sensitivity Threshold

Each receiver has a *threshold level*—a minimum level of signal where the receiver just starts to operate. The receiver cannot detect signals below this threshold. The receiver antenna system (receiving antenna plus transmission line) must deliver a signal that is at or above this threshold for the wireless link to begin to operate. A typical threshold for an 11-Mbps 2.4-GHz wireless link receiver is around –85 dBm. The smaller (the more negative) this number is, the more sensitive the receiver is. For example, a receiver that has a threshold of –90 dBm is more sensitive than a receiver that has a threshold of –85 dBm.

NOTE   There is a tradeoff between receiver sensitivity and receiver data rate. Generally, the higher the data rate of the receiver, the less sensitive the receiver is. For example, a receiver that has a threshold of –85 dBm at a data rate of 2 megabits per second (2 Mbps) might have a threshold of only –80 dBm at a data rate of 11 Mbps. If you compare the sensitivities of two different receivers, be sure you compare them at the same data rate (or bandwidth) setting.

Fade Margin

The reason for calculating a wireless link budget is to design and build a reliable wireless link. Microwave signals normally interact with many objects in their environment, as discussed throughout this chapter. Therefore, fading is a normal condition for all microwave links. To overcome the effects of this fading and to provide reliable service, every microwave link needs a certain amount of extra signal, over and above the minimum receiver threshold level. This extra signal is called the *fade margin*. Another term sometimes used for this extra signal is *system-operating margin (SOM)*. Most wireless equipment manufacturers recommend a minimum fade margin of at least +10 dB to ensure reliable link performance. In general, the longer the link, the more fluctuation in signal levels and the greater the fade margin needs to be. Figure 2-25 shows a sample link budget calculation, including the calculated fade margin.

Figure 2-25   *Link Budget and Fade Margin Calculations*

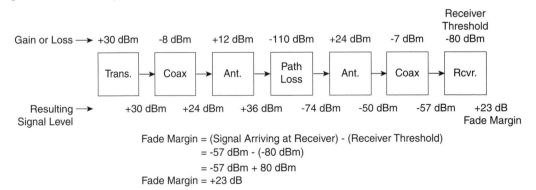

By calculating the fade margin, you can predict the reliability of a wireless link. The 2-mile long link shown in Figure 2-25 has a fade margin of +23 dB. +23 dB is 13 dB more than the 10 dB fade margin needed to make this link perform reliably; therefore, you can conclude that this link is going to deliver excellent reliability.

TIP   It is important that you measure the fade margin of every link that you install. Even though the calculated fade margin might be 10 dB or more, it is possible that installation mistakes or local noise conditions could reduce the performance of your real-world links. After you measure the fade margin, you can be sure that the link will operate reliably. Chapter 7, "Installing Outdoor Wireless Systems," covers the fade margin measurement process in detail.

Doubling the Link Distance

Doubling the distance of a wireless link requires four times more signal power, not twice the power like intuition would suggest. Wireless signal power declines as the square of the distance covered. Doubling the distance of the wireless link requires 2^2, or four times, the power. Four times the power is +6 dB (as shown in Figure 2-13).

After you have measured the fade margin on a link, you can predict how far the link can be extended. For example, the fade margin on the 2-mile 2.4-GHz link in Figure 2-25 is +23 dB. Doubling the distance requires four times (+6 dB) more power. Starting from the 2-mile fade margin of +23 dB and subtracting 6 dB leaves a remaining fade margin of +17 dB. This is 7 dB more than the minimum required fade margin of 10 dB; therefore, you can double the distance of this link to 4 miles and still have a reliable link. Of course, these figures are true only if both the 2-mile and the 4-mile link have unobstructed wireless LOS paths.

If you calculate or measure a fade margin of less than 10 dB (or whatever value of fade margin the manufacturer of your equipment recommends), you need to increase the power or reduce the loss of one or more of the system elements shown in Figure 2-25. You can increase the transmitter power, reduce the transmission line loss, use a larger antenna, or use a more sensitive receiver. Any of these improvements will increase the fade margin and improve the reliability of your link.

Tips for Planning Long Wireless Links

The longer a wireless link, the more important it is to properly design and plan the link so that it will provide you with reliable performance. The following sections provide some reminders to help you plan longer, reliable wireless links. Consider your links that are longer than about 7 miles (11 km) to be long links.

Antenna Height

As you know, the earth is curved. The distance to the radio horizon is 7.75 miles (12.5 km) for an antenna that is mounted 30 ft (9 m) above the ground, assuming a k-factor of 4/3.

Longer link distances require that you mount your antennas higher above the ground to extend your radio horizon. You can calculate the distance in miles to the radio horizon by multiplying 1.415 times the square root of the height of your antenna (in feet) above the ground. You can calculate the distance in kilometers to the radio horizon by multiplying 4.124 times the square root of the height of your antenna (in meters) above the ground.

Fresnel Zone

You know that a wireless wave needs a clearance (Fresnel) zone from objects that it passes close to. You also know that the size of this Fresnel zone is largest in the middle of a wireless path and that the Fresnel zone size increases both with longer distances and with higher frequencies.

The longer your link, the higher above the earth your antennas need to be mounted so that the part of your wireless wave closest to the earth can maintain an adequate Fresnel zone clearance above the earth.

Atmospheric Refraction (k-Factor)

You have learned that the k-factor varies depending on the temperature, the water vapor, and the barometric pressure of the atmosphere. The k-factor is usually greater than 1, bending microwave signals around the earth and extending the radio horizon beyond the visual horizon by approximately 15 percent. Sometimes, however, the k-factor can be less than 1, causing microwave signals to bend away from the Earth and causing the radio horizon to be closer than the visual horizon.

The longer a wireless link, the more regions of the atmosphere the wireless wave passes through and the more frequently the k-factor changes. These k-factor changes result in more frequent changes in your wireless path and more frequent fading. You need to allow a higher fade margin.

Link Budget

You remember that a reliable wireless link requires each receiver to receive a signal that fits both of the following conditions:

- Is above the receiver threshold
- Is high enough above the threshold to fade (usually at least 10 dB) and still remain above the threshold

The transmitter power, transmission line loss, antenna gain, and receiver sensitivity might need to be adjusted to maintain an adequate fade margin. The longer your wireless link, the more variation in signal strength and the more fade margin you need.

A rule-of-thumb that I like to use is to add 1 decibel of additional fade margin (above the original 10 dB) for every additional mile beyond 10 miles of link distance.

Long-Link Strategies

To successfully design, plan, install, and test long links, consider doing some (or all) of the following:

* Get help from wireless equipment vendors to select equipment and antenna systems with appropriate fade margins.

* Consult advanced wireless engineering textbooks (see the books in Appendix B, "Wireless Hardware, Software, and Service Provider Organizations").

* Consult with people (both paid and unpaid) who have more hands-on wireless experience than you do.

* Install the links carefully; pay particular attention to mounting the antennas firmly and aligning them correctly.

* Allow more time to test longer wireless links before placing them into service.

* Monitor your long links to be sure that they are providing reliable service.

* Enjoy the journey. Although long wireless links require you to spend more time and energy to do it right, the rewards for you in personal satisfaction are substantial and long lasting. Have fun with wireless — after all, whether you realize it or not, wireless is having fun with you.

Review Questions

1 How does the wavelength of a wireless signal change as the frequency of the signal increases?

2 When a 2.4-GHz signal encounters an obstruction, what happens?

3 Does ionospheric reflection occur at microwave frequencies?

4 How is wireless power measured?

5 In the abbreviation dBm, what does the "m" stand for?

6 If 1 Watt equals +30 dBm, then 2W equals how many dBm?

7 The main lobe of a non-isotropic antenna radiates power in which direction?

    A   In one horizontal direction

    B   In two horizontal directions

    C   Equally in all horizontal directions

    D   Both A and C

8 If you can stand at one antenna and see the antenna at the other end of a wireless link, do you have a line-of-sight wireless path?

9 Tripling the distance on an unobstructed wireless link requires increasing the power how many times?

CHAPTER 3

Choosing Your Network Architecture

This chapter helps you evaluate the four major wireless network architectures and choose the most appropriate architecture for your network. Specifically, this chapter does the following:

- Describes four wireless network architectures: point-to-point, point-to-multipoint, cellular, and mesh

- Explains the advantages and disadvantages of each of these architectures

- Provides examples of each architecture

- Assists you in evaluating, drafting, and designing your own wireless network using one or more of the four architectures

Point-to-Point Architecture

The point-to-point architecture is the simplest of all four wireless network architectures. It connects one single point to another single point, as illustrated by Figure 3-1.

Figure 3-1   *Point-to-Point Architecture*

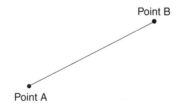

Advantages of Point-to-Point Architecture

The advantages of point-to-point architecture include the following processes that are faster, simpler, and less costly when compared to other wireless network architectures:

- Antenna selection

- Line-of-sight (LOS) determination

- Site surveys
- Hardware costs
- Facility costs
- Installation
- Testing
- Support

Antenna Selection

Point-to-point wireless networks should use directional antennas whenever possible. Directional antennas focus and radiate the signal in just one direction. This directivity has two important advantages: maximizing signal strength and minimizing noise pickup. In a point-to-point network, each endpoint needs to radiate a signal in only one direction; therefore, every point-to-point network should use a directional antenna at each endpoint. Selecting a directional antenna is a simple, straightforward process compared to selecting an antenna for a point-to-multipoint network, for example.

TIP   Chapter 5, "Selecting Antenna Systems," contains more information about antenna selection. Please resist the urge to use omnidirectional (omni) antennas in point-to-point networks. Omnis minimize cost and shorten the installation process slightly, but they are more susceptible to interference and they cause unnecessary interference to other wireless networks. Always use directional antennas for both ends of point-to-point links.

LOS Determination

Between each network location, you need a wireless LOS path.

NOTE   Remember from Chapter 2, "Understanding Wireless Fundamentals," that a wireless LOS path means that there is *both* an unobstructed visual path *and* an unobstructed Fresnel Zone clearance between the two antennas.

A point-to-point wireless network requires *only one* LOS path. Because only one path is needed, confirmation of this single LOS path is a fairly quick process. More complex network architectures require the confirmation of *many* simultaneous LOS paths; this confirmation is a longer, more complex process.

Site Surveys

There are two types of site surveys:

- **A physical site survey**—Should be performed for every location on a wireless network

- **A radio frequency (RF) site survey**—Should be performed for each hub site on a wireless network

---

NOTE   Chapter 4, "Performing Site Surveys," describes in detail how to perform both types of site surveys.

A point-to-point wireless network requires that you perform physical site surveys for only the two network endpoints. Neither endpoint is a wireless hub site that would require a more complex and time-consuming RF site survey. It is faster and less complex to perform the site surveys required for a point-to-point network than for most other wireless architecture.

Hardware Costs

The endpoint of a point-to-point network communicates with only one other endpoint. Compare this to the more complex hub site of a point-to-multipoint network that communicates with 2 to 30 (or more) endpoints. If only a few network endpoints need to be connected, hardware and software costs are lower for point-to-point network equipment when compared to more complex network architectures.

Facility Costs

Facility costs include the following:

- Renting or leasing space for wireless equipment
- Renting or leasing tower or roof space for wireless antennas
- Electrical power and backup power systems

These costs are lower in a point-to-point network, which requires less equipment space, rooftop space, and backup power.

Installation

Installation costs are lower in a point-to-point network because you need to install only two network endpoints, consequently minimizing the costs for the following:

- Installing the wireless equipment
- Installing the antennas, antenna cabling, and antenna mounting hardware
- Installing the amplifiers (if used)
- Managing the installation process

Testing

Testing is an essential step for every new wireless network. Testing is necessary to ensure that the network is ready to provide reliable wireless service. The test process for a point-to-point network is shorter and less complex compared to the test process needed for a more complex architecture.

Support

Network monitoring and network support are necessary functions in every wireless network. A license-free network can experience sudden throughput deterioration caused by noise, interference, antenna problems, and equipment problems. It is less expensive to support a small point-to-point network than it is to support a larger, more complex network architecture.

Disadvantages of Point-to-Point Architecture

Many successful network deployments eventually result in an expansion of the network to serve more end users. The disadvantages of a point-to-point network architecture occur because this expansion process includes several requirements that might be difficult or costly to satisfy. These requirements include the following:

- LOS path availability
- Backbone bandwidth availability
- Antenna system expansion
- A low-noise hub site
- Ability to upgrade equipment

LOS Path Availability

All current license-free wireless networks operate in the microwave frequency range and transmit at relatively low power levels. When a microwave signal encounters an obstruction, the signal experiences a combination of the following:

- Attenuation
- Reflection
- Diffraction

In every case, the signal is attenuated (reduced in power). Usually, the attenuated signal is too weak to provide a reliable wireless link. To preserve enough signal strength to provide a reliable link, it is important to have an unobstructed LOS path between network endpoints.

Typically, expanding a point-to-point network results in it becoming a point-to-multipoint network. Point-to-multipoint architecture is described in more detail in the next section, but briefly, it consists of one hub location that connects to more than one end user location.

Expansion of a point-to-point network into a point-to-multipoint network is not possible if LOS paths do not exist between one of the old endpoints and all (or most) of the new end user locations. Determining if the needed LOS paths exist requires site surveys and sometimes requires path testing.

TIP   When performing site surveys for a new point-to-point wireless network, always evaluate each network endpoint to see if it could serve as a future hub site for an expanded point-to-multipoint network. For example, a site that is mostly surrounded by trees and nearby hills would have few LOS paths in other directions. The site would not be a good candidate for a future hub location.

Backbone Bandwidth Availability

The expansion of a point-to-point network to become a point-to-multipoint network requires additional backbone bandwidth at the hub site to meet the needs of the additional users. This backbone bandwidth might be either LAN bandwidth (in the case of a corporate network) or Internet access bandwidth (in the case of an Internet service provider [ISP]). A point-to-point network that does not have additional backbone bandwidth available cannot be easily expanded.

Antenna System Expansion

The hub site of a point-to-multipoint network serves many users in several different directions, often using different radios and different frequencies. A hub site antenna system consists of several antennas. When a point-to-point network needs to be expanded, additional antenna space might be difficult to obtain for the following reasons:

- The space might not be physically available on the rooftop.
- Building management might not allow additional antennas because of concerns about the building's appearance.
- The cost of leasing additional rooftop space might be too high to be affordable.
- Zoning regulations might limit the number, height, or appearance of rooftop antennas.

TIP	When you negotiate an agreement to install a point-to-point antenna system, try to include permission to install additional antennas, if needed, in the future.

Low-Noise Hub Site

Proper operation of a wireless network occurs only when the wireless equipment receives a signal that is substantially stronger than the noise and interference. A strong signal alone does not make a wireless link work well; a strong signal together with a low noise level make a wireless link work well. In other words, a high ratio of signal to noise (signal-to-noise ratio, or SNR) makes the network work well.

NOTE	*Noise* is everything that is not the desired signal. Noise includes undesired signals, industrial noise, natural noise, and so forth.

A point-to-point network uses a directional antenna that is aimed toward only one other antenna. This directivity maximizes the received signal and minimizes interference and noise coming from all other directions.

Upgrading a point-to-point network to a point-to-multipoint network results in changing the antenna system from a very directional one to a less directional one. The new antenna covers a wider area; therefore, it picks up more noise and interference. If the new level of interference and noise is too high, the SNR might be too low for reliable point-to-multipoint operation.

TIP	Make it a habit always to look and plan ahead. When you perform a physical site survey for a point-to-point network, consider performing radio frequency (RF) site surveys also. By examining the level of wireless noise, you can determine if the noise level is low enough to allow a point-to-multipoint hub to be placed there in the future.

Ability to Upgrade Equipment

The features and configuration capability of wireless equipment varies widely. It is always good to re-use wireless equipment instead of throwing or giving it away when the network is upgraded.

Some point-to-point equipment can be reconfigured to work in a point-to-multipoint network, but other equipment cannot be reconfigured. If you expect that your point-to-point network might need to be upgraded to a point-to-multipoint network, be sure to select equipment that has reconfiguration capability.

Examples of When to Use Point-to-Point Architecture

The following examples describe situations in which a point-to-point architecture is the most appropriate choice.

Two Network Locations Only

Point-to-point architecture is best when you have only two locations that need to be connected and the network most likely will not be expanded in the future. Point-to-point architecture minimizes the costs, deployment time, and experience level needed to get your network up and running.

Longer-Than-Normal Links

If you need a network link that is longer than normal, point-to-point architecture is the best choice.

NOTE   Ahhh, but just how long is a normal link, you ask? In general, a normal link can be as short as one block or as long as 10 miles (16 km).

If you are planning a link that is longer than normal, such as a 15- or a 30-mile (24- to 48-km) backbone link, plan on point-to-point. A long link needs the following:

- High-gain antennas to focus all the signal strength toward the other end
- Directional antennas to reduce the interference and noise coming from all other directions
- Antennas mounted high above the ground to prevent the earth from intruding into the Fresnel zone

The antenna systems used for a point-to-multipoint network are too broad to use on a long point-to-point link. Their gain is too low and their beamwidth is too wide to provide the high signal strength and low noise that a long point-to-point link needs.

High Noise Level

When a particular location has a high noise level, it is likely that only a point-to-point link will work at that location. A high-noise location needs the higher signal levels and lower noise levels that only a directional high-gain antenna can provide. A point-to-multipoint antenna system would be overcome by the noise.

Path Obstructions

Often, a site has many nearby obstructions, such as tall mountains or tall surrounding buildings. A site like this might work as an endpoint on a point-to-point network or even as an endpoint on a point-to-multipoint network. The site might not be a good location for a point-to-multipoint hub site.

Point-to-Multipoint Architecture

A point-to-multipoint wireless network can be an economical way of providing connectivity from a single hub site to many end user locations. The wireless equipment at the hub site is referred to as the *access point*. The equipment at each end user location is generally referred to as the *customer premises equipment (CPE)* or *client equipment*. Point-to-multipoint architecture is often used, for example, to provide connectivity between buildings that are located in a campus environment. Another use of point-to-multipoint architecture is to provide wireless Internet access service from one ISP location to many end user locations. Depending on the number of locations that need to be connected, the hub site might be divided into several sectors to increase network capacity.

NOTE   Think of a sector as one slice of a whole pie. Each sector faces in one specific direction and serves only the users who are located in that direction.

Each sector usually has its own dedicated radio, antenna system, and frequency. Figure 3-2 shows a diagram of a typical point-to-multipoint network with no sectorization.

Figure 3-2   *Point-to-Multipoint Architecture (No Sectorization)*

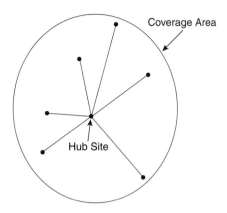

Figure 3-3 shows a diagram of a typical point-to-multipoint network with a three-sector hub site.

Figure 3-3   *Point-to-Multipoint Architecture (Three Sectors)*

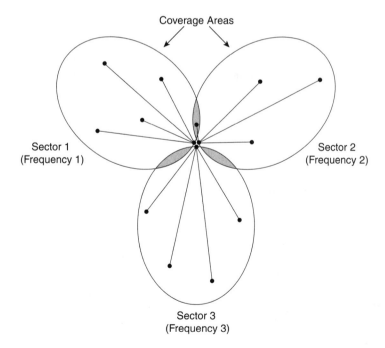

A point-to-multipoint network can have one to six (or more) sectors. Most networks have two or three sectors. Although no specific rules exist for deciding how many sectors to build, it is important to plan to meet both the current and the future bandwidth needs of your users. If you have 100 heavy business users on an 11-megabit per second (Mbps) wireless network, you should plan to build more than one 11-Mbps sector to avoid network congestion and slow performance. If, on the other hand, you have only five residential users on an 11-Mbps network, one sector might be enough to meet the bandwidth needs of these users.

Advantages of Point-to-Multipoint Architecture

The advantages of point-to-multipoint architecture are as follows:

- Cost effective for many users
- Scalable
- Open for the testing of new technology

Cost Effective for Many Users

Point-to-multipoint architecture is a cost-effective way to serve many end users from one central site; all the end users share the same central site equipment. When a new user needs to be added to the network, the only new equipment that needs to be purchased is for that one new user. No new hub site equipment is needed. Compare this to a point-to-point network in which *two* radios would be needed if *one* new user needed connectivity to an existing point-to-point wireless network.

Scalable

A point-to-multipoint network is easily scaled up for more users. Every time a new hub site radio (or hub site sector) is added, several end user locations can be added.

Open for Testing of New Technology

A point-to-multipoint network that has a sectorized hub site makes the testing and introduction of upgraded hardware or software possible. For example, with a three-sector hub, new software can be installed and tested on just one of the three sectors. End users on the other two sectors can continue to use the older software until the new software has been tested and verified. When the new software proves to be stable, it can be installed on the other two sectors.

Disadvantages of Point-to-Multipoint Architecture

The disadvantages of point-to-multipoint architecture, when compared to point-to-point architecture, include the following:

- Bandwidth management
- Antenna selection
- LOS determination
- Site surveys
- Initial hardware costs
- Facility costs
- Installation costs
- Testing
- Support

Bandwidth Management

The bandwidth management process is more complex within a point-to-multipoint network because many users are sharing the access point (or sector) bandwidth.

Antenna Selection

Access point antenna selection is more demanding in a point-to-multipoint network. If the area to be covered is a relatively small area (one mile [1.6 km] in diameter, for example) and if the number of end users is small (for example, 20 or less), a simple one-sector access point using an omnidirectional antenna might be all that is needed. More often, however, the following conditions are present:

- The area to be covered is several miles/km in diameter with trees, buildings, or other obstructions present.

- The number of end users is 20 or more, and the number of end users is expected to increase.

- The level of interference is high, as it likely will be if other unlicensed networks exist in the same general area.

When any of these conditions occurs, proper design and selection of the antenna system components are especially important. Improper antenna design or selection limits network throughput and prevents the network from delivering satisfactory wireless service.

LOS Determination

The requirement for LOS paths to all the potential end users complicates the selection of a hub site location for a point-to-multipoint network. The time needed to verify the existence of these line-of-sight paths can be substantial. The more potential end users that are on the network, the more time that will be needed to verify LOS.

NOTE   As this chapter is being written, many wireless manufacturers have begun to advertise wireless equipment with near-line-of-sight or non-line-of-sight (both abbreviated as NLOS) capabilities. The NLOS definition is vague and is used loosely at this time.

Few point-to-multipoint NLOS systems have actually been installed and operated under real-world conditions at the present time; therefore, it is not yet possible to verify the accuracy of these advertising claims. For more information, please see the NLOS discussion in Chapter 6, "Evaluating and Selecting Wireless Equipment."

Site Surveys

Compared to a point-to-point network, a point-to-multipoint network serves many more end users; therefore, the network site survey times are longer. More importantly, the time needed to perform adequate hub site surveys and to select the best hub site locations is longer. Chapter 4 describes the physical and radio frequency (RF) site survey processes.

Initial Hardware Costs

The initial hub site (access point) hardware costs for a point-to-multipoint network are higher than for a point-to-point network. These higher costs occur because of the need for more antennas, antenna cables, connectors, equipment cabinets, power supplies, and backup power systems. Often, the cost of the access point wireless equipment is also higher. Total hardware costs (including CPE) for a point-to-multipoint network with 20 users can range from $8000 to more than $100,000.

Facility Costs

An access point (hub) site probably costs more to use per month than a point-to-point site. Rental or leasing rates might be higher due to the possible need for more equipment and rooftop antenna space, as well as the greater amount of electrical power consumed.

Installation Costs

The installation costs for a point-to-multipoint access point site are higher than for a point-to-point site. The reason is simple; the labor cost is higher to install more equipment, cabling, antenna systems, and power systems.

Testing

An access point in a point-to-multipoint network serves many customers located over a wide geographic area. The test time needed to confirm reliable coverage over this area can be substantial. Reliable wireless coverage requires more than end users being able to hear the access point. It also requires the access point being able to hear the end users. It might take days, weeks, or months to test and adjust an access point so that it provides reliable two-way service throughout the coverage area.

Support

The support costs to maintain a point-to-multipoint network are substantially higher than for a point-to-point network. These support costs include monitoring network performance, maintaining network hardware, responding to possible interference problems, and maintaining network security.

Examples of When to Use Point-to-Multipoint Architecture

Point-to-multipoint architecture is the best choice when many end users are located in the same general area, such as in the same small city or in the same part of a larger city.

Cellular Architecture

When point-to-multipoint networks are connected to the same backbone network and designed to allow the same frequencies to be re-used in different areas, the result is a cellular network. The backbone network might be either wired or wireless. Figure 3-4 shows a diagram of a cellular network that includes three point-to-multipoint networks.

Figure 3-4 *Cellular Architecture*

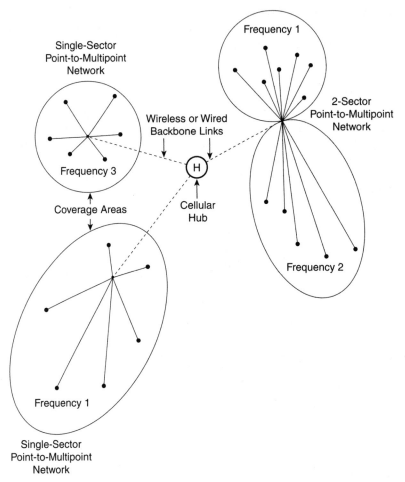

Advantages of Cellular Architecture

The advantages of using a cellular architecture are as follows:

- Expands the geographical coverage area
- Increases the network capacity
- Leverages the use of network resources
- Provides redundant end user coverage
- Allows roaming

Expands the Geographical Coverage Area

Each point-to-multipoint network (or sector) within a cellular network is considered to be one cell. A cellular network with multiple cells can cover a larger geographical area than a single point-to-multipoint network. A wireless Internet service provider (WISP) that wants to extend coverage to a new area can add a new wireless (or wired) backbone lnk and then install one or more new wireless access points in the new area.

Increases the Network Capacity

Each additional cell in a cellular network increases the number of end users that the network can serve. For example, a cellular network with two cells can serve twice as many end users as a single point-to-multipoint network.

Leverages the Use of Network Resources

A cellular network allows the sharing of network resources between large numbers of end users. These resources include backbone bandwidth network administration, maintenance, and monitoring. These resources are typically supplied from the same network hub location.

Provides Redundant End User Coverage

Cells in a cellular network might be designed to overlap each other. If cells do overlap, end users might be able to obtain service from an adjacent cell if one cell is temporarily out of service. Sometimes, this requires re-aiming the end user's antenna. These resources are typically supplied from the same network hub location.

Allows Roaming

Roaming refers to the capability of an end user to move out of the coverage area of one cell and into the coverage area of another cell while retaining network connectivity. For example, cellular telephone networks are designed to provide roaming capability for mobile telephone users. In contrast, only a few outdoor networks that are used to provide Internet access service offer roaming.

NOTE   The 802.11b access points typically provide a roaming feature. This roaming feature works well within small, well-designed, indoor wireless LANs. This same roaming feature does *not* usually provide satisfactory roaming between large, outdoor wireless cells.

Disadvantages of Cellular Architecture

There is one primary disadvantage of a cellular architecture: it is important that nearby cells re-use the same spectrum space without interfering with each other. During installation, it is important to verify that mutual interference between cells is low.

Re-Using Limited Spectrum

License-free wireless bands have a limited amount of frequencies (spectrum space). A cellular architecture must be designed to re-use this spectrum space in a noninterfering fashion. Cells that use the same frequency (in a direct sequence spread spectrum system) or the same hopping sequence (in a frequency-hopping spread spectrum system) must be isolated from each other far enough so that interference between the cells does not reduce the throughput of the cells.

Verifying That Interference Is Low

One crucial task during the installation of a cellular network is to identify and eliminate interference between cells that are close together (and even between cells that are farther apart). Throughput testing confirms that interference between cells is low enough for satisfactory network operation.

Cells that use the same frequency should be throughput-tested simultaneously. The test process is as follows:

Step 1   Perform a throughput test (upload a file) from the farthest end user location to the access point location for one cell. Make a note of the throughput.

Step 2   Go to the nearest adjacent cell that uses the same frequency or hop sequence. Perform the same throughput test from the farthest end user location to the access point of the second cell. Make a note of the throughput.

Step 3   Perform the two throughput tests simultaneously and note the throughput from each end user location. If the throughput stays the same for both end user locations during the simultaneous test, enough isolation between the cells exists for satisfactory operation.

Step 4   If the throughput between either end user location and its corresponding access point is reduced when both tests are running simultaneously, you must increase the isolation between the access point antenna systems. Increasing the isolation might be as simple as redesigning one of the cell site antenna systems or as complicated as moving the cell site locations farther apart.

TIP	Be sure to allow additional test time when you are building and testing a cellular network. Take the time needed to test and minimize interference between cells. Failure to confirm during installation that the cells do not interfere with each other might make it necessary to interrupt service to the end users later and to redesign the network.

Examples of When to Use Cellular Architecture

Cellular architecture is the best choice when more end users exist than a single point-to-multipoint network can cover or when end users are located in different geographical areas—areas that just one point-to-multipoint network cannot cover. Cellular architecture is the most frequently selected method of expanding a point-to-multipoint network.

Mesh Architecture

Mesh architecture is a multipoint-to-multipoint architecture with one or more Internet interconnection points. In a mesh network, each network node can connect to any other network node that is turned on and within wireless range. Mesh networks are usually deployed in areas where many end users are located relatively close to each other, such as from one block up to one mile apart.

Each mesh network node performs two functions:

- As a wireless router/repeater
- As an end node

Packets can travel through several intermediate wireless nodes to reach the desired end user node. If one or more of the intermediate nodes is down, the packet is dynamically rerouted through other intermediate nodes. Figure 3-5 shows a diagram of a mesh architecture network.

Figure 3-5   *Mesh Architecture*

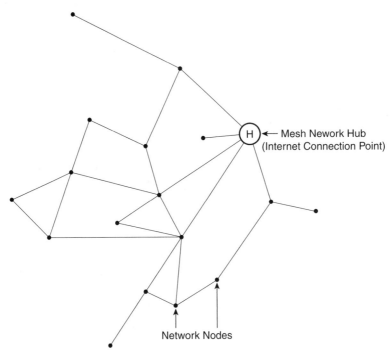

H ← Mesh Nework Hub
(Internet Connection Point)

Network Nodes

Advantages of Mesh Architecture

The advantages of mesh architecture are as follows:

- Near-line-of-sight coverage
- Routing redundancy
- Simpler network design process
- Simpler antenna installation

Near-Line-of-Sight Coverage

A clear LOS microwave path is always desirable between nodes in a wireless network. In many areas, clear LOS paths are difficult to achieve due to obstructions such as trees and buildings. In areas where LOS paths are partially obstructed, mesh architecture might allow reliable connectivity. This occurs because the network nodes are placed close enough together to allow reliable node-to-node-to-node communication in spite of the obstructions attenuating the signal strengths. The denser the obstructions, the higher the signal attenuation and the closer together the mesh nodes need to be placed.

Routing Redundancy

In a mesh network, every wireless node is a wireless router or repeater. Operating as a router, each node is capable of dynamically calculating the best available path to each distant node. If one node is down (due to failure, being turned off, or being blocked by an obstruction), network traffic is rerouted through other nearby nodes. This on-the-fly rerouting capability provides a measure of network routing redundancy.

Simpler Network Design Process

Point-to-multipoint and cellular network architectures require a moderately complex network design process to ensure that LOS paths exist between each end user location and the wireless access point. The network design process for a mesh architecture network is somewhat simpler. The node-to-node-to-node capability of a mesh network, where each node serves as a relay point, simplifies the network design process. As long as the network designer ensures that each node can communicate with at least one or two nearby nodes, network design can proceed without needing to verify the existence of longer LOS paths.

Simpler Antenna Installation

In a point-to-point or cellular network architecture, each end user location normally uses an antenna that is highly directional and that points back toward the wireless access point. This is desirable because of the need to maximize the signal strength and minimize the interference between the end user and the access point. Successful installation of this directional antenna requires that the appropriate high gain antenna be selected, mounted at or above a specific height, and then pointed in the specific direction of the access point. Each antenna installation must be completed with a fairly high level of precision and accuracy. In contrast, the antenna installation at a mesh network end user does not require the same high level of precision. In a mesh network, the typical end user antenna is not a directional antenna; it is an omnidirectional (omni) antenna. An omni allows the end user node to communicate in more than one direction so it can connect to more than one other node. The same omni antenna can be used at each end user location; it can normally be mounted at a standard (rooftop) height and does not need aiming in a particular direction.

Disadvantages of Mesh Architecture

The disadvantages of mesh architecture are as follows:

- More wireless nodes needed
- Progressive network deployment process
- Difficult bandwidth management

More Wireless Nodes Needed

In a mesh architecture, wireless paths are shorter than in other network architectures. This means that if the number of network nodes is equal, the coverage area of a mesh network is less than the coverage area of a point-to-multipoint network.

Progressive Network Deployment Process

A mesh network relies on the availability of point-to-point-to-point wireless repeating. This means that if a wireless node is installed beyond the range of the nodes that have already been installed, the new node will not be able to connect to the mesh network to obtain service. To prevent this problem, you must deploy a mesh network progressively within a particular service area. Deployment must begin near the Internet access point and continue outward toward the far edge of the mesh.

Difficult Bandwidth Management

Each end user node in a mesh network has dual roles:

- Wireless router or repeater
- End user node

The wireless bandwidth available to each end user node is shared between providing Internet access for that specific end user and providing backbone access for the other end users who are connecting to the Internet through that node. The more hops that exist between an end user and the Internet access point, the less bandwidth that is available to that end user. Managing this shared bandwidth dynamically with continuously changing customer bandwidth needs and backbone bandwidth needs is a challenge for the mesh network software.

Examples of When to Use Mesh Architecture

Mesh architecture is most appropriate when a number of end users are clustered closely together and numerous LOS obstructions exist. Throughput requirements of the users should also be fairly modest, such as up to a few hundred kilobits per second (kbps). One such environment would be a residential housing development where many trees obstruct the LOS paths between the houses. The short path lengths, alternate routing paths, and relatively modest throughput needs of the residents would make a mesh network the appropriate architectural choice.

Selecting the Preliminary Network Architecture

The presence of LOS paths between the proposed network locations is the major determining factor in selecting a network architecture and designing your network. Your final network might be a combination of the four architectures described in this chapter—that is perfectly all right. The terrain and the obstructions in every area are unique. This means that your final network architecture will also be unique. It will be constructed with LOS paths that fit around and over the obstructions in your area.

To select the most appropriate network architecture for your wireless WAN and design your actual wireless network, follow these steps:

Step 1 Map the locations of the end users.

Step 2 Evaluate point-to-point architecture.

Step 3 Group users by proximity.

Step 4 Evaluate point-to-multipoint architecture.

Step 5 Evaluate cellular architecture.

Step 6 Evaluate mesh architecture.

Step 7 Draft preliminary network architecture.

Step 8 Confirm hub site availability.

Step 9 Confirm end user site availability.

Step 10 Confirm site usability.

Steps 1 through 6 will help you select the most appropriate network architecture for your wireless WAN. Steps 7 through 10 will help you design your actual wireless network.

Step 1: Map the Locations of End Users

Obtain a topographical (topo) map that covers all the areas where potential network end users are located. A topographic map shows the terrain elevation at each location. Figure 3-6 shows a representation of a topographic map for the (fictional) area of Pleasantown, in the state of Harmony.

Figure 3-6   *Topographic Map of Pleasantown*

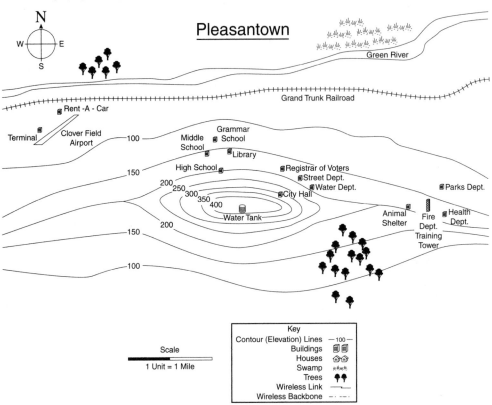

TIP   Topographic maps are available from map stores, bookstores, or (in the United States) the offices of the U.S. Geological Survey (USGS). For some areas, mapping software is available that makes it easy to prepare a custom topographic map for your area. See the "Wireless Link Planning Software" section of Appendix B, "Wireless Hardware, Software, and Service Provider Organizations," for a list of sources for maps and mapping software.

It is helpful to know the elevation of each end user location as well as the elevation of the terrain between the locations. This information helps to determine if an LOS path exists between the locations. On your map, mark the position and the approximate elevation of each end.

Step 2: Evaluate Point-to-Point Architecture

If only a few end-user locations exist, point-to-point architecture is often the best architectural choice. For example, Figure 3-7 shows the area around the Pleasantown airport.

Figure 3-7   *Point-to-Point Network*

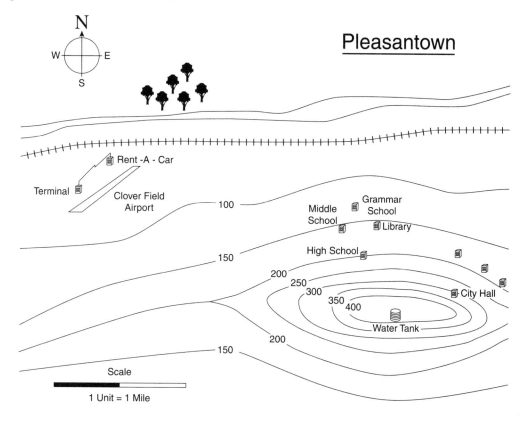

The airport terminal and the airport rent-a-car location need a broadband wireless network connection. These are the only two points that need to be connected. They are both at the same elevation and no obstructions stand between them. The LOS path, simple site survey, and low hardware cost make this an ideal situation for a point-to-point network. If your situation is roughly similar to this example, point-to-point architecture should be your choice. If, however, you have more than a few network end point locations, point-to-point might not be your best choice. Go to Step 3 to continue the evaluation and selection process.

Step 3: Group Users by Proximity

The existence of LOS paths is the most significant factor that affects your network architecture. There is a higher likelihood that end users who are located close to each other will have an unobstructed LOS path to a common access point location. Keeping this in mind, look at Figure 3-6 again. A number of end user locations exist that are close together and have shared LOS paths to access point locations.

In downtown Pleasantown, the grammar school, middle school, high school, and library are within one mile of each other. Also downtown, the Registrar of Voters, City Hall, Street Department, and Water Department are close together. On the east side of town, the animal shelter, the Fire Department training tower, the Health Department, and the Parks Department are within one mile.

Now, look at your own map and see if there are end user locations that are close together and that can be grouped together. If you have one or more such groups, plan on using either point-to-multipoint, cellular, or mesh architecture. Go to Step 4 to continue the architecture evaluation.

Step 4: Evaluate Point-to-Multipoint Architecture

Point-to-multipoint architecture provides economical service to a number of end users who all have an unobstructed LOS path to one high-level access point site. Figure 3-8 provides an example.

At the east edge of Pleasantown, the Animal Shelter, Health Department, Parks Department, and Fire Department training center are all located close together. The top of the Fire Department training tower is high enough to provide an LOS path to each of the other three locations. Together, these four locations can be grouped together into one single point-to-multipoint network. The access point antenna for the network can be mounted on top of the training tower.

On your map, identify any group (or groups) of users who appear to have LOS connectivity to a shared access point location. Consider this group as a potential point-to-multipoint network. The following list directs you to the next step:

- If you have just one group of users and they all appear to have an LOS path to a shared access point location, plan on using a point-to-multipoint architecture. Go to Step 7.

- If you have more than one group of users, each with its own access point location, go to Step 5.

- If many of your end users don't have an LOS path to an access point location, go to Step 6.

Figure 3-8 *Point-to-Multipoint Network*

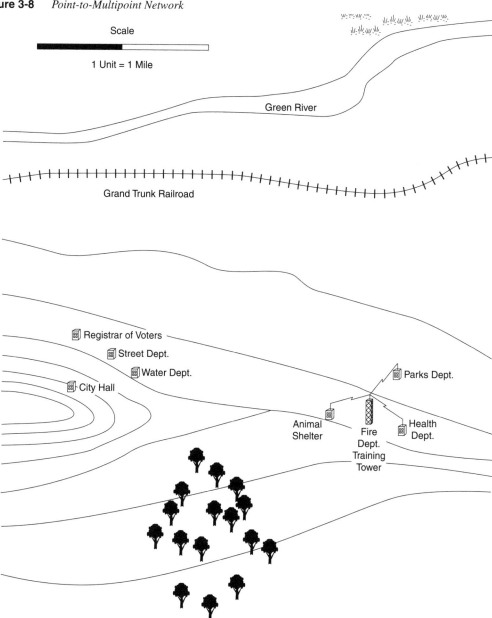

Step 5: Evaluate Cellular Architecture

Sometimes, an area might have more than one point-to-multipoint network, with each network served by its own access point. If several of these access point locations are then connected, the result is a cellular network.

Multiple Point-to-Multipoint Networks

Figure 3-8 identified one point-to-multipoint network at the east edge of town (Fire Department, Parks Department, Health Department, and Animal Shelter). If you look at the end user locations near the center of town in Figure 3-9, you see several other potential point-to-multipoint network possibilities.

Figure 3-9   *Multiple Point-to-Multipoint Networks*

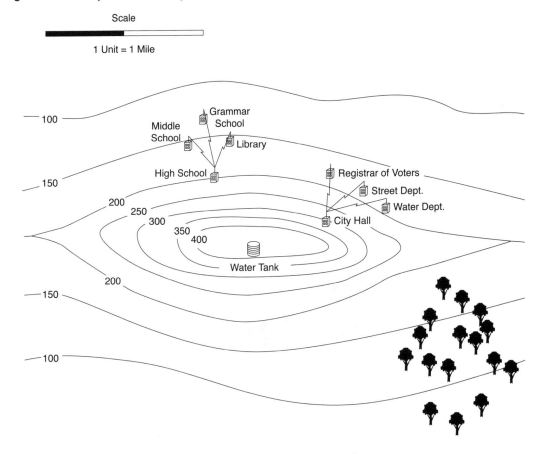

City Hall is located on the side of the hill approximately at a 300-foot (91 m) elevation. The Registrar of Voters, Street Department, and Water Department are each about one mile from City Hall and the elevation of each is about 175 feet (53 m). From the roof of City Hall, there is an LOS path to each of the other three locations. Together, these four locations can be combined into one point-to-multipoint network. The access point can be placed inside City Hall and the antenna can be placed on the roof.

Another point-to-multipoint network exists near the high school. From the roof of the high school (elevation 200 ft [61 m]), LOS paths exist to the library, grammar school, and middle school. An antenna system on the high school roof can supply connectivity to the other three locations.

Access Point Connectivity

Pleasantown now has three new access points, one for each of the three new point-to-multipoint networks. The access point antennas are on the Fire Department training tower, the City Hall roof, and the high school roof. If these three access points are connected together through a common location, a cellular network is created. Refer to Figure 3-10 to see if this is possible.

Figure 3-10 *Cellular Network Options*

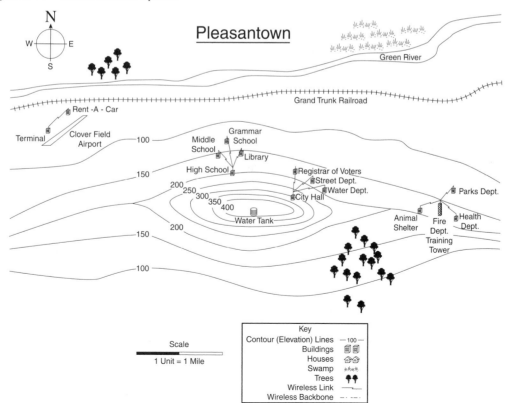

Do any locations exist in Pleasantown that have LOS paths to all three existing access points?

- The Fire Department training tower might be one possibility, but the LOS path from there to the high school is long (about 3.5 miles [5.6 km]), and the path is obstructed by City Hall.

- City Hall has LOS paths to both the Fire Department training tower and the high school. City Hall is one candidate to serve as the hub of a cellular network that would connect and serve all three of the point-to-multipoint networks in town.

- Another cellular network hub location is possible. The water tank on the top of the hill is located at an elevation of 400 ft (122 m). From the top of the tank, it is easy to see the high school, City Hall, and the Fire Department training tower. The tank can serve as the hub of a cellular network. Because the hilltop is the highest point around Pleasantown, it would also allow future expansion of the cellular network to new locations as the area grows.

On your map, identify any locations that appear to provide wireless connectivity to all your wireless access point locations. If you can identify one or more cellular hub site locations, plan on using a cellular architecture for your broadband wireless WAN, and then go to Step 7. If cellular architecture doesn't fit your area, go to Step 6.

Step 6: Evaluate Mesh Architecture

Occasionally, a group of potential wireless network end users are located close together, but they don't have LOS paths to a shared access point. Under these conditions, none of the previous network architectures provide reliable wireless service. One alternative is to evaluate mesh architecture as a possible solution.

Recently, Forest Shadows Estates was carved out of the woods southeast of Pleasantown. Many Forest Shadows Estates residents want broadband Internet access, but they are beyond digital subscriber line (DSL) range, and the cable television company does not offer Internet access.

Because of the number of trees in the area, none of the houses have an LOS path to any of the wireless access point locations in Pleasantown. Some houses have an LOS path to another house and some houses do not. The distances between the houses are short; therefore, in spite of the high attenuation caused by the trees, enough wireless signal remains to allow each house to connect to at least one other house. Mesh architecture can provide connectivity to the Internet if at least one point on the mesh network can be connected to the Internet. Two possible ways to bring Internet connectivity to a hub point on a Forest Shadows Estates mesh network are as follows:

- Purchase a leased line from the local telephone company. The line will cost $500 each month, or a total of $6000 each year.

- Erect a tower and install a point-to-point wireless link connecting the mesh network to the water tank on the hill. If the water tank was already acting as the hub of the cellular network that served Pleasantown, it will be a simple matter to add connectivity from the water tank to a new tower in Forest Shadows Estates. The cost of the tower and the wireless link to the water tank will be $6000.

- Either broadband option will work to connect the Forest Shadows Estates residents to the Pleasantown WAN. The subdivision builder evaluated these two options and decided to pay for the building of the tower and the installation of the wireless link; the results are illustrated by Figure 3-11.

Figure 3-11 *Mesh Network Connected to Cellular Network*

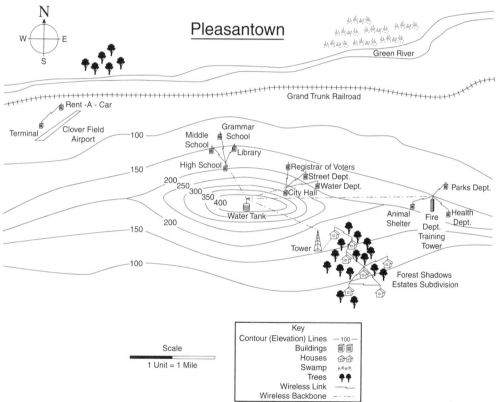

- The builder reasoned that it would be better to pay $6000 one time, own the equipment, and charge the residents each month for Internet access. "Besides," he thought, "the new interstate highway will soon be built and it will pass along the edge of Forest Shadows Estates. I'll be able to lease antenna space on my new tower to three or four cellular telephone companies, and that will bring me an additional three or four thousand dollars of income each month."

- If your potential end users are located close to each other but they have no LOS path to an access point, mesh architectures can successfully connect all or most of your end users. Keep in mind that backbone connectivity is also required to and from at least one node on the mesh network. Go to Step 7.

Step 7: Draft Preliminary Network Architecture

By now, you are aware of the terrain in your area and you know the major obstructions that you need to go around or over. You should have a clear idea which network architecture is best for your proposed WAN. Keep your network design as simple as possible, although it is okay to combine several architectures if that is what you have to do to provide service to all of your end users. Draw straight lines on your map to connect your proposed hub and end user locations.

Measure Compass Headings

Measure the approximate compass headings from the hub site(s) to the end user sites.

TIP   Use a protractor placed over your map. If you are using mapping or topographic software, use the compass tool to determine the headings.

The heading from end user site to hub site will be 180 degrees opposite to the heading from the hub site to the end user site. Start with the estimated heading from hub to end user and either add or subtract 180 degrees. (Choose either one—whichever is easier for you to visualize and calculate. The result is the same.) For example:

A heading of 50 degrees from hub to end user will have a heading of 230 degrees (50 degrees plus 180 degrees equals 230 degrees) from end user to hub. A heading of 300 degrees from hub to end user will have a heading of 120 degrees (300 degrees minus 180 degrees equals 120 degrees) from end user to hub.

Measure Distances

Use the scale of miles on your map with a ruler or the mapping software compass tool to determine the distance from hub sites to end user sites and mark these distances on your map. If you are using point-to-point or mesh architecture, estimate and mark the distances between end user locations.

Make a note of any path distances that appear to be beyond the common range of wireless equipment. Although you have not yet selected the wireless equipment that you will use, some general rules follow:

- Path lengths greater than approximately 7 miles (11.3 km) frequently need some kind of special attention, such as higher antennas, larger antennas, or extra amplification (when legal).

- Point-to-point networks can span distances as long as 30 miles and sometimes longer. To achieve these distances, there must be *no obstructions* to the LOS path, and the end points must be substantially higher than the height of the terrain. Five hundred feet or more of antenna height might be needed. Long links like this are easiest to build if one or both ends of the link are located on hilltops or on the tops of tall buildings.

- Long links that have obstructions, such as mountains, along the way need intermediate repeater locations.

Inspect LOS Paths

Physically drive (or walk) between your hub site locations and your end user locations. If you have a point-to-point or mesh network, drive between end user locations. The purpose is to look for obstructions such as tall buildings, tall trees, water tanks, bridges, or radio towers that were not visible on your map. These tall obstructions could cause attenuation and make the path unusable.

If you find obstructions, mark their location and their approximate height on your map. Calculate the Fresnel Zone clearance needed at that point along the wireless path.

TIP   Use the formula and the example in Figure 2-24 in Chapter 2 to calculate the Fresnel Zone clearance needed.

If your inspection reveals the presence of significant obstructions, you must revise your network architecture. You can either add intermediate repeater sites or redesign the network to use shorter LOS paths.

Make a Frequency Plan

In a point-to-multipoint network with more than one sector or in a cellular network, the same frequency (direct sequence spread spectrum) or hopping sequence (frequency hopping spread spectrum) might be re-used on more than one link or sector. It is important to isolate network segments that share a frequency or hopping sequence from each other. Lack of proper isolation results in interference and throughput reduction. See Chapter 5 for information about isolating antennas on different sectors.

Step 8: Confirm Hub Site Availability

If you are using point-to-point architecture, go to Step 9. Otherwise, you will be using a network architecture that requires one or more hub sites. Inquire as to who owns or manages the buildings where the hub sites are located. Contact the building manager, explain your interest in placing wireless equipment there, and request a meeting to discuss performing a site survey to determine if the site qualifies as a good hub site location.

Step 9: Confirm End User Site Availability

Inquire as to who owns or manages the buildings where the end user sites are located. Contact the building manager, explain your interest in placing wireless equipment there, and request a meeting to discuss performing a site survey to determine if the site qualifies as a good end user site location.

Step 10: Confirm Site Usability

Before concluding that a hub site or an end user site is acceptable, you must perform a site survey. A physical site survey includes determining where and how to mount the antennas, run the cabling, and accomplish the other physical details surrounding the installation. Perform a physical site survey for *all installations*. An RF site survey uses wireless test equipment, including a spectrum analyzer, to examine the RF environment and to confirm that wireless noise or interference is not too high to prevent the successful operation of the new network. Perform an RF site survey for all hub sites and backbone node locations.

Chapter 4 contains a detailed description of both the physical and the RF site survey process. It is important to perform both physical and wireless site surveys before finalizing the design of your network. The site surveys reveal any factors that would prevent successful use of a site, such as the lack of LOS paths, the lack of appropriate antenna-mounting locations, or high noise levels. Chapter 4 also helps you with suggestions about how to revise your network architecture if your site surveys reveal that network revisions are needed.

Review Questions

1 If you have one pair of backbone locations that need to be connected, which network architecture is the most appropriate?

2 What type of antenna—omnidirectional or directional—does a point-to-point network normally use?

3 When a microwave signal strikes an obstruction, what always happens to it?

4 When a point-to-point network is expanded, what architecture is usually chosen? Why?

5 Why is SNR important in a wireless network?

6 What network architectures use sectors?

7 What are the consequences of selecting the wrong access point antenna system for a point-to-multipoint network?

8 What architecture is used to allow frequency re-use while connecting several point-to-multipoint networks?

9 What is the primary disadvantage of cellular architecture?

10 What type of network architecture can be used if end users are located close together and have partially obstructed (non-LOS) paths between each other?

11 What type of routing does a mesh network perform?

CHAPTER 4

Performing Site Surveys

During your preliminary network design process, you selected a draft network architecture based on your preliminary conclusions about the existence of line-of-sight (LOS) paths between specific network locations. Now, you need to evaluate your potential wireless equipment locations to determine if they meet the qualifications that allow you to proceed and to successfully install wireless equipment there. These potential locations might be buildings, towers, or possibly even hilltops with no buildings or wireless equipment. This chapter helps you perform two types of site surveys:

- Physical site surveys
- Radio frequency (RF) site surveys

Performing effective site surveys allows you to determine the following things:

- If the site is 100 percent perfect for your network
- If the site would be acceptable for your network with a few changes to the site, to your network design, or both
- If it is possible to make changes to the site to better meet the needs of your proposed network
- What modifications to make to your network design to fit your network to the site
- If the site is not acceptable for your network because changes to the site or to your network design would be too expensive
- If RF path testing or coverage testing should be performed to gather more information and to determine if the site is suitable
- The specific installation details that must be documented now but used later by installation personnel

Physical Site Surveys

Physical site surveys examine the physical environment of the building, tower, or other location where you want to place either a point-to-multipoint access point or a point-to-point end node. The physical site survey helps you accomplish the following tasks:

- Verify that the locations where you want to place your wireless nodes will actually allow you to place wireless equipment there.

- Determine the best location inside the building or inside the tower equipment vault to place the wireless equipment.

- Verify that your postulated LOS paths actually exist.

- Determine where and how to mount your antenna systems to make successful use of the LOS paths.

- Determine how to design and route the cabling to the antenna system.

- Determine how to protect against damage from lightning by properly grounding the antenna system.

- Document your physical findings and make further recommendations for additions or changes to the preliminary network design.

Reviewing the Preliminary Network Design

Before you travel to a physical site survey location, take time to review the preliminary network design that you created in Chapter 3, "Choosing Your Network Architecture." Make a note of the following:

- The directions that your antennas need to point *from* the site that you are preparing to survey

- *How high* above ground your antennas must be mounted so that the tallest obstacle along your LOS paths does not intrude into more than 40 percent of the Fresnel zone

---

NOTE   It is tempting to skip over this calculation and hope that the antennas will be high enough and that your links will work. Don't fall for this temptation, though. Calculate the Fresnel zone clearances needed, as described in Chapter 2, "Understanding Wireless Fundamentals." If you do not do this now, your wireless network might not provide reliable performance or it might not work at all.

- Determine the approximate antenna gains needed. When you know the gain, you know the approximate physical size of the antenna. Knowing the size helps you evaluate potential antenna-mounting locations and antenna-mounting hardware.

TIP   If you need to calculate the approximate antenna gain, use the link budget formula in Chapter 2.

Contacting Site Management

The first step in performing a physical site survey is to obtain permission from the building or tower manager to check the site to see if it would be a suitable location to place an antenna.

NOTE   You might be performing a physical site survey of an existing wireless tower site instead of a building. The principles are the same, although instead of looking for a flat roof or building wall to mount the antenna on, look for the best location on the tower to mount your antenna.

Locate the building manager, identify yourself, and explain your interest in placing a wireless system in the building or on the tower. You will most likely be asked to speak with the facility manager. Be prepared to provide the following information:

- Your name and your company name
- Who will use the wireless system
- The size and location of the wireless equipment that connects to the antenna system
- The size, appearance, location, and weight of the antenna system

TIP   It is helpful to actually bring an antenna with you if possible, or at least to bring a drawing or a picture of the proposed antenna. Most wireless antennas are fairly small, and by showing the antenna size, you help to eliminate concern that the antenna will detract from the appearance of the building.

- How the antenna could be mounted to or on the building
- How the cabling connects the antenna to the wireless equipment
- Whether your wireless equipment will or will not interfere with wireless equipment that already exists on or in the building

TIP   This is a good time to ask about the existence of any other wireless equipment in the building or on the tower. When you know about other wireless equipment, you know more about the wireless environment. This knowledge can alert you to the possibility of interference to or from your proposed wireless installation. See Chapter 8, "Solving Noise and Interference Problems," for detailed information about interference.

- The information you need to obtain by doing a physical survey and, if needed, a radio-frequency (wireless) site survey of the building

If management agrees, schedule a day and a time to perform a physical site survey. Allow at least two hours minimum to complete the survey.

If the site already has a number of wireless systems installed or if you plan to install a hub site with one or more wireless access points, schedule several additional hours to perform a wireless site survey.

Physical Site Survey Preparation

Plan to take the following information and equipment with you when you perform the physical site survey:

- A knowledge of the zoning requirements for the city, town, or jurisdiction in which the site is located.

- Distance and direction information to the sites that you hope to provide the wireless link to. You should have this information from your earlier network design work.

- Fresnel zone clearance distances from obstructions along the wireless path.

- A notebook, a pencil, and a pen to record your physical site survey findings.

- Gloves to protect your hands when climbing.

- Sunglasses to protect your eyes from ultraviolet light damage.

- A hat to protect your face from excessive exposure to sunlight, which can lead to skin cancer. Also, if you expect to be on the roof for a considerable period of time during the middle of the day, consider applying sunscreen to your face and hands before going onto the roof.

- A jacket. On a cold day, the rooftop of a building can be much colder and windier than at street level.

- Water. The temperature on the roof of an office building can be 10 to 20 degrees Fahrenheit (5.5 to 11 degrees Celsius) above the ambient temperature, so you can suffer from heat exhaustion on a hot day if you don't drink lots of water.

- A magnetic compass to determine the exact direction toward the other wireless sites.

- A Global Positioning System (GPS) receiver to calculate and display exact distances and antenna direction headings.

- A digital camera to photograph the building, the roof area, and the view in each direction from the roof.

- A flashlight to help you see in dark basements, attics, and crawlspaces.

- A five-foot stepladder to see into (and possibly crawl into) ceiling areas.

Locating a Controlled Equipment Environment

The first step in performing your physical site survey is to find the best location to place the wireless equipment. Some wireless equipment mounts outdoors—at or near the antenna—and connects to the indoor network with fiber-optic cable or with Category 5 (Cat 5) Ethernet cable. Most wireless equipment, however, mounts indoors and connects to the antenna system with coax cable. Therefore, in every case, you need to select an indoor location to house some physical equipment. The indoor location that you choose must provide the following:

- **Accessibility**—The location must allow reasonable access to the equipment for installation and servicing.

- **Security and access control**—The location must prevent unauthorized personnel from gaining access to the equipment and perhaps turning it off or removing it.

- **Power availability**—Sufficient AC or DC power must be available to power the equipment.

- **Temperature control**—The location must not get hot enough or cold enough to exceed the operating temperature limits of the equipment.

- **Humidity control**—The location must not be too wet or too humid.

- **Dust control**—The location should be reasonably clean and dust free to prevent dust or dirt from collecting inside the wireless equipment and causing premature failure.

- **Minimal distance to antenna**—The area should be located as close as possible to the area where the antenna system is located to minimize signal loss in the cabling.

- **Access to cable routing paths**—The equipment location must have access to cable routes that go to the area where the antenna system will be installed. The cable routes might consist of conduit, cable raceways, crawlspaces, drop-ceiling areas, air plenums, or other cabling paths.

TIP   If other wireless equipment is installed in the building, ask where it is installed. If cabling access to that location is good, consider placing your equipment in the same location.

Minimizing the Distance Between the Equipment and the Antenna

In most cases, the performance of your wireless network improves the closer the wireless equipment is mounted to the antenna. This occurs because the shorter the length of the antenna cable, the more signal that reaches the equipment.

As much as possible, choose an indoor location that is as close as possible to the antenna location. For example, if you have a choice between a location that is 60 feet (18 meters) from the antenna and a location that is 350 feet (106 meters) from the antenna, choose the 60-feet-away location because the performance and range of your wireless network is maximized.

If you are evaluating a communications tower as an antenna location, avoid going too high on the tower. Plan to go only high enough to cover the area where your customers are located. Going too high increases your costs for cabling, installation labor, and maintenance labor. In addition, the cost of mounting on a tower frequently is more expensive the higher you go. Going too high also increases the exposure of your system to additional noise and interference.

Gaining Access to the Roof

Most building roofs contain air conditioners and ventilation systems. To install and service these systems, most buildings have a way to reach the roof from inside the building. Roof access methods include stairways to the attic, doors, and roof hatches from the attic to the roof, and ladders attached to a wall. Occasionally, you will find a building with *no* existing roof access. In situations like this, it might be necessary to place your own ladder against an outside wall of the building and climb to the roof.

TIP   Be sure to make a note of situations in which your installation crew will need to ladder the roof themselves. They will need to bring a long ladder with them, and they will need more time to complete the installation because they must use ropes to raise and lower antennas, tools, and equipment up onto the roof.

Routing the Cables

Try to locate the shortest path from the indoor equipment location to the outdoor antenna location. Use existing cable paths whenever possible. One of the most challenging parts of the physical site survey is finding a way to route the cable from the outside of the building to the inside.

TIP   Building managers and owners are concerned about preventing damage caused by water leaking into their buildings. Tell the building manager that you would prefer not to drill holes (and especially not vertical holes that rainwater could pass through) to bring your cabling inside. The manager will appreciate that you are aware of and that you respect the needs of their company.

If possible, try to find and use an existing cable entry hole into the building. These existing holes might be holes for other cables, ventilation grates, electrical conduits, or roof jacks. The building manager can often advise you of existing cable routing paths and answer your questions about which routes are acceptable.

Surveying the Roof

When you are on the roof, take a good look around. Locate any existing antenna installations. Note how the other antennas are mounted to or on the building and notice where their cabling runs. Make a drawing of the rooftop and indicate the height of the roof above ground. Add the locations of the other antennas and any large pieces of rooftop equipment.

TIP   Note the location of existing AC power outlets. These will come in handy later, such as during installation when drills need to be recharged or test equipment needs to be plugged in.

Determining Where to Point the Antenna

From the review of your preliminary network design, you know the compass headings where your antennas need to point.

Turn your magnetic compass until the north (N) mark is under the marked end of the compass needle. The needle is pointing toward magnetic North. Mark an arrow on your rooftop drawing showing where North is relative to the sides of the building. The mark at the top center of the compass dial shows the direction that you are facing.

Turn the compass dial until the compass heading for your antenna is at the top center of the dial. Slowly turn your body until the marked end of the compass needle once again is under the N mark. You are now facing in the direction that your antenna needs to point. Mark this heading on your rooftop drawing and walk toward that side of the building to look for places to mount your antenna.

If your antenna is to be mounted on a square or a triangular tower, examine the tower legs and the flat tower faces and select the leg or the face that is pointing the closest to your desired antenna direction.

Determining Where to Place the Antenna

You can place and mount your antenna using several good methods. A flat, clear, horizontal roof area on the side of the building that your antenna needs to face is probably the best mounting location. A flat vertical wall that faces the direction that your antenna needs to point can also be used. The peak or the ridgeline of a roof is the worst location to mount an antenna. Figure 4-1 shows examples of some of the best mounting locations.

Figure 4-1   *Antenna-Mounting Location Examples*

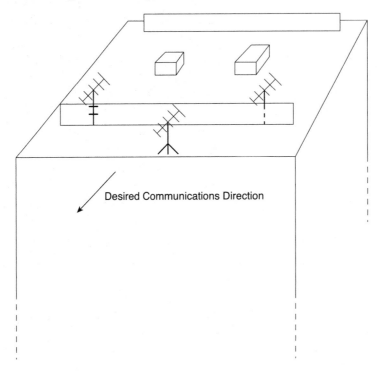

Desired Communications Direction

If the roof has industrial equipment such as air conditioners or ventilation equipment, select your antenna-mounting locations to be some distance away or in a location where the equipment is behind the antennas. This way, the equipment won't block the LOS path.

NOTE   Chapter 5, "Selecting Antenna Systems," has additional information about antenna-mounting hardware. Chapter 7, "Installing Outdoor Wireless Systems," has more information about installing the antenna support hardware. If you want to become more familiar with these details, look through those chapters now.

Be aware of the visual impact that your antennas will have. Whenever possible, choose a location that will make your antennas less visible from the street level.

Avoiding Nearby Obstacles

From your roof, note any nearby obstacles in the direction that your antenna will point, such as nearby trees or buildings. If the obstacles are higher than (or almost as high as) your antenna, the LOS path that your system needs is obstructed. Add these obstacles to your rooftop drawing, noting the direction, approximate height, and approximate distance. If these obstacles are present, you must either move your antenna to a different, less obstructed part of the roof or raise your antenna until it is above the obstacles.

Avoiding Power Lines

If power lines run along the side of the building near the roof, you must choose an antenna-mounting location far enough away from the power lines so that the antenna and the antenna support mast cannot hit the power lines if the antenna falls.

WARNING   Each year, people are burned and killed when antennas fall and hit power lines. DO NOT EVEN THINK of placing an antenna or a support mast close enough to power lines so that it could hit the lines if it fell over or was blown over.

Avoiding Distant Obstacles

If distant obstacles, such as tall buildings or hills, exist along your LOS path, you likely are already aware of them from your preliminary network design work. If these obstructions intrude into your Fresnel zone, they add additional loss, which can prevent your link from working.

From the rooftop of a four-story building, you can often identify tall buildings up to 10 or more miles (16 km) away. In the morning on a clear day, you might be able to identify tall hills and mountains 25 or more miles (40 km) away.

From your roof, note any distant obstacles and add them to your drawing with the approximate distance, height, and direction. Moving your antenna to a different area of the roof will probably not help you avoid these obstacles. You will need to raise your antenna higher to clear them.

Determining Antenna Height

To determine how high your antenna needs to be above the ground, start with the height above ground of the roof, and then do the following:

- If nearby obstacles exist that you cannot stay clear of by moving your antenna to a clearer area of the roof, add the height needed to clear the obstacle.

- Remembering that 60 percent of the Fresnel zone needs to be clear; if any distant obstacles exist that intrude into more than 40 percent of your Fresnel zone, add the additional height needed for Fresnel zone clearance above the obstacle.

- If your path is longer than approximately 7 miles (11 km), you might need to add additional antenna height to clear the earth bulge, as described in Chapter 2.

- Knowing the total height that your antenna needs to be above the ground, subtract the roof height from the total antenna height. The result is the height that your antenna needs to be mounted above the roof.

Selecting the Antenna-Mounting Structure

You now know the following about your proposed antenna system:

- The direction that the antenna needs to point

- The location on the roof where the antenna will be clear of other antennas, nearby obstacles, rooftop equipment, and power lines

- The height that the antenna needs to be above the roof

- The availability of flat roof areas and vertical walls, which can serve as possible antenna-mounting locations

Make a note of the area that you recommend the antenna system be mounted in. Indicate this area on your rooftop drawing.

Grounding the Antenna System

To be safe as well as legal, all outdoor antenna systems must be properly grounded and protected from lightning.

NOTE   At press time, the National Electrical Code (in the United States) requires that every antenna mast be grounded. Coaxial cable shields must also be grounded. Each conductor of a Cat 5 cable running indoors from an outdoor antenna must be protected with an antenna discharge unit (a lightning arrestor) where the cable enters the building.

The following section is an overview but not a complete treatment of the subject of grounding and lightning protection. The purpose is to give you a basic introduction to lightning protection so that you can determine where to route the ground wire for your antenna system. For more information about the grounding requirements in your area, do the following:

- Consult your local building or planning department to learn what local rules and regulations are in place.
- Talk with an electrician to gain the benefit of his local experience.
- Refer to the National Electrical Code for the latest guidelines.
- Use the additional grounding standards information sources listed in Appendix B, "Wireless Hardware, Software, and Services Provider Organizations."

Providing Protection from Lightning

A lightning protector (lightning arrestor) works by providing a low-impedance path to ground for the high-voltage, high-current electrical energy contained in a lightning strike. All outdoor wireless antenna systems must contain a lightning protector or surge suppressor.

Without a lightning protector, the energy from a direct or a nearby lighting strike travels to the ground by passing through (and damaging or destroying) the wireless equipment and the wired network equipment. The building housing the equipment can also be damaged, and the people within the building can be injured. Even an installed lighting protector cannot provide proper protection unless it connects to a good ground connection.

Locating the Grounding Point

Locating the best grounding point is one of the most challenging parts of performing a site survey because it can be difficult to find a good ground point that allows a short, straight, large-diameter ground wire to be run from the antenna system to the ground. Figure 4-2 shows the ideal grounding scenario.

Figure 4-2 *Ideal Grounding and Lightning-Protection Scenario*

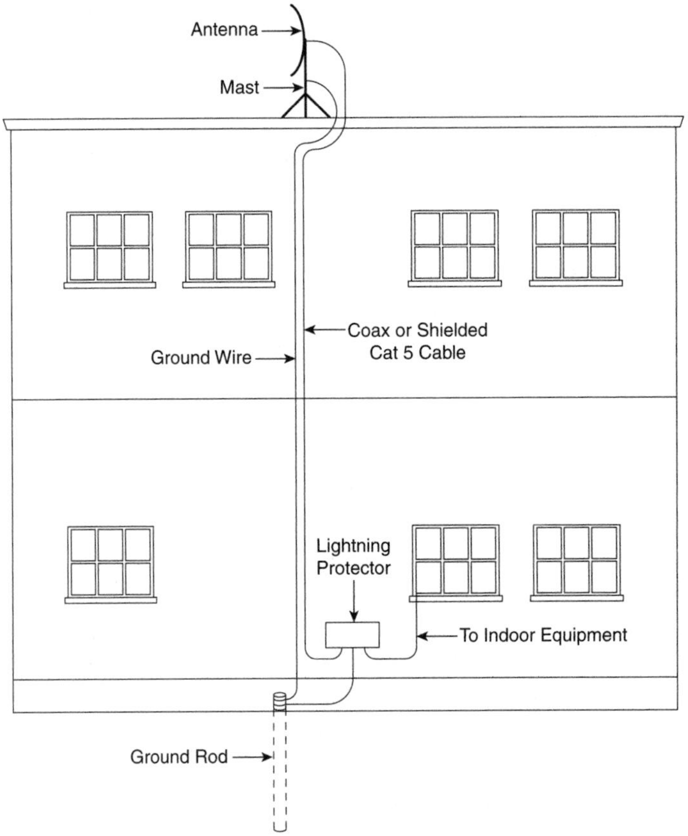

The best ground wire route is to run the shortest possible large-diameter ground wire straight down from the antenna system to an 8-foot (2.4 m) ground rod.

In some situations, the rooftop antenna is located too far away from the earth to allow you to run a short ground wire. One alternative is to ground the antenna system to the building. If there is a rooftop penthouse with air conditioning or ventilation equipment inside, you might be able to attach the ground wire directly to the building's structural steel. Ask the facility manager to help select the best, most direct ground attachment point.

TIP Resist the urge to use a rooftop electrical ground point such as the frame of an air conditioner or a connection to metal electrical conduit. These electrical ground connections are usually long and indirect and are not designed to provide proper protection from lightning. You must either locate a suitable lightning-protection ground point or plan to have one installed when the antenna system is installed.

TIP   The lightning protector must also be grounded. The most effective location for the lightning protector is at the point where the antenna cable (or the Ethernet cable, if power-over-Ethernet [PoE] equipment is used) enters the building. Again, for effective protection, use an 8-foot (2.4m) ground rod.

Revising the Preliminary Network Design

Based on your physical site survey findings, it might be necessary for you to revise your preliminary network design. Use the suggestions in Table 4-1 as a guide to overcome common site problems.

Table 4-1   *Solutions to Physical Site Problems*

Problem		Solution
LOS Path Problems	There is no LOS path on a single backbone link or end user link.	Revise that link to use an intermediate relay or repeater location.
	There is a lack of several LOS paths to or from a hub site.	Choose a higher hub site location, one with better LOS paths to the end user locations.
Hub Site Antenna Problems	There is no appropriate location to mount antennas at a hub site.	Erect a short tower on the roof to provide additional antenna-mounting space; if that is not possible, move the hub site to a different location.
	More than 100 feet separate the hub site wireless equipment and the antenna system.	Find a new equipment-mounting location closer to the antenna system; or Use an indoor or outdoor wireless equipment architecture that can tolerate long cable runs; or Budget to use more expensive, larger-diameter, lower-loss coax.
	The hub site antenna system design is difficult.	Get help from a more experienced wireless system designer.
Rooftop Cost Problem	The cost for roof space is too high.	Investigate the use of other lower-cost high-elevation locations, such as private homes or businesses, where you can trade Internet access for roof space.

Physical Criteria Evaluation and Conclusion

Your physical site survey findings need to be preserved and communicated. The information that you develop will determine if the site is physically suitable for your wireless network. If the site is acceptable, your survey information can be a guide during the installation process. This is why it is important to clearly document all your findings, comments, and recommendations.

Table 4-2 provides one example of a form that you can use to collect your site survey information. You can modify this form to meet your specific needs. Use the tearout card at the end of this book to make copies of this form.

Table 4-2   *Sample of Physical Site Survey Data Form*

Surveyor Name		**Phone/E-Mail**	
Site Address		**Site Owner**	
Site Manager		**Phone/E-Mail**	
Facility Manager		**Phone/E-Mail**	
Existing Wireless Equipment		**Existing Antenna Locations**	
New Equipment Location		**Power Source**	
Path Length		**Fresnel Zone Clearance**	
Roof Height		**Roof Access Location**	
Antenna Location		**Antenna Height Above Ground**	
Antenna Mounting Hardware Needed		**Antenna Heading/Tilt**	
Nearby Obstructions		**Distant Obstructions**	
Cable Type and Length		**Cable Entry Point**	
Cable Route			
Grounding Locations (Mast and Building Entrance)		**Ground Wire Route (Mast and Building Entrance)**	
Lightning Protection Description		**Lightning Protection Location**	
Site Evaluation	**Good**	**Acceptable**	**Not Acceptable**
Comments and Recommendations			
Follow-Up Issues			
Drawings Attached			

Radio Frequency (RF) Site Surveys

The physical site survey process inspects the physical environment where your wireless equipment will potentially be installed. If your physical site survey finds the site acceptable, then your next step is an RF site survey. The RF site survey examines the outdoor wireless environment that your network must work within.

It is a good policy to do an RF site survey for each potential new installation because the license-free frequencies are shared bands. There is always the possibility of interference from other wireless systems.

The consequence of installing a wireless network incorrectly in an area with a high level of interference is simply that the *throughput of your network will be reduced*. Under worst-case conditions, your throughput might be less than if you were using a 14.4-kbps dialup modem. If you plan to install a hub site for a point-to-multipoint network, an RF survey is a necessity. The risk of having your new network not work properly is just too high. Don't take a chance; do the RF site survey and maximize your likelihood of installing a reliable, high-throughput network.

At this point, you're probably wondering if there are ever any situations where you can skip the RF survey without running too much risk that your new system won't work. Yes—you can skip the RF site survey if you install a point-to-point link (or the customer end of a point-to-multipoint link) and you know that the following conditions are true:

- No other wireless systems are in the area on the same frequency to cause interference.
- A clear LOS path exists to the other end of the link.

Overview of the RF Site Survey Process

The purpose of an RF site survey is to accomplish the following:

- Determine if signals are already present in the area that are strong enough to cause interference to your new system
- Document the signal type, strength, direction, and polarization of the other signals present
- Evaluate the site to see if the wireless environment has a low enough level of interference and noise to allow your new wireless system to operate reliably there

You might wonder why it matters what other signals are present. It matters because interference to your system can occur from other systems that are already present in the same area where you want deploy your new system. If you experience interference, the opposite will probably also be true—your system will cause interference to the other system. If you know about other nearby systems, you can plan to deploy your system in a way that minimizes interference and allows successful, high throughput operation of both systems.

NOTE You can find much more information about minimizing interference in Chapter 8.

RF Site Survey Test Equipment

RF site survey test equipment ranges from PC-based utility programs to full-featured RF spectrum analyzers. You need the following equipment to perform an RF site survey:

- The physical site survey equipment listed earlier in this chapter.

- A spectrum analyzer with an instruction manual. The spectrum analyzer must cover the frequency bands that you plan to use. In some cases, a PC-based site survey utility can be used in place of a spectrum analyzer.

- If your equipment is not battery powered, you need 100 to 200 ft (30 to 60 m) of AC extension cord.

- A 30 dB attenuator that can be placed in the coaxial cable between the antenna and the spectrum analyzer.

- A 6 dBi omnidirectional antenna to check for signals coming from all directions.

- A 10–14 dBi panel antenna to check for signals coming from specific directions.

NOTE   If you already know what type of antenna your link will use, plan to test with that antenna during your site survey.

- A wireless sniffer, protocol analyzer, or site survey utility.

TIP   A wireless protocol analyzer can be added to supplement, but not replace, a spectrum analyzer. For example, an 802.11b protocol analyzer or packet sniffer can be helpful if you plan to deploy multiple 802.11b access points in the middle of a medium-to-large city. The protocol analyzer can help you determine the number of other 802.11b access points in the vicinity, their frequency, and their approximate direction. You should still perform an RF site survey with a spectrum analyzer to locate sources of non-802.11b signals and strong signals outside of the 2.4-GHz band.

How a Spectrum Analyzer Works

A spectrum analyzer is a very-wide-band receiver that can be adjusted to receive across either a wide or a narrow range of frequencies. Spectrum analyzers visually display the signal energy that they find at each frequency. A wide receive range can look at a wide band of frequencies simultaneously, such as from 2400 MHz to 2500 MHz. A narrow receive range examines a single frequency or a single signal all by itself, such as 2442 MHz.

Spectrum Analyzer Input

The spectrum analyzer is a sensitive receiver that is designed to detect low signal levels received from whatever antenna you connect to the input. For example, a signal level of + 20 dBm (100 mW) or higher can overload a spectrum analyzer and permanently damage it. This damage is expensive to repair. To protect the input circuitry, many spectrum analyzers have built-in input attenuators that can be switched ON to reduce the amplitude of strong signals.

TIP

It is a good habit to begin each of your RF site surveys by switching the built-in attenuator ON. After you check the signal levels and you see that none of the levels is high enough to cause damage, you can switch the attenuator OFF.

If your spectrum analyzer does not have a built-in input attenuator, you can buy a low-cost 30-dB attenuator and manually insert it between the antenna and the input connector. When you see that no exceptionally strong signals are present, you can remove the attenuator and continue with your testing.

Refer to the instruction manual that came with your spectrum analyzer to find the maximum safe input level.

Spectrum Analyzer Output

The output from the spectrum analyzer is a graph of signal strength versus frequency. The horizontal (x-axis) of the spectrum display shows the frequency range that is being received. The x-axis is usually divided into 10 divisions. For a wide sweep range, these divisions are adjusted to be large. For example, a setting of 10 MHz per division results in a total receiving range of 100 MHz. For a narrow sweep range, the divisions are adjusted to be small. A setting of 10 kilohertz (kHz) per division results in a receiving range of 100 kHz.

The center frequency on the x-axis is also adjustable. This is either the single frequency being examined or the center of the frequency band being examined.

The vertical (y-axis) of the spectrum display shows the signal strength (amplitude). The y-axis is frequently divided into 8 or 10 divisions. Moving down the y-axis, each line marks a signal level that is 10 times lower (10 dB lower) than the division above it. These signal levels generally range from about 0 dBm (1 mW) down to –100 dBm.

By looking at both the display axis simultaneously and observing the signal's shape (also called spectral output), it is possible to determine the signal strength, the center frequency, the width of the signal, and (with practice) the type of modulation being used.

By using a directional antenna and rotating the antenna in different directions while watching the signal level, you can tell the direction that a signal is coming from.

By shifting your directional antenna from horizontal to vertical polarization while watching the signal level, you can tell whether a signal was transmitted from an antenna that was horizontally polarized or vertically polarized.

NOTE   For additional information about antenna polarization, see the discussion in Chapter 5.

Inspecting a Band of Frequencies

Most RF site survey work consists of examining a wide band of frequencies to determine if other signals are present in or near the frequency band that you plan to use.

NOTE   This is a bit like using a wide-angle lens (such as a 24 mm or a 28 mm lens) on a 35 mm camera. You see a wide area without seeing all the little details of everything in the picture.

The following examples provide practice setting the spectrum analyzer and seeing what the output looks like.

The standard North American FM radio broadcast band ranges from 88 MHz to 108 MHz. FM radio broadcast signals are not spread spectrum signals, but they are easy to see on the spectrum analyzer. That's why they are used in these first two examples.

Figure 4-3 shows the spectrum analyzer output that would be visible when viewing the FM broadcast band in a major city where you will see from 20 to 40 different stations.

Figure 4-3   *Wide Spectrum Analyzer Frequency Coverage Display*

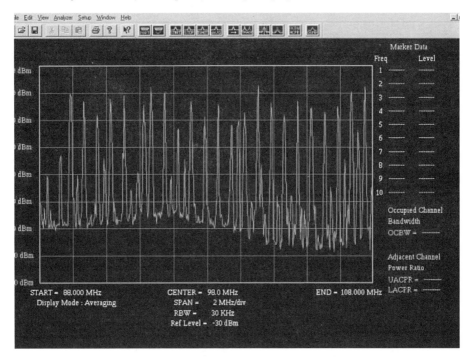

The center frequency is 98 MHz and the span (the frequency range between each x-axis line) is 2 MHz per division. There are 10 horizontal divisions, so the total frequency coverage is 10 times 2 MHz for a total range of 20 MHz. The lowest frequency being received is 88 MHz and the highest frequency is 108 MHz.

Inspecting a Single Frequency

Switching from the inspection of a wide band of frequencies to the inspection of a narrow band of frequencies is easy. Adjust the span control to 200 kHz per division. The center frequency is the same (98 MHz), but the overall frequency coverage is now 2 MHz (10 divisions times 200 kHz per division for a total range of 2 MHz). Figure 4-4 shows the resulting display.

Figure 4-4 *Three-Signal Spectrum Analyzer Coverage Display*

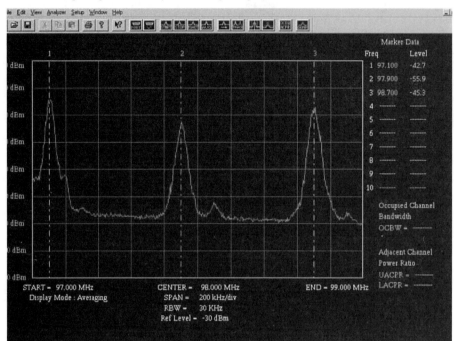

Instead of 40 stations, only the three stations near the 98 MHz center frequency are visible. From left to right, these stations are at 97.1 MHz, 97.9 MHz, and 98.7 MHz.

If you reduced the span per division still further, you would see even more details of the signal at the center frequency. In Figure 4-5, the span is reduced to 50 kHz per division and the center frequency is set to 98.7 MHz (the frequency of the right-hand station in Figure 4-4).

NOTE   This is like using a telephoto lens (such as a 200 mm lens) on a 35 mm camera. You see a magnified view of one object without seeing much of the landscape or the context that surrounds that object.

Figure 4-5   *Single-Signal Spectrum Analyzer Coverage Display*

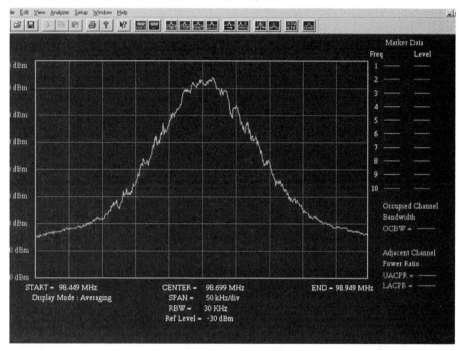

Figure 4-5 shows only the signal of the station at 98.7 MHz. With these spectrum analyzer settings, you can study the characteristics of this one signal more closely. You already know that the modulation type is FM, but you can also determine the following:

- **Signal strength**—The display shows that the signal has a peak signal strength of approximately –34 dBm.

- **Direction**—If you rotate the spectrum analyzer antenna until you see the signal strength peak and then use your compass to determine the direction that the antenna is pointing, you will know the direction that the signal is coming from.

- **Polarization**—If you rotate your antenna from horizontal polarization to vertical polarization and back to horizontal, you can determine if the signal was transmitted from an antenna with a horizontal or a vertical polarization. The position (horizontal or vertical) of your spectrum analyzer antenna that results in the highest signal strength is the same polarization as the signal's transmitting antenna.

Spectrum Analyzer Peak-Hold Feature

The spectral output of a spread spectrum signal is not constant. Spread spectrum modulation was originally designed for use by the military to spread out wireless signal energy and make it harder to detect and decode the intelligence. The varying modulation of a spread spectrum signal causes the signal to continuously change in frequency and in signal strength. After you learn the general shape of spread spectrum signals, you can determine the modulation type of signals that you see.

Unless you have a very expensive spectrum analyzer designed specifically to analyze spread spectrum signals, you must practice using the peak-hold feature on your spectrum analyzer. This feature displays a second output trace that captures the peak signal strength and holds these peak values so that you can examine the signal shape more carefully. Without the use of this feature, it is difficult to see enough of a spread spectrum signal to determine much about it. Using the peak-hold feature allows you to arrive at more accurate and more useful conclusions.

Please go back and look at Figure 4-4 for a moment. It shows three FM broadcast signals. The frequency and the phase (phase is related to frequency change) of each of these signals changed slightly as the signal was modulated. By activating the peak-hold feature of the spectrum analyzer, you get a fuller picture of the signal shapes. In Figure 4-6, peak-hold was turned ON for the same three signals shown in Figure 4-4.

Figure 4-6 *Spectrum Analyzer Peak-Hold Function*

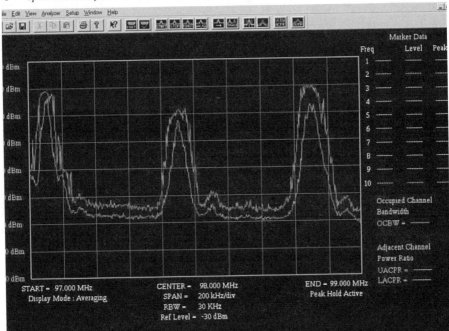

The lower trace in Figure 4-6 shows what the three signals looked like at one moment in time. The upper trace shows (and holds) the peak value that each signal reached during the entire time that the signals were sampled (about 20 seconds). Using peak-hold for your RF site surveys results in a clearer picture of the type of signals that are present.

Inspecting Real-World Signals on a Spectrum Analyzer

From a downtown rooftop in many cities, you can see a variety of signals on (and near) the license-free bands. Many signals are inside the bands and some signals are below or above the band. You need to be aware of all signals because sometimes signals just outside the band can affect your ability to receive signals inside the license-free bands.

One disadvantage of using a PC-based site survey utility instead of a spectrum analyzer is that the utility doesn't have the ability to receive outside of the band. You run the risk of missing strong signals outside the band that could reduce your wireless throughput.

TIP   If you plan to deploy a system on an existing tower that has many transmitters already installed and operating —be advised that this is the most challenging RF environment that you can encounter. If you plan to use a site like this, you must do a thorough RF site survey with a spectrum analyzer. The chances of high levels of RF energy overloading your receiver and reducing your throughput are high.

In addition to your RF site survey, be ready to take other evasive measures; in other words, be ready to add additional filtering to your system to help it perform reliably. See Chapter 8 for information about using bandpass filters.

The majority of the signals that you will encounter outdoors in the license-free bands will be either direct sequence spread spectrum (DSSS) or frequency-hopping spread spectrum (FHSS). Occasionally, you will encounter a combination of several of these signals on the same band at the same time. The following sections show you what these signals look like.

Direct Sequence Spread Spectrum

A DSSS signal is easy to identify when you use the peak-hold feature to allow the signal spectra to fill out. The signal is approximately 22-MHz wide from side to side. The more data the signal is carrying, the faster and wider the display fills. When no data is being carried, no (or little) signal is present. The weaker the signal, the more time it takes to see it and identify it.

Figure 4-7 shows two strong (approaching –60 dBm) DSSS signals in the 2.4 GHz band. One signal is on Channel 1 (2412 MHz) and the other is on Channel 6 (2437 MHz). The peak-hold trace (the upper trace) reveals the two hill-shaped signal spectra.

Figure 4-7   *DSSS Spectrum Analyzer Signal Display*

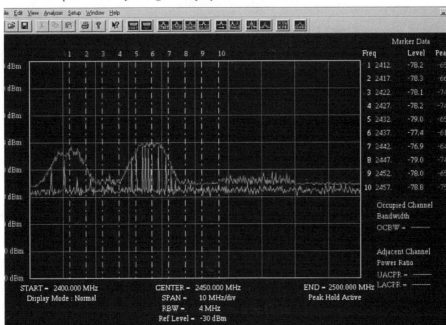

Frequency Hopping Spread Spectrum

An FHSS signal is easy to identify by using the peak-hold feature. The signal hops from 1-MHz channel to 1-MHz channel, throughout the band. The spectrum analyzer peak-hold trace looks like the teeth on a comb, with a signal peak every few MHz, as shown in Figure 4-8.

Detecting Other Signals on the Spectrum Analyzer

Occasionally, you will see other signals and modulation types that you cannot identify or classify. It is important to record and document these other signals. The license-free bands are shared bands that are legally used by a wide variety of end users.

Figure 4-8   *FHSS Spectrum Analyzer Signal Display*

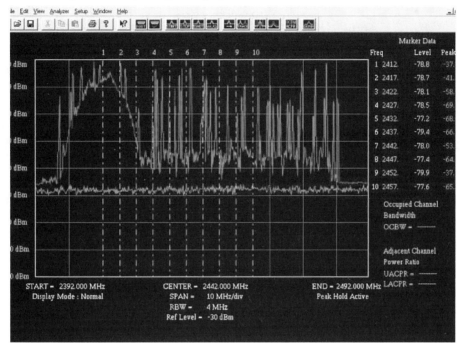

The FCC originally designated these bands for license-free industrial, scientific, and medical (ISM) use on a shared basis with military and licensed amateur radio users.

Additional signal types that you might see include the following:

- Newer forms of DSSS and FHSS modulation, such as multicarrier direct sequence and wide-band frequency hopping

- Wide-band non-spread spectrum signals in the 5-GHz Unlicensed National Information Infrastructure (U-NII) bands

- Military communications and radar systems

- Licensed amateur radio public service and experimental systems

Performing an RF site survey with a spectrum analyzer helps you to accomplish the following:

- Know in advance the RF level in a specific band.

- Work around the RF signals that you see.

- Avoid delays during deployment of your network.

- Avoid creating interference problems for others.

- Promote successful license-free operation by communicating and cooperating with others.

Chapter 8 contains many tips and techniques that can help you deploy your wireless networks cooperatively and successfully.

RF Site Survey Principles

Following are some principles to help you prepare your RF site survey inspection procedure:

- First, if you have never used a spectrum analyzer before, it is best to experiment with it first in your office or shop. Learn how to operate it and practice identifying different types of signals. Learn how to use the peak-hold feature and how to protect the spectrum analyzer from being overloaded and damaged by strong signals.

- Plan to do your RF survey using a two-person test team. Your assistant might suggest questions and test ideas that did not initially occur to you; besides, it is easier to haul all the test equipment up to a roof (or a hilltop) if two people share the workload.

- Plan and list your RF survey steps in advance. Think in terms of taking wireless snapshots of the area. Think about where your end locations are and how your sectors will cover those end locations. You need to check the strength, the antenna polarization, and the signal types present in each of your sectors. For example, if you plan to deploy a three-sector access point on a rooftop in a medium-size city, plan to do the following:

  1 **Take an overall look**—Use the omnidirectional antenna to look at the number and level of signals present within a band of frequencies starting below and ending above the band that you plan to use. For example, if you plan to use 2.4 GHz equipment, you should examine the frequency band from 2.3 GHz to 2.5 GHz. This step allows you to quickly locate strong signals in the band and adjacent to the band.

  2 **Look at each sector**—Use the panel (or directional) antenna to look for signals within the band and within each of your sectors. First, search for signals using the antenna that is oriented for vertical polarization and then search for horizontally polarized signals. This step allows you to identify the presence and the polarization of signals within each of your sectors.

  3 **Take a detailed look**—Narrow the spectrum analyzer frequency sweep and use the panel antenna to take a detailed look at any strong in-band signals that you discover. These signals can interfere with the system that you plan to install. Save a file or a screen shot of these strong signals along with information about their direction, antenna polarization, and the length of the sample interval.

4 Vary the sampling interval — Use both long sampling intervals and short sampling intervals. The more quickly a spectrum analyzer display fills up with signals, the more intense the level of RF activity. Experiment using sampling intervals as short as 15 seconds and as long as 30 minutes.

- Do one or two practice sessions from a high, outdoor location before your first real RF site survey. These practice sessions allow you to become familiar with the outdoor RF environment where more than one signal is present simultaneously. You will become comfortable with your RF survey process before your actual site survey when a facility manager could be looking over your shoulder, asking you questions, and judging your professionalism.

- Schedule your actual RF site surveys to take place during the busiest part of the workday, when RF activity and RF interference is highest. Good test periods are in the morning from 8:30 to 10:30 a.m. (0830 to 1030) and after lunch from 1:00 to 3:00 p.m. (1300 to 1500). The more potential wireless signals that are present during your testing, the more meaningful your test results will be. Allow at least two to four hours for each survey location. It is important to have enough time to set up and thoroughly investigate and document the signals that are present.

- Choose your test location to be as close as possible to the location where you would like to permanently install your antenna system; for example:

  1 If your antenna system will be on a building rooftop, test from the section of the roof that has the clearest possible view (ideally, 360 degrees). Nothing on the roof should obstruct the LOS path toward your endpoint locations.

  2 If you are testing on a hilltop, find a clear spot that is about 100 feet away from towers or buildings. The towers and buildings can obstruct the LOS paths of incoming signals.

  3 If you need to locate your antenna system on an existing tower to obtain a LOS path, use an antenna with a radiation pattern that is similar to your actual antenna. If practical, place the test antenna in the same tower location where your real antenna will go. Your test antenna should be exposed to the same local and distant RF environment that your real antenna will be exposed to.

NOTE   If you are not certified as a tower climber, you need to hire a properly certified tower climber to safely climb the tower and mount the test antenna. Even with a certified tower climber, it is still your responsibility to make sure that the climber always uses the appropriate safety equipment.

RF Site Survey Process

Before you begin your RF site survey, here are some additional explanations about the way wireless equipment works. These explanations help you understand what to look for and why.

Observing Signal-to-Noise Ratio (SNR)

The *signal-to-noise ratio (SNR)* is the single most important condition that must be met before a wireless signal can be successfully received and decoded. Simply stated, the level of the received signal must be high enough and the noise level low enough to allow the receiver to separate the signal from the noise. If the signal level is too low or the noise level is too high, the incoming data will be lost. The more often that incoming data is lost, the slower the network throughput and performance. On the other hand, the higher the SNR, the better and faster the network performs.

At this point, it is important to understand what the definition of noise includes. Noise is everything other than the desired signal; therefore, noise is the total of natural noise, manmade noise, signals from other networks, and even signals from other access points in your own network. Again, noise is everything other than your one desired signal at every moment in time (every receiver timeslot).

Access Point Vulnerability to Noise

A low SNR at any point in a wireless network results in slow (or, in the worst case—no) data throughput on that particular wireless link. The worst place to have a low SNR is at the hub site (the access point) of a point-to-multipoint network. The reason should be obvious. If an access point (AP) receiver is bombarded with high noise levels, that AP will find it difficult to receive and decode the signals from all the network endpoint transmitters in the network. The throughput to and from all the users of the network will be drastically slowed down.

Unfortunately, point-to-multipoint access points are the most vulnerable to noise for the following reasons:

- They are often located near the center of a metropolitan area where they are exposed to a high concentration of noise sources.

- They are usually located atop high buildings where they can pick up noise from a long distance away.

- They use wider beamwidth antennas (when compared to the narrower beamwidth of point-to-point antennas) that receive noise from a wider and larger area.

The more noise that an AP receiver is exposed to, the lower the SNR will be and the stronger the signals must be for them to be received and decoded. For the signals to be stronger (remember that the amount of power radiated from the antenna systems is limited by the

Federal Communications Commission), the endpoint locations must be closer to the AP location. Therefore, the higher the noise level that an AP receiver is exposed to, the shorter the distance it can communicate and the smaller the cell radius or sector size. This is why it is important to do a site survey and verify that the hub site noise levels are reasonably low. If the noise levels are too high, the range of your newly installed access point might be low, perhaps as low as one-half mile.

Locating Nearby Out-of-Band Noise Sources

Out-of-band noise sources are (as the name suggests) not in the same frequency band that you plan to use. Most often, these transmitters are located just below or above the band and transmit with high power. Following are some examples:

- Paging transmitters
- Cell site transmitters
- Multichannel, Multipoint Distribution Service (MMDS), Multipoint Distribution Service (MDS), and Instructional Television Fixed Service (ITFS) transmitters
- AM, FM, and television broadcast transmitters
- Commercial two-way radio transmitters, especially if they operate near the intermediate frequency (IF) used by your equipment

---

NOTE   Chapter 6, "Evaluating and Selecting Wireless Equipment," describes IF-based equipment in more detail.

Out-of-band interference sources can be strong, either physically nearby or on a nearby frequency. They can overload your receiver and decrease the receiver's sensitivity to desired signals. This in turn reduces the network range and slows the network throughput.

By locating these interference sources early in your network design process, you can do the following:

- Recommend additional test time during installation.
- Recommend the use of a bandpass filter to minimize possible throughput reduction from receiver overload.
- Recommend moving your equipment further away from the high-power transmitters.

Locating In-Band Noise Sources

In-band noise sources are on frequencies within the same ISM or U-NII frequency band that you plan to use. Here are some potential in-band noise sources:

- FHSS networks used by Internet service providers (ISPs) and by corporate, governmental, and educational organizations
- DSSS networks used by ISPs and organizations
- Broadband non-spread-spectrum wireless equipment used in the 5-GHz U-NII bands
- Amateur television (ATV) repeaters used by licensed radio amateurs
- Microwave ovens, cordless phones, Bluetooth and HomeRF devices, indoor wireless access points, wireless video cameras, and other license-free wireless consumer devices

By detecting these noise sources early, while it is still possible to modify your network design, you can minimize the impact of noise and interference. Table 4-3 provides techniques to help your network coexist peacefully with various noise sources.

Table 4-3   *In-Band Noise Source Coexistence Techniques*

In-Band Noise Source	Coexistence Technique
FHSS networks	Locate your access points away from the existing FHSS access point locations. Plan to use antenna systems with the opposite polarization. If you are planning a FHSS network, coordinate your hopping sequences with the existing FHSS network. Be aware that if you deploy a DSSS network without adequate RF isolation, you will experience a severe throughput reduction.
DSSS networks	Locate your access points away from the existing DSSS access point locations. Plan to use antenna systems with the opposite polarization. If you are planning a DSSS network, coordinate your frequencies with the existing DSSS network. Be aware that if you deploy an FHSS network without adequate RF isolation, you will experience a throughput reduction.
Broadband non-spread-spectrum U-NII equipment	If possible, select your frequencies so they do not overlap the existing U-NII network frequencies. Locate your access points away from the existing U-NII equipment access point or endpoint locations. Plan to use antenna systems that have the opposite polarization.

Table 4-3   *In-Band Noise Source Coexistence Techniques*

ATV repeaters	If using DSSS, choose operating frequencies that do not overlap the ATV frequencies; specifically, do not choose frequencies that overlap the repeater audio subcarrier or video carrier frequencies. Locate your access points away from the ATV repeater location. Communicate with and coordinate with the repeater operator. Remember: This is a licensed repeater and it has priority over your network operation.
License-free wireless consumer devices	In general, when used indoors, these devices do not have a big impact on the operation of your (properly designed) outdoor network. To minimize impact, avoid locating your access point antenna systems close to areas where these devices exist. For example, avoid placing your antennas near an employee lunchroom where microwave ovens are frequently in use.

If your RF site survey reveals a substantial amount of in-band noise, you can do the following:

- Suggest that the operators of the existing networks be contacted regarding frequency or antenna coverage coordination.

- Recommend additional test time during your network installation process to correct any noise problems that arise.

- Recommend redesigning your network and moving your wireless equipment (or at least your AP locations) further away from the existing wireless networks.

Locating 802.11b Access Points

The use of 802.11b DSSS access points is rapidly increasing. These access points were originally designed for use on indoor wireless LANs. More and more frequently, ISPs, community network proponents, and experimenters take these access points, add external antenna systems, and deploy the access points in outdoor locations. In large cities, quite a few of these access points are likely deployed. Your spectrum analyzer can detect these access points as long as the access points are handling traffic. Their transmissions are indistinguishable from any other DSSS transmissions.

Before you decide to deploy an 802.11b (or other DSSS) network in a particular area, you should know how many 802.11b access points are already deployed. A PC-based site survey utility or 802.11b packet sniffer provides this information. Use your panel antenna to discover how many access points are within RF range in each of the directions that you plan to deploy your network antennas.

Documenting RF Site Survey Findings

Your RF site survey must collect enough information to make an intelligent decision about where (and with what antennas) to deploy or, possibly, not to deploy your network. The documentation needed to make this decision should include your printed spectrum analyzer output files marked with the following information:

- Date when the data was collected
- Time of day when the data was collected
- Spectrum analyzer sample times (Was it a 60-second sample or a 60-minute sample?)
- Antenna used to collect the data
- Antenna heading used to collect the data
- Antenna polarization used when the data was collected

No Spectrum Analyzer? Now What?

If you do not have access to a spectrum analyzer or even to a PC-based site survey utility, you still have four choices:

- Rent a spectrum analyzer for two weeks or for a month. This is a good choice if you think you might need to buy one in the future. The rental has the advantage of allowing you to become familiar with one (or more) different models.

- Plan to perform a wireless path test using the actual equipment that you plan to deploy. If this path testing is successful, you can be reasonably sure that the equipment will perform the same way after it is permanently installed. The disadvantage of this choice is that you might have to buy the equipment before you can do the path test. Path testing is described later in this chapter.

- Make the decision to recommend that the site be used even though no RF site survey could be performed. You might make this recommendation if you are located in a rural location where few (or no) wireless systems are deployed. Keep in mind, however, that there is always some risk that interference might be present that will affect the throughput of the network that you install.

- Hire a company that is experienced in performing RF site surveys to perform a site survey for you and with you.

RF Criteria Evaluation and Conclusion

Before you make a decision to select a wireless site based on the results of an RF site survey, take a moment to review the following benefits and shortcomings of the site survey process.

The benefits of performing an RF site survey are as follows:

- It helps you gather information about the RF environment that your new network faces.

- It stimulates you to think about alternative network deployment scenarios.

- It allows you to make reasoned judgments and recommendations about whether to use a particular site.

The shortcomings of the RF site survey process are as follows:

- Each RF environment and wireless equipment combination is unique; therefore, there are no absolute Go/No-Go answers, only relative answers.

- The wireless environment can change after the site survey. New networks can be deployed or existing networks can be removed from service.

RF Site Acceptance

You have designed and conducted an RF site survey, collected and documented data, read the explanation of SNR, and reviewed the shortcomings of the RF site survey process. Now you must decide if a site is acceptable for your network. The best site survey data that you have to help you make your decision is the SNR that you observed, as shown in Figure 4-9.

Figure 4-9   *SNR Spectrum Analyzer Signal Display*

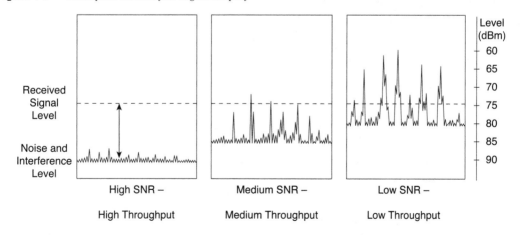

In the real world, the average received signal typically ranges from a low of approximately –85 dBm to a high of approximately –65 dBm. In the Figure 4-9 example, the average received signal level is shown by the dashed line to be –75 dBm.

In the left panel, the noise level is low and the resulting SNR is high. If your spectrum analyzer results look generally like this, you can deploy your network and expect high throughput with little or no problem from noise.

In the center panel, the noise level is moderate. Occasional noise peaks reach and slightly exceed the –75 dBm receive signal level, but they do not occur during every receive data packet and their level is not too high above –75 dBm. If your spectrum analyzer results look generally like this, you can deploy your network and expect good throughput. If you make some effort to reduce the noise level, you should be able to achieve high throughput.

In the right panel, the noise level is high. Noise peaks frequently far exceed the –75 dBm receive signal level. If your spectrum analyzer results look generally like this, your deployed network will deliver low throughput. If you make heroic efforts to reduce the noise level, you should be able to achieve medium throughput, at least until the noise level increases further. In this situation, your best course of action is to attempt to find a site where the noise level is lower.

Table 4-4 provides additional information to help you arrive at a decision about the feasibility of deploying your wireless network at a particular site. If you want still more information before making a final decision, go to the following section and perform path testing or coverage testing.

Table 4-4 *Site Selection Feasibility*

Factor	Excellent	Good	Poor
RF Environment	Friendly—There are no noise sources or only a few obvious noise sources. High SNR values and high throughput can be expected.	OK—There is more than one strong out-of-band interferer and there are only one or two strong in-band interference sources. Medium SNR values and medium throughput can be expected.	Heavy Interference—There are many in-band noise sources. Low SNR values and low throughput can be expected.
Location Desirability	Ideal—This is the best possible site to locate the wireless network equipment.	OK—This location is not perfect, but network coverage and performance are acceptable from this location.	Poor—Physical or RF factors make this location too difficult or expensive to use.
Alternative Locations	Available—Several other locations are available. This location can be selected but does not have to be selected.	Possibly available—Alternative locations might be available. This location might have to be selected.	None—No other alternative locations are available. This location must be selected or no network can be deployed.
More Information and Testing Needed?	No—A definite decision to select this location can be made right now.	Probably—This site could be selected now without further testing and could be made to work.	Yes—More information must be obtained before this site could be selected.

Performing Path Testing or Coverage Testing

There are times when performing path testing or coverage testing using the actual wireless equipment that you plan to deploy might be necessary to provide additional information to support your eventual Go/No-Go deployment decision.

Performing Path Testing

Your RF site survey might not have provided an absolute Go/No-Go answer to the noise and interference question. Questions might remain about the following:

- The duration and intensity of the noise and interference over longer periods of time
- What antenna you should use
- The noise-resistance features of the wireless equipment that you plan to use

In these situations, perform a path test using the selected wireless equipment and antenna. This allows you to test the actual network performance. When the path test is running, be sure to perform throughput testing in both directions and to document the results. For more information, please see Chapter 7 for details about testing point-to-point wireless links.

Performing Coverage Testing

Perhaps, you would like to deploy an access point hub site but you are unsure whether the interference level from other wireless networks in the area would prevent successful performance of your network. Perhaps, you would like to deploy an access point to serve an area that has many trees or many buildings and you are not sure how much of the area your access point will actually cover. In these two situations, it is best to perform a coverage test.

To perform the coverage test, temporarily install an access point with the antenna system that you believe will provide good coverage of the area. Then, use actual customer premises equipment (CPE) and drive around the coverage area. Test the throughput at each location. Document the areas where throughput is excellent, good, borderline, or nonexistent. Plot these results on a map. You now have a coverage footprint for that equipment/antenna combination. You can make changes to the antenna system and retest the coverage. Use your results to determine the areas that you can serve successfully. For more information about testing point-to-multipoint wireless links, see Chapter 7.

Negotiating a Site Lease

After your physical and RF site surveys, if a decision is made to use the site, you need to negotiate a site agreement. The following sections provide some tips that you can use as you prepare to reach agreement with the site owner or manager. These tips are based on a win-win scenario where both you and the site owner benefit from the agreement.

Lease Rates

Monthly lease rates can vary widely depending on the market area where a site is located. In a rural area, you might find rates as low as $200 per month. In a city with high buildings and high population levels, monthly rates might be $1000 per month or higher. This occurs because—at least in the United States—building owners have become accustomed to receiving these high rates from cell phone companies. The owners might not be willing to reduce their price for small ISPs or institutional users.

One possible way to reduce your monthly costs is to ask the building or tower owner if he can use Internet connectivity at the site. If the owner agrees, you might then be able to negotiate a agreement to pay a lower lease rate in return for providing free Internet access to the site.

Finally, when roof space on a building is limited, building managers generally give preferential treatment to tenants who already lease office space within the building as opposed to potential new tenants who only want to lease roof space for antennas and wireless equipment.

Avoiding Interference

When negotiating a contract for space in or on a building, it is appropriate to advise the site manager about the license-free nature of your equipment. You could suffer from interference if other license-free equipment is placed nearby on the roof without first consulting and coordinating with you. Ask that a provision be included in your lease to allow you to approve or disapprove such additional use.

The building management will probably also ask for assurance from you that the wireless equipment that you deploy will not cause interference to equipment that others have already deployed. Be ready to meet with the owners of any equipment already in place and to provide this assurance to building management. Managers of communications antenna tower sites adhere to this principle strictly. The new potential tenant is always responsible for eliminating interference problems caused by their equipment.

Access to Equipment

Try to negotiate 24-hour, 7-day per week equipment and antenna access. Accessing your equipment to provide maintenance and adjustments is required so that you can provide quality service to your wireless customers or end users.

Insurance Requirements

Most locations require you to have liability insurance to cover any possible damage that your equipment might cause. Site owners are rightly concerned about possible damage from water leaks or falling antennas. Most often, liability coverage in the amount of $1 million is required. Costs for this coverage can start below $1000 per year but are often higher.

Consult with several insurance agents in advance to obtain quotes or to confirm that your business insurance policy provides coverage.

Many sites might also ask you to show proof that you carry worker's compensation insurance. This protects the owners from being sued if one of your workers experiences an injury while working on their site.

Work Requirements

Each location will have its own combination of rules and regulations regarding who can perform antenna and equipment installations. In many cases, your personnel will perform all the installation work. In some buildings, the cabling might have to be installed by electrical contractors who are approved by building management. In some cities, you might be required to use union members to install your equipment. Your installation will proceed most efficiently if you accept and respect whatever work regulations are in place.

Tower Site Requirements

A communications tower site is a specialized environment. Many different communications systems are located closely together and need to be managed carefully to ensure that they all operate properly. Site requirements for locating your antenna system on an existing tower can be rather rigid. You can expect to encounter the following:

- **Tower mounting position limitations**—Your choice of where you can mount your antennas on the tower might be limited. Tower management will advise you which mounting positions are open and available. To minimize your installation, maintenance, and monthly costs, plan to mount your antenna(s) at the lowest level that provides complete coverage of your service area.

- **Additional hardware costs**—If you are the first to place antennas at a certain tower height, you might be asked to pay for antenna-mounting hardware, such as antenna support brackets. The brackets (or arms) allow several antenna systems to be mounted horizontally at the same level.

- **Installation personnel requirements**—Many tower sites require that only properly trained tower riggers perform antenna installations. This is more than just a safety issue. Tower management wants to minimize the chance that an improperly installed antenna could fall and damage other antennas on the tower.

- **Strict interference protections**—It is rather unlikely that your low-power license-free equipment will cause interference to any other tower equipment. Once in a while, however, interference can be caused by spurious signals that your equipment generates. If this should ever occur (again, it is rather rare), you will be asked to pay the costs to filter or correct the problem.

Review Questions

1 A physical site survey includes determining how to route cable from the wireless equipment to the antenna. True or false?

2 Before you perform a physical site survey, you should know how high above the ground your antennas need to be mounted. True or false?

3 If there is already wireless equipment operating on a building, you will first discover it during your RF site survey. True or false?

4 Minimizing the distance between your wireless equipment and your antenna system is important. Why?

5 If power lines run near a roof edge, is it okay to mount your antenna near that roof edge? Why or why not?

6 What is the biggest consequence from installing a wireless system in an area with a high noise level?

7 If you have a wireless protocol analyzer, you do not need a wireless spectrum analyzer. True or false?

8 If the operation of license-free equipment causes interference to the operation of licensed amateur radio equipment, the operator of the license-free equipment is responsible for correcting the interference problem. True or false?

9 The length of the spectrum analyzer sampling interval doesn't tell you anything about the level of RF interference in a particular area. True or false?

10 In general, the higher the signal-to-noise ratio on a wireless link, the higher the wireless throughput. True or false?

11 What part of a point-to-multipoint wireless network is the most vulnerable to a high noise level? Why?

CHAPTER 5

Selecting Antenna Systems

Your selection of the proper antenna system is the biggest factor in the success of your wireless network. This chapter helps you select the most effective antenna system for your wireless wide-area network (WAN). This chapter discusses the following topics:

- How antennas focus power
- Basic antenna types
- Antenna polarization and how to use it
- Reasons to combine antennas and how to combine them
- Reasons to isolate antennas and how to isolate them

In a wired Ethernet, the Ethernet cable directs the signal. Ethernet packets can go only where the Ethernet cable goes. In a broadband wireless WAN, the antenna directs the signal. Wireless packets can only go where the antenna system radiates them.

Your antenna system must radiate signals only toward your end users. In addition, to be effective, your antenna system must have the following characteristics:

- Be mounted high enough to achieve a line-of-sight (LOS) path
- Have enough gain to provide reliable link performance
- Be mounted correctly and held in position securely
- Reject noise and interference from other signals and networks

Using Antennas to Focus Power and Reduce Interference

You already know that antennas focus power to and from the end users while reducing interference from other networks and other directions. The next few sections discuss the electromagnetic building blocks that antennas use to focus power. In addition, you will see how to reduce interference using antenna polarization.

Antenna Building Blocks: Lights, Mirrors, and Lenses

Antennas achieve their directivity by using a combination of properly sized and properly spaced antenna elements. These elements are electromagnetic building blocks. Combining the elements in different ways produces different antenna radiation patterns. In some designs, the antenna elements are electrically connected to each other, forming a driven array. In other designs, the elements are placed close together but with no electrical connection, forming a parasitic array.

All antennas use a driven element. The driven element is always electrically connected (via coaxial cable) directly to the wireless equipment. Antennas achieve gain when the driven element is combined with additional element building blocks that reflect, direct, or concentrate the signal.

It is helpful to use the concept of lights, lenses, and mirrors to illustrate how different antenna designs achieve gain as the antenna elements work together to focus transmitted and received energy.

Driven Element: The Light

To create light, a source of electrical energy (such as a battery) is connected to a light bulb. The light bulb converts the electrical energy into light energy.

To create a wireless signal, a source of radio frequency (RF) energy (a transmitter) is connected to the driven element of an antenna. The driven element converts the RF energy into radiated electromagnetic energy—a wireless signal. Every antenna system must have at least one driven element to initiate this energy conversion.

A dipole antenna is one-half wavelength ($\Lambda/2$) long and is frequently used as a driven element. A dipole mounted vertically above the earth radiates energy equally in all horizontal directions. This energy forms a torus (donut-shaped) pattern around the antenna. When the dipole is horizontal to the earth, the donut-shaped pattern becomes bidirectional, radiating energy in just two horizontal directions, off the two sides of the dipole. Figure 5-1 shows a top view of this bidirectional radiation pattern, as well as the bidirectional pattern of light energy radiated from a fluorescent light tube.

Both the horizontal dipole and a horizontal fluorescent light radiate most of their energy off the sides. They radiate little or no energy off the ends. When this bidirectional property is combined with other antenna elements or, in the case of the fluorescent light tube, with other optical elements, a more concentrated, more focused beam of energy results.

Figure 5-1   *Bidirectional Radiation Patterns*

Top View(s)

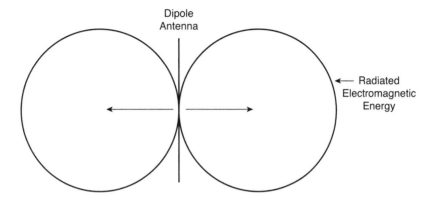

Bidirectional Patterns-Energy Radiated in Two Directions

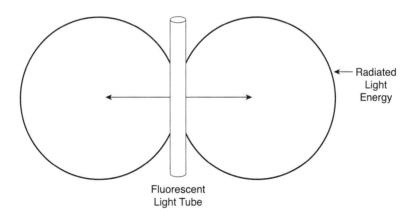

Figure 5-2 shows two vertical antennas. The lower antenna has a single dipole, half-wavelength-long driven element. The top antenna has four half-wavelength-long driven elements. The four driven elements are mounted one above the other and connected together electrically. Because all four driven elements are in a single line, this antenna is called a collinear array.

Figure 5-2 *Multiple-Driven Element Radiation Patterns*

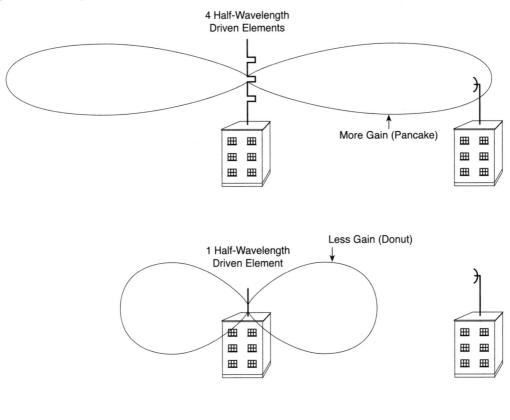

Side View(s)

When two or more driven elements are electrically connected and placed end-to-end (a collinear array), the vertical radiation pattern changes. The donut-shaped pattern flattens out into a pancake shape. The pancake-shaped pattern extends farther away from the antenna than the donut-shaped pattern.

Stated technically, the antenna with the pancake-shaped pattern has more gain compared to the antenna with the donut-shaped pattern. The transmitter power supplied to the antenna hasn't changed, but the end-to-end driven elements concentrate that transmitter power into a narrower but longer coverage area (a narrower vertical beamwidth). A receiver located inside this coverage area can be located farther away from the antenna and still receive a good signal.

NOTE	Another way to look at this is to imagine that the donut around a single half-wave vertical antenna is a jelly donut. When more half-wavelength elements are added, it is like a giant foot came along and stepped on the donut, squashing it down. The jelly squirts out beyond the donut. The radiation pattern of a gain antenna is like the jelly in the donut—it spurts out farther and flatter than the donut. The energy radiated from a four-half-wavelength-long collinear array spurts out about twice as far as the energy from a single half-wavelength-long vertical antenna.

Reflector: The Mirror

Some antenna designs use a reflector along with the driven element. A reflector is an antenna element that is about 5 percent longer than the driven element. The reflector is placed parallel to the driven element and about one-quarter wavelength ($\lambda/4$) away from the driven element, as Figure 5-3 shows.

There is no electrical connection between the driven element and the reflector. When electromagnetic waves leave the driven element, they encounter the reflector. Because the reflector is both physically and electrically longer than the waves, the waves bounce off of the reflector and turn back toward the driven element. The reflected waves join the non-reflected waves to form a stronger signal pattern in the direction away from the reflector. The effect is similar to placing a curved mirror behind a light bulb. Most of the light energy is reflected in one direction, away from the curved mirror.

Together, the driven element and the reflector combine to make the antenna more directional, with more gain in the forward direction and less gain in the backward direction.

Figure 5-3   *Effect of a Reflector*

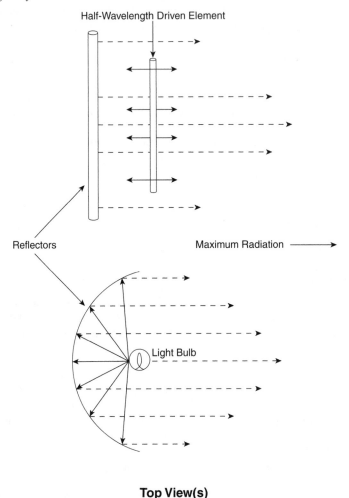

Half-Wavelength Driven Element

Reflectors

Maximum Radiation ⟶

Light Bulb

Top View(s)

Director: The Lens

Some antenna designs use a director along with a driven element. A director is an antenna element that is about 5 percent shorter than the driven element. The director is placed parallel to the driven element and about one-quarter wavelength ($\lambda/4$) away from the driven element. There is no electrical connection between the driven element and the director. When electromagnetic waves leave the driven element, they encounter the director. Because the director is physically and electrically smaller than the waves, the waves tend to travel toward the director. The director concentrates the waves into a tighter beam. This is similar to using a lens in front of a light bulb to concentrate the light energy, as shown in Figure 5-4.

Figure 5-4   *Effect of a Director*

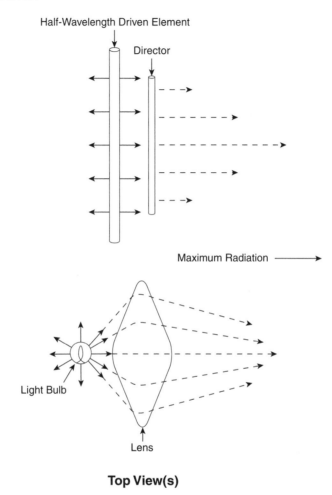

Top View(s)

The director has a concentrating effect on the electromagnetic waves similar to the way a lens concentrates light waves. The waves are concentrated in the direction of the director. This gives the antenna directivity and gain in the forward direction.

NOTE   Many antennas make use of both reflectors and directors. When both of these elements are combined with the driven element, the result is a highly directive high-gain antenna. The Yagi antenna (discussed shortly) is one example.

Antenna Polarization

This section describes antenna polarization and provides several examples to help you select the best polarization for your particular wireless system environment.

Definition of Antenna Polarization

Two electromagnetic fields leave a transmitting antenna and arrive at a receiving antenna: an electric field (also referred to as the E-field) and a magnetic field (also referred to as the H-field). The E-field and the H-field are perpendicular (at a 90-degree angle) to each other, and each field is also perpendicular to the direction that the electromagnetic wave is traveling.

The E-field exists in the same plane (with the same orientation) as the plane of the antenna elements. By definition, the plane of the E-field is the polarization of the antenna. If the antenna elements are vertical relative to the surface of the earth, the E-field is vertical and the signal is vertically polarized. If the antenna elements are horizontal relative to the surface of the earth, the E-field is horizontal and the antenna is horizontally polarized.

In your networks, you can use any of the following four types of polarization to maximize reception of desired signals while reducing noise and interference from undesired signals:

- Vertical polarization
- Horizontal polarization
- Circular polarization
- Cross polarization

Vertical Polarization

Vertical polarization is used in many wireless WAN deployments. Figure 5-5 shows the orientation of the E-field of a vertically polarized antenna relative to the antenna and relative to the surface of the earth.

Figure 5-5   *Vertical Polarization*

Top View

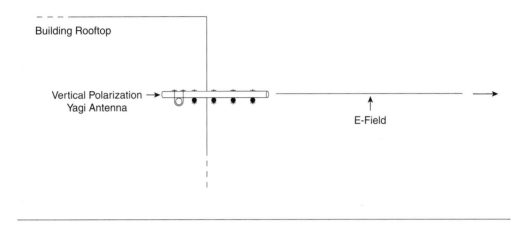

Side View

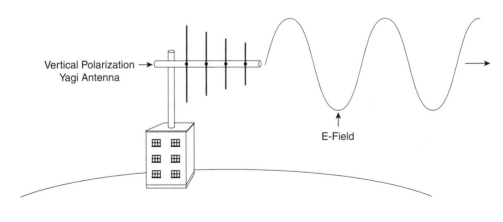

With a vertically polarized antenna, the E-field is vertical, relative to the surface of the earth.

Horizontal Polarization

Horizontal polarization is used in some wireless WAN deployments. Figure 5-6 shows the orientation of the E-field of a horizontally polarized antenna relative to the antenna and relative to the surface of the earth.

Figure 5-6   *Horizontal Polarization*

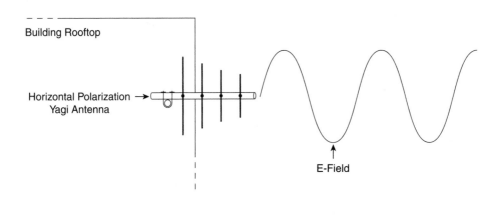

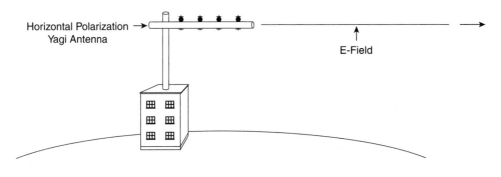

With a horizontally polarized antenna, the E-field is horizontal, relative to the surface of the earth.

Circular Polarization

Occasionally, circular polarization is used in a wireless WAN. Figure 5-7 shows the orientation of the E field of a circularly polarized antenna relative to the antenna.

Figure 5-7   *Circular Polarization*

Side View and Top View (Identical)

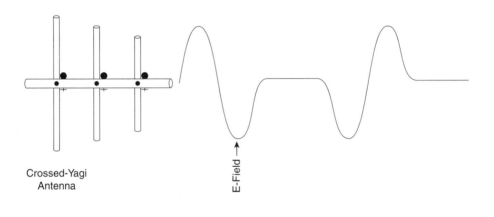

Crossed-Yagi
Antenna

E-Field

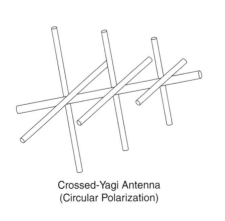

Crossed-Yagi Antenna
(Circular Polarization)

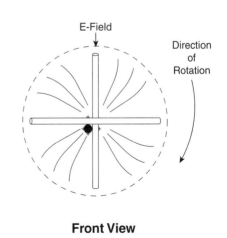

E-Field

Direction
of
Rotation

Front View

With a circularly polarized antenna, the E-field is constantly rotating relative to the antenna. Depending on the antenna construction, the E-field might be either right-hand circularly polarized or left-hand circularly polarized, depending on the direction (or sense) of rotation. The E-field from a right-hand circularly polarized antenna rotates clockwise as it leaves the antenna. The E-field from a left-hand circularly polarized antenna rotates counterclockwise as it leaves the antenna.

Cross Polarization

Cross polarization and circular polarization sound similar but they are not the same thing. As explained in the previous paragraph, circular polarization describes the orientation of the rotating E-field relative to the antenna. In contrast, cross polarization occurs when the E-fields of two antennas are at right angles to each other, such as when one antenna is horizontally polarized and one antenna is vertically polarized. Another example of cross polarization is when one antenna is right-hand circularly polarized and the other antenna is left-hand circularly polarized.

Most antennas have a cross-polarization discrimination (XPD) of about -20 dB. This means that the antenna discriminates against (attenuates) cross-polarized signals by about 20 dB. A signal attenuated by 20 dB is reduced to about 1/100th of its original power level. For this reason, you need to use the same antenna polarization at both ends of your wireless link or suffer a 20-dB reduction in signal strength.

Sometimes, you can use XPD to your advantage. If you need to reduce the level of an interfering signal, you can orient both (or all) of your antennas to be cross polarized relative to the polarization of the interfering signal. You will reduce the level of the interfering signal by 20 dB or 99 percent, as shown in Figure 5-8.

Figure 5-8   *Cross Polarization*

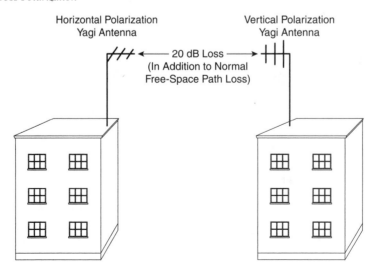

In addition to using cross polarization to reduce the level of interfering signals, you can use cross polarization to do the following:

- **Reuse frequencies**—You can cross polarize your antennas to reduce noise from other parts of your own network, thereby allowing you to reuse the same frequency at other access points (APs).

- **Avoid overload**—You can cross polarize to attenuate strong out-of-band signals and thereby reduce overloading and desensitization of your receiver. Desensitization reduces the size of your system coverage area.

Polarization Selection Examples

The examples in the three sections that follow illustrate typical uses of vertically polarized, horizontally polarized, and circularly polarized antenna systems.

Example 1: Cost-Effective Deployment

Initially, for a fast, simple, and low-cost deployment, a vertically polarized omnidirectional (omni) antenna is often used, as shown in Figure 5-9.

Figure 5-9   *Vertically Polarized Omnidirectional Antenna*

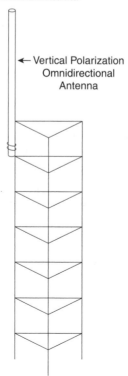

A vertical omni is the fastest, lowest-cost way to deploy an outdoor wireless WAN. If the antenna is mounted high enough to be clear of nearby obstacles, it is relatively easy to cover a circular area with a radius of two or three miles.

There are, however, several significant disadvantages to using an omni:

- **Exposure to noise**—Using an omni exposes the AP receiver to a high level of noise. All the vertically polarized noise and interference sources within the antenna coverage area are received all the time. You cannot discriminate against or reduce any of the noise sources.

- **Coverage area limitations**—Using a low-to-moderate gain omni (+6 to +10 dBi) limits the coverage area to a few miles. Using a higher gain omni (such as +15 dBi) enlarges the coverage area in theory but, in practice, the flatness of the pancake radiation pattern concentrates most of the energy toward the far edge of the coverage area. This makes it difficult to simultaneously cover the end users who are located closer to the antenna.

Because of these limitations, using a vertical omni as a quickly deployed, low-cost antenna system is not recommended except in a small town where there are no significant present (or future) noise and interference sources.

Example 2: Noise Reduction

Compared to the previous vertical omnidirectional antenna example, a better, more noise-resistant AP antenna system uses three horizontally polarized sector antennas, as Figure 5-10 shows.

Figure 5-10 shows an AP with three sectors. Each sector covers about 120 degrees and uses a horizontally polarized sector antenna.

Horizontal polarization reduces the noise and interference coming from the vertically polarized antennas by 20 dB. This occurs because of the cross polarization discrimination (XPD) between the horizontally polarized and the vertically polarized antenna systems.

The three-sector antenna system has an additional advantage compared to an omnidirectional antenna system. An omni is exposed to noise from a 360-degree coverage area. Each sector of a three-sector system is exposed to noise only from a 120-degree coverage area. The noise reduction advantage should be 2/3, or 66 percent.

Downtilting provides even more noise reduction and signal-to-noise ratio (SNR) improvement for the three-sector system. Downtilting allows orienting the main lobe of each sector antenna down away from the horizon and toward the majority of end users in that sector. This increases the signal level to and from end users in the sector while reducing the distant noise coming from beyond the sector.

Figure 5-10   *Horizontally Polarized Sector Antennas*

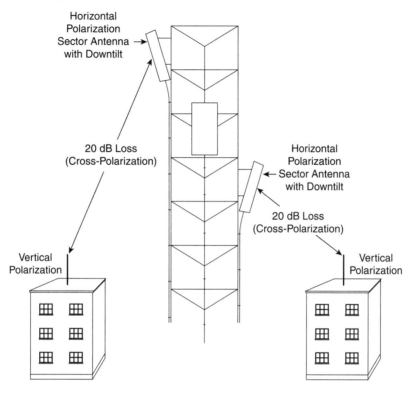

NOTE   A more detailed description of sector antennas is coming up in the next few pages, so stay tuned in.

One final advantage of a sectorized antenna system is that it can start out with one radio and one three-way power splitter to connect all three sectors to the one radio. Removing the splitter and adding two more radios expands the AP to serve three times the number of users without needing to change the antenna system in any other way.

Example 3: Multipath Resistance

In an urban environment with many buildings, many incoming signal reflections are possible, and multipath can be a problem. Circularly polarized antenna systems, as Figure 5-11 shows, can prove beneficial.

Figure 5-11   *Circularly Polarized Antenna in a Multipath Environment*

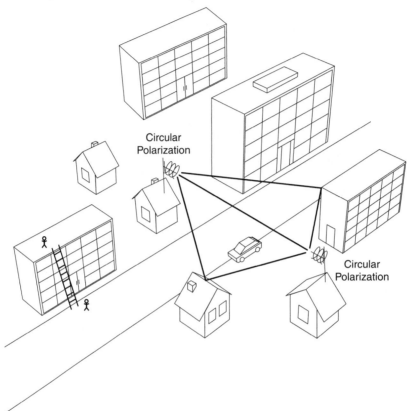

When a circularly polarized signal is reflected, the polarization sense changes. For example, a right-hand circularly polarized signal becomes left-hand circularly polarized. Circular polarization can reduce multipath effects because a once-reflected signal arrives at the receiving antenna with a reversed polarization sense. The XPD of the circularly polarized receiving antenna attenuates the reflected signal by -20 to -30 dB. This severely attenuated multipath signal is too weak to interfere with the direct signal and cause receiver errors.

TIP   Use circular polarization conservatively and only in environments where multipath appears to be a bigger problem than noise and interference. Circular polarization provides only -3 dB of XPD from horizontally and vertically polarized signals. By using circular polarization, you will experience interference from and cause interference to any nearby horizontally and vertically polarized antenna systems.

Surveying Common Antenna Types

You need to be able to identify different types of antenna systems for the following reasons:

- **Antenna selection**—To select the best antenna for your particular application, you need to know what antenna types are available and what the characteristics are of each type.

- **Interference reduction**—You will most likely deploy a wireless network in an area where one or more other wireless networks already exist. You need to be able to identify the antenna type, polarization, and coverage pattern that these existing networks are using. This information allows you to select antennas for your own network that will minimize interference from (and to) the existing networks.

The sections that follow describe the antenna types that are most frequently used for outdoor wireless WANs:

- Omnidirectional antennas
- Yagi-Uda (Yagi) antennas
- Corner reflector antennas
- Parabolic antennas
- Panel antennas
- Helix antennas

Omnidirectional Antennas

An omni antenna radiates equally in all horizontal (azimuth, or compass) directions, but it exhibits directivity in the vertical direction by concentrating energy into a donut or pancake-shaped pattern.

Most often, omnidirectional antennas are vertically polarized, although horizontally polarized omnis are also available. Horizontally polarized omnis generally cost more because their construction is more complex and they are manufactured in smaller quantities.

Figure 5-12 shows both vertically polarized and horizontally polarized omni antennas.

Figure 5-12   *Omnidirectional Antennas*

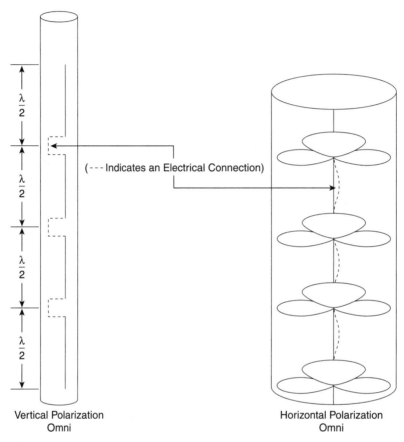

The vertically polarized omni consists of four vertical 1/2 wavelength (λ/2) driven elements, placed end to end, and connected electrically. The main lobe of the omni is shaped like a pancake, with a gain of about +6 dBd (decibels referenced to a λ/2 dipole) or +8 dBi (decibels referenced to an isotropic antenna) for stations that are located within the main lobe.

The horizontally polarized omni consists of four cloverleaf-shaped antennas, placed one above the other and connected electrically. This omni pattern, although horizontally polarized, is also pancake shaped with a gain of +6 dBd (or +8 dBi).

NOTE   Figure 5-12 shows one typical design of a horizontal omni. There are also other horizontal omni designs.

Yagi-Uda (Yagi) Antennas

The Yagi-Uda (usually called simply a Yagi) antenna is named after Hidetsuga Yagi and Shintaro Uda. This antenna consists of a dipole driven element, usually with a single reflector and one or more directors. Figure 5-13 shows a Yagi antenna.

Figure 5-13   *Yagi-Uda (Yagi) Antenna*

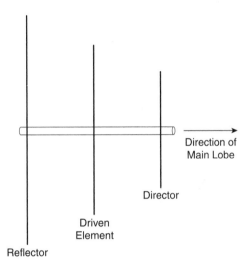

A Yagi antenna is made up of the following antenna building blocks:

- The driven element (DE) is a $\lambda/2$ dipole.

- The reflector is slightly longer than the driven element, has no electrical connection to the DE, and acts like a mirror to reflect the radiated energy back toward the DE.

- The director is slightly shorter than the DE, has no electrical connectivity to the DE, and acts like a lens to focus the radiated energy away from the DE.

The main lobe of the Yagi extends out from the front; the front is the end of the antenna that the director is on. A Yagi can be mounted either vertically or horizontally, depending on the polarization that you need. Figure 5-13 shows a three-element Yagi; however, Yagis are often constructed with many more elements. At 2.4 GHz, Yagis with 10 or even 20 elements and gains as high as +20 dBi are available.

Corner Reflector Antennas

A corner reflector consists of a dipole-driven element mounted in front of a parasitic (no electrical connection) reflector. Instead of a straight reflector, like a Yagi, the corner reflector is a sheet of metal bent into a corner shape, as shown in Figure 5-14.

Figure 5-14   *Corner Reflector Antenna*

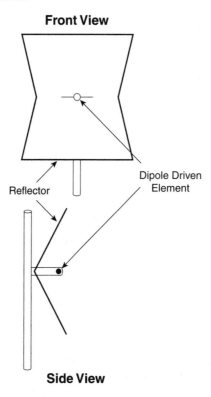

The main lobe of a corner reflector extends out from the front (the driven element) side of the antenna. The angle of the reflector can be 45, 60, or 90 degrees. The antenna in Figure 5-14 is horizontally polarized because the driven element is horizontally polarized. By rotating the entire antenna 90 degrees, the main lobe becomes vertically polarized. The gain of a corner reflector might be as high as +15 dBi.

NOTE   Occasionally, you might see a corner reflector design that uses a series of rods or rib-shaped elements for the reflector instead of a solid metal reflector. The rods are arranged in a corner pattern just like a solid metal reflector. These antennas perform about the same as a solid-back corner reflector, but they are lighter and present less resistance in high winds.

Parabolic Reflector Antennas

A parabolic reflector antenna (or dish antenna) usually consists of a dipole-driven element mounted in front of a parabolic-shaped reflector. Some more expensive parabolic antennas use a waveguide feed instead of a dipole-driven element. Figure 5-15 shows two parabolic antennas, one with a solid reflector and one with a grid reflector.

Figure 5-15   *Parabolic Antenna*

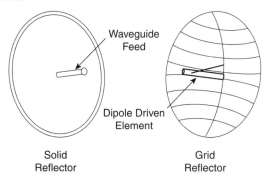

The main lobe of a parabolic antenna extends out from the front (the driven element) side of the antenna. By rotating the mount of a parabolic dish 90 degrees, you can select either vertical or horizontal polarization.

The larger the diameter of the reflector, the higher the gain of the antenna. Typical 2.4-GHz parabolic antenna gains range from +18 to +24 dBi.

A grid parabolic has less wind resistance, a lower front-to-back (F/B) ratio, better XPD, and a lower cost than a solid parabolic antenna.

Panel Antennas

A panel antenna typically consists of an array of driven elements mounted in front of a flat, metallic reflector. The entire antenna is covered with a plastic or fiberglass cover. A panel antenna is usually only a few inches wide. Depending on the gain, the height and width might vary from 6 inches (15 cm) on a side up to and beyond 30 inches (76 cm) on a side. Figure 5-16 shows two panel antenna examples.

Figure 5-16   *Panel Antennas*

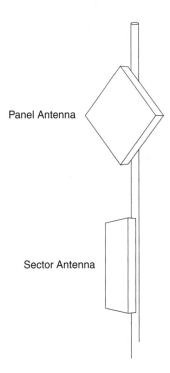

The horizontal and vertical beamwidths of the main lobe of a panel antenna might or might not be symmetric. An example of a symmetric beamwidth is an antenna with a 30-degree horizontal and a 30-degree vertical beamwidth. A non-symmetric example is a sector antenna with a 60-degree horizontal beamwidth and an 8-degree vertical beamwidth. Keeping these respective beamwidths in mind, a panel can be rotated 90 degrees to utilize either horizontal or vertical polarization. This type of panel antenna is often called a sector antenna because it is specifically designed for use in sectorized AP antenna systems.

Panel and sector antennas have moderate to high gains, from +8 to +20 dBi. They have a clean, uncluttered appearance, moderate prices, and are available with a wide variety of radiation patterns. For these reasons, panel antennas are gaining wide acceptance for use in wireless WANs.

Helix Antennas

The helix is a circularly polarized antenna with a circular, helically wound driven element that is shaped like a spring. The driven element usually has from 5 to 20 turns; each turn is one wavelength (λ) in circumference, with individual turns spaced one-quarter wavelength apart along the length of the antenna. The driven element is mounted in front of a metallic reflector that can be either circular or square and either solid or mesh, as Figure 5-17 shows.

Figure 5-17   *Helix Antenna*

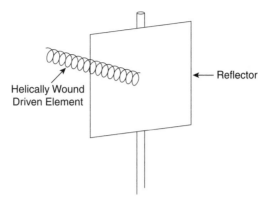

Depending on the direction that the driven element is wound, the helix produces either left-hand or right-hand circular polarization. Helix antennas have typical gains of +12 through +17 dBi; the more turns, the higher the gain.

TIP   Remember this when using circular polarization: The antennas on both ends of the link need to use the same circular polarization sense (both right-hand sense or both left-hand sense).

Combining Antenna Systems

There are a number of reasons to combine antennas or to connect more than one antenna simultaneously to the same piece of wireless equipment. Often, antennas are combined to modify the directivity and the gain of an antenna system. For example, the horizontally polarized omni in Figure 5-12 is made up of four horizontally polarized omni antennas placed (stacked) close together and electrically connected. When these four antennas are stacked together to create one antenna system, the gain goes up by +6 dB and the vertical beamwidth of the main lobe narrows by a factor of four. (Donut-to-pancake—remember?) You might have situations in which you need to combine antennas to create a custom coverage pattern.

Multipath fading is sometimes a problem in wireless WANs. To reduce the problem of multipath, some wireless equipment includes the capability to monitor two antenna inputs and to switch to the signal from the best antenna on a packet-by-packet basis. A two-antenna system is called a diversity antenna system. At some point, you might need to set up a diversity antenna system. The sections that follow describe techniques and provide examples to help you successfully combine antenna systems or set up diversity antenna systems.

Feeding Power to Combined Antenna Systems

You can use a number of methods to feed power to combined antenna systems. The power feed technique that is the most practical for wireless WAN use is to use a *power divider* (sometimes called a *power splitter*). Power dividers are used to feed equal amounts of power to individual antennas within an antenna system. Figure 5-18 provides an example of a two-port power divider.

Figure 5-18   *Using a Power Divider*

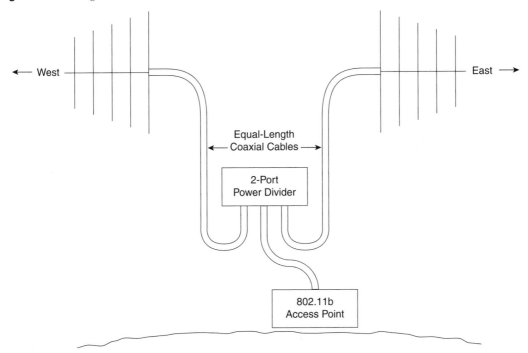

Figure 5-18 shows a two-port power divider dividing the power from one 802.11b AP and sending one-half of the power to each antenna. Two, three, and four port dividers are commonly available.

Bidirectional Antenna Systems

In Figure 5-18, the AP is operating as a low-cost repeater. It is located on a mountain to provide a backbone connection between two communities. It repeats between one community that is located to the east and one community that is located to the west.

An omnidirectional antenna would be a poor choice for this repeater because much of the energy would be radiated (and wasted) in directions other than east and west. To avoid interference from other directions and to maximize link distances to the east and the west, a custom antenna system is needed that focuses the radiated energy toward only the east and the west. The antenna system in Figure 5-18 provides the necessary bidirectional coverage.

The spacing between the two antennas is not critical as long as the two antenna patterns don't interact with each other. If the two antennas are mounted back to back on the same tower or mast and separated vertically by at least 10 feet (3 meters), the antenna system should perform as expected.

NOTE   Keep in mind that splitting power between two or more antennas reduces the range of each antenna. Also, using a single access point as a repeater reduces the throughput by 50 percent.

Diversity Antenna Systems

The primary fading mechanism affecting outdoor microwave links is multipath fading. To minimize system outages due to fading, some wireless equipment incorporates a diversity antenna-switching feature. Diversity means having a signal available from a second (diversity or alternate) antenna system. If the signal from the main antenna system fades or is degraded, the signal from the diversity antenna system can be selected.

Space diversity is the primary diversity technique used in low-cost wireless LAN equipment. This requires that the main and the diversity antennas be separated far enough so that when the signal arriving at the main antenna fades, the signal arriving from the diversity antenna does not. To achieve this uncorrelated fading behavior in an outdoor WAN deployment, a vertical separation between the antennas of 10 to 200 wavelengths is required. At 2.4 GHz, this is a vertical separation of 4 feet to 80 feet (1.2 meters to 24 meters). The more the separation, the better the reduction in multipath fading. Figure 5-19 shows a diversity antenna system.

Figure 5-19   *Diversity Antenna System*

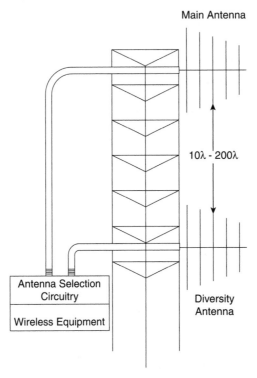

Many 802.11b access points include a diversity feature. These access points were originally designed for indoor use, although many organizations and service providers now deploy them in outdoor WANs. Before activating the diversity feature on your access point, you should do the following:

- Study your documentation carefully so that you understand how your particular equipment implements diversity switching.

- Avoid the temptation to use different types of antenna systems or to point the two antenna systems in different directions. The diversity feature is not designed to function properly this way.

TIP   If you need to cover two different directions with one access point, use two antennas—a two-port power divider and the primary antenna port on your AP. Disable the diversity feature.

- Determine the best spacing to use for deploying the diversity antenna. A rural or suburban point-to-point link benefits from vertical separation between the main and the diversity antenna. A point-to-multipoint antenna system in an urban area benefits from horizontal separation to discriminate against multipoint reflections from buildings.

- Plan to mount the AP as close as possible to the antennas and midway between them. This reduces the cost of antenna cabling.

- If in doubt, disable diversity and use one antenna.

Isolating Antenna Systems

The scarcest and most valuable resource that is needed by individuals and groups who want to deploy license-free broadband wireless WANs is license-free spectrum—frequencies that can legally be used without spending hundreds of thousands of dollars to buy a license.

The quantity of available license-free frequencies is not increasing, but the number of people who want to use these frequencies is increasing. The result is that the same spectrum space will be used repeatedly. The knowledge and the ability to re-use frequencies and to avoid interference determines who is successful in the license-free wireless business and who is not. Any interested individual can put an outdoor wireless system on the air; however, providing reliable service with it is not a plug-and-play operation.

This section suggests techniques that allow you to re-use the license-free frequencies successfully by isolating antenna systems from each other.

Benefiting from Antenna System Isolation

Moving antenna systems away from each other creates isolation between the systems. As the antennas move farther apart, the signal level that each antenna receives from the other antenna is reduced. Armed with this knowledge, you can use physical antenna separation to provide isolation between different parts of your network, and you can also isolate your network from other networks. Antenna system isolation provides the following major benefits:

- Noise reduction from other networks
- Noise reduction from your own AP transmitters network

Noise Reduction from Other Networks

Antenna separation between your antenna(s) and the antennas of other, nearby networks allows you to operate on the same frequencies that the other networks are using. For example, using direct-sequence spread spectrum (DSSS) in the 2.4 GHz band, there are only three non-overlapping channels; these are channels 1, 6, and 11. If you are using these frequencies and a neighboring network is also using one or more of them, the networks interfere with each other. The networks can interfere with each other even if they are 5 to 10 miles (8 to 16 km) apart. Without effective antenna isolation, packets from each network collide and the throughput of both networks suffer.

In addition to packet collisions between your network and other license-free networks, you can also experience slow network performance caused by licensed transmitters. All wireless receivers are susceptible to being overloaded by strong, nearby signals. Licensed transmitters that are located on the same site as your license-free equipment might be legally transmitting with fairly high power levels. Even though they are not transmitting on the same exact frequencies that you are using, they might overload your receiver and cause your incoming packets to be lost. The result is the same as interference from other same-frequency trans-mitters—your network throughput decreases. Antenna isolation is the easiest, lowest-cost method to minimize noise and interference problems as you design, deploy, and operate your wireless WAN.

Noise Reduction from Your Network

When you deploy more than one sector at the same physical location, noise caused by your transmitters in your other sectors can cause receiver desensitization, coverage area reduction, and decreased throughput. This is true whether you are using direct-sequence spread spectrum or frequency-hopping spread spectrum equipment.

If you are deploying direct-sequence spread spectrum (DSSS) equipment, you might reach the point where you need to use more than three frequencies at the same physical location. If you deploy a second wireless access point, you will most likely need to re-use one or more of the three non-overlapping frequencies (channels 1, 6, and 11). In either of these situations, using antenna isolation techniques, you will be able to successfully re-use frequencies.

If you are deploying more than one sector of FHSS equipment, you will be following the manufacturer's recommendations to utilize the same hopping set but different hopping sequences for co-located sectors. This practice minimizes but does not eliminate the throughput reduction caused by collisions between your sectors. The use of effective antenna isolation techniques reduces these collisions further.

The following sections help you determine how much isolation you can obtain by separating antennas both vertically or horizontally.

Vertical Separation Isolation

Separating antennas vertically on a mast or on a tower is fairly straightforward. It requires mounting the antennas (the antennas might or might not be similar to each other) one above the other. This method requires no extra hardware.

Isolation between the two antenna systems is obtained via two mechanisms. The total vertical separation isolation is the sum of these two mechanisms. Figure 5-20 demonstrates the mechanisms, and the list that follows describes them in more detail.

Figure 5-20   *Vertical Separation Isolation*

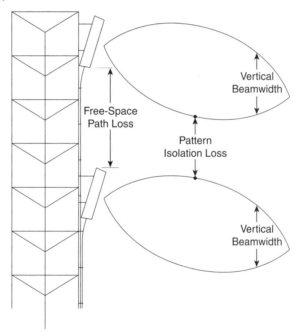

- **Free-space path loss (FSPL)**— You will remember from the discussion of free-space path loss in Chapter 2, "Understanding Wireless Fundamentals," that free-space path loss is the price that must be paid to enjoy the magic of wireless communications. Of all the wireless energy that leaves a transmitting antenna, only a tiny percentage ever arrives at the receiving antenna. Most of the energy is simply lost in space. Now (when you need some antenna isolation) is the time that this loss can be your gain. After leaving an antenna, a 2.4-GHz signal experiences about 49 dB of FSPL in the first 10 feet (3 meters). In other words, only about 1/100,000 of the signal remains after it has traveled 10 feet.

NOTE	Experienced wireless engineers differentiate between an antenna's near field and an antenna's far field. In an antenna's near field, the signal strength varies in a more complex fashion, and other nearby objects can affect the signal strength. Both an antenna's published specifications and true FSPL calculations apply only in the antenna's far field. For the purpose of this book, however, the discussion of antenna isolation is still a useful one and close enough to reality that it is a practical design and planning tool.

- **Pattern isolation loss**—If both antennas have clean radiation patterns without significant minor lobes extending upward or downward and a fairly narrow vertical beamwidth, a significant amount of additional isolation is possible between the patterns of the antennas.

Table 5-1 shows the approximate total vertical separation isolation values that can be obtained when the FSPL isolation and pattern isolation loss are combined.

Table 5-1   *Vertical Separation Isolation Values (dB)*

Vertical Separation in Feet (Meters)	Total Antenna-to-Antenna Isolation (in dB @ 2.4 GHz)
1 (0.3)	43
2 (0.6)	55
3 (0.9)	62
4 (1.2)	67
5 (1.8)	74
10 (3.0)	83
15 (4.6)	90
20 (6.1)	95
50 (15.2)	112
100 (30.5)	124

Horizontal Separation Isolation

Obtaining horizontal separation isolation for antennas mounted on the roof of a building is straightforward, as Figure 5-21 shows. One extra support mast is required compared to mounting both antennas on the same mast.

Figure 5-21   *Horizontal Separation Isolation*

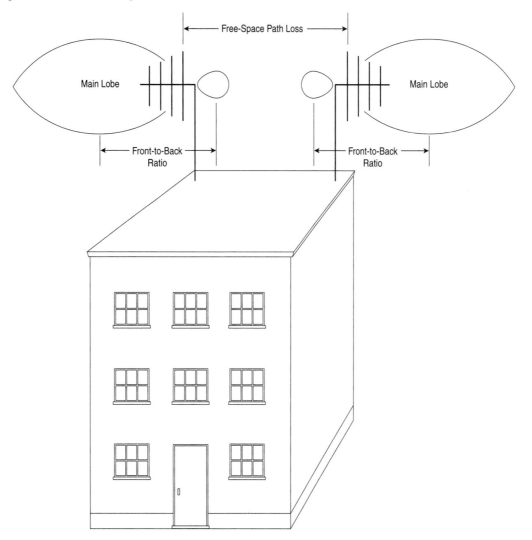

In Figure 5-21, the rooftop antennas are mounted back to back. The maximum isolation possible from horizontal separation is the sum of the front-to-back ratios of both antennas plus the free-space path loss shown in Table 5-2.

NOTE   What is the front-to-back (F/B) ratio, you ask? This is a good place to define it. F/B ratio is another power ratio in dB—just like the power ratios using dB that you looked at earlier in this book. The F/B ratio is the ratio between the energy in the main (front) lobe of an antenna divided by the energy in the back lobe of the antenna. Good antennas focus and radiate most of their energy from the front of the antenna and very little of their energy toward the back. The higher the F/B ratio (for example, +20 dB or +30 dB), the better the antenna and the less interference that will be experienced to and from signals in back of the antenna.

Table 5-2   *Horizontal Separation Isolation Values (dB)*

Horizontal Separation in Feet (Meters)	FSPL Isolation (in dB @ 2.4 GHz)
1 (0.3)	29
2 (0.6)	35
3 (0.9)	39
4 (1.2)	41
5 (1.8)	43
10 (3.0)	49
20 (4.6)	55
30 (6.1)	59
50 (15.2)	63
100 (30.5)	69

Cross-Polarization Isolation

Earlier in this chapter, Figures 5-8 and 5-10 provided examples of using XPD isolation. XPD isolation is mentioned again here in the context of the other antenna-isolation techniques. Keep XPD isolation in mind and use it frequently as you design and deploy your outdoor wireless WANs. It can add up to –20dB of additional isolation.

Obstruction Isolation

To maximize and maintain the performance of your network, it is sometimes necessary to use obstruction isolation. Buildings and other large objects reduce the strength of microwave signals through absorption, diffraction, and reflection.

When you need additional isolation between antenna systems, position the antennas in such a way as to place a building (or part of a building) between the antennas, as shown in Figure 5-22.

Figure 5-22 *Obstruction Isolation*

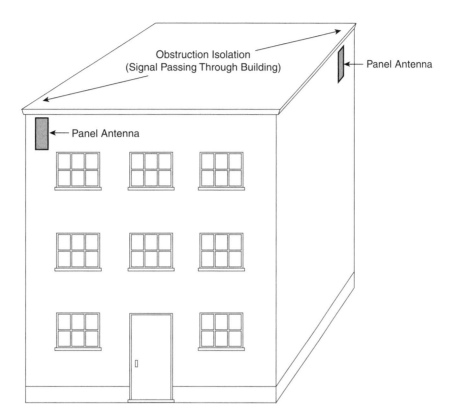

The construction of each building is different, so it is difficult to estimate the amount of isolation that a building provides. If you estimate an average of –8 dB for each exterior wall and –4 dB for every interior wall, the isolation provided by the building in Figure 5-22 might total between –30 and –40 dB.

Sector Antenna Systems

Chapter 3, "Choosing Your Network Architecture," described sectors as similar to pieces of pie, but sectors are never exactly wedge shaped. In practice, sectors can be shaped like a circle, an oval, a fan blade, or whatever shape you need to cover a specific area. Figure 5-23 shows examples of access point locations with sector antenna systems consisting of one, two, three, and six sectors. Your antenna system for each sector needs to be selected and aligned to maximize the coverage within that sector and minimize the noise and interference from all other sectors and areas.

Figure 5-23 *Sector Coverage Examples*

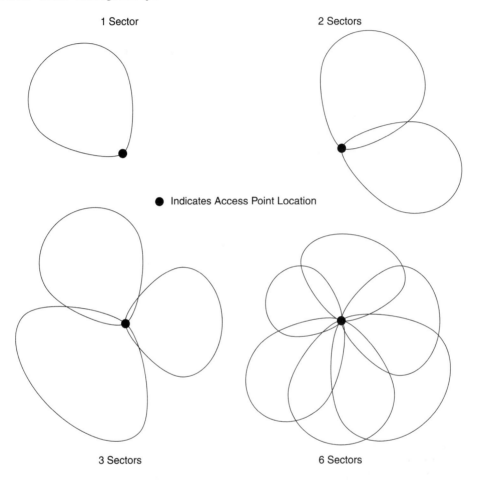

1 Sector

2 Sectors

● Indicates Access Point Location

3 Sectors

6 Sectors

When you choose to build a sectorized access point, you gain the following advantages:

- **Scalability**—You can increase the capacity of your system. You can start small, perhaps with just a single sector serving a few users. As the number of users grows, you can add more sectors. By converting omnidirectional coverage to three-sector coverage, you can triple the capacity of your hub site.

- **Reliability**—You can select the gain and the pattern of each sector antenna to provide the highest signal level for end users in that sector. You can also choose the polarization and adjust the downtilt of each sector antenna to reduce interference from other networks. By designing a good sector antenna system and installing the sector antennas correctly, you reduce the noise level and improve the reliability of your service within each sector.

Selecting Sector Antennas

Sectorization always yields dividends compared to a non-sectorized antenna system. For the best performance from your sectorized system, consider the suggestions in the sections that follow as you design your system and select your antennas.

Low-Noise Access Point Location

Although a sectorized system handles noise and interference far better than a non-sectorized system, it is still important to select a low-noise access point location. Even the best sector antenna design might not provide satisfactory service if it is installed in a high-noise location.

TIP   For help in choosing a low-noise location, review the wireless site survey information in Chapter 4, "Performing Site Surveys."

Sector Orientation

Coordinate the orientation of your sectors to provide effective, scaleable coverage of your service area. For example, if many of your end users are concentrated in a downtown area, plan to use more than one sector to cover that area. For example, if you decide to use a total of three sectors to cover the downtown area, then each sector should cover 1/3 of the total area. If the total downtown area extends 180 degrees when viewed from your access point location, each sector antenna should have a horizontal beamwidth of 45 to 60 degrees.

Sector Radius

The radius of each sector plays a direct role in choosing the proper antenna for that sector. A sector with a small radius requires a low-gain sector antenna. A sector with a large radius needs a high-gain antenna. Use the formula for link budget in Chapter 2 to determine how much gain you need to cover your sector. Remember to allow a fade margin of at least 10 dB.

Polarization

Choose the polarization of each of your sector antennas. Each sector should be cross polarized when compared to the polarization of the strongest source of noise and interference within that sector. It is okay to use different polarizations in different sectors.

Horizontal Beamwidth

Choose the horizontal beamwidth of each sector to be from 75 to 100 percent of the width (in degrees) of the sector. There is no absolutely correct formula; however, one rule of thumb is to choose a sector antenna with a horizontal beamwidth equal to *75 percent of the sector width*; for example, a 45-degree horizontal beamwidth antenna is often chosen for a 60-degree sector.

Remember from Chapter 2 that horizontal beamwidth describes the width of an antenna's main lobe at the half-power points. This means that an antenna with a 60-degree horizontal beamwidth still radiates a substantial amount of power beyond a 60-degree angle.

TIP

If you prefer to have a substantial overlap between sectors to provide a little redundant area coverage when frequency re-use is not an issue, choose a horizontal beamwidth equal to the sector width.

Vertical Beamwidth

Choose the vertical beamwidth of each sector antenna based on the radius of the sector. A sector that has a larger radius needs a wider vertical beamwidth to cover the sector. A sector that has a smaller radius needs a smaller vertical beamwidth.

Downtilt

Choose sector antennas that can be mechanically downtilted to allow you to center the main lobe of the antenna in the middle of the coverage area of each sector. More downtilt is needed in sectors that have more elevation differential between the end users and the sector antenna. For example, in a 5-mile radius sector, an antenna that is mounted 500 feet higher than the elevation of the end users must be downtilted more than a sector antenna that is mounted only 150 feet higher than the end users.

F/B Ratio

Select a sector antenna with the highest possible F/B ratio consistent with the cost of the antenna. Higher F/B ratios result in more interference rejection off the back of the antenna. More interference rejection allows a higher signal-to-noise ratio and better performance in the forward direction.

Size, Weight, and Appearance

Choose a sector antenna that has a size and weight that can be safely and securely mounted in or on the available mounting area or tower.

Choose an antenna that has an appearance that is acceptable to the management of the site where the antenna is to be located.

TIP   If you need to paint an antenna to make it blend in with a building, be sure to select paint without metallic content. Metal in the paint reduces the performance of the antenna.

Quality and Cost

Sector antennas range in cost from $50 to more than $500. Choose a sector antenna that balances quality and cost. A more expensive, higher-quality antenna will have the following features:

- Higher-quality materials for a longer life
- A cleaner radiation pattern with fewer side lobes to cause interference
- More constant performance characteristics across the band, including gain and standing wave ratio (SWR)
- A mounting system that is easier to install and adjust
- Fewer internal parts to minimize the chances of failure

Other Antenna System Components

An antenna system has several other parts, such as these:

- **Feed system**—The feed system carries power to and from the antenna. The feed system is coaxial cable (coax) or, in rare instances, waveguide.
- **Coaxial connectors**—Connectors transfer power between different sections of the feed system.
- **Mounting hardware**—Mounting hardware connects the antenna to the antenna supports. The mounting hardware must hold the antenna firmly in place, including any uptilt or downtilt. Mounting hardware also secures feedlines to masts, towers, and buildings.
- **Covering**—Antenna coverings are called radomes.

The sections that follow cover the antenna system components in greater detail.

Feed Systems

99 percent of the time, an antenna feed system consists of coaxial cable plus connectors, jumpers, and lightning arresters. 1 percent of the time, a feed system consists of waveguide. Waveguide is heavy, expensive, and low loss compared to coax. A full description of waveguide is beyond the scope of this book; however, in brief, waveguide is like running a rectangular, circular, or elliptical metal pipe up a tower to connect the radio and the antenna. Wireless energy is carried inside the waveguide until the energy reaches the antenna.

Consider the following coax characteristics when selecting the proper coax for your antenna feed system:

- Impedance
- Loss
- Size
- Type
- Power-handling capability
- Upper frequency limit

The sections that follow cover each characteristic and provide recommendations for selecting coax transmission line that is suitable for your purposes.

Impedance

Most radios are designed with an antenna impedance of 50 ohms (50 Ω). The coax for these antenna systems needs to have a characteristic impedance of 50 Ω.

NOTE It is becoming increasingly popular to integrate a radio directly into an antenna and run Ethernet cable from the outdoor radio/antenna combination down to the indoor network equipment. This configuration avoids the coaxial cable losses that would otherwise occur. These integrated systems use shielded outdoor Category 5 (Cat 5) Ethernet cable and no coaxial cable.

Loss

Coaxial cable is rated in decibels (dB) of loss per 100 feet at each frequency. For example, good quality, low-loss 0.4-inch (1 cm) diameter cable (the most frequently used size) has a loss of about –7 dB per 100 feet at 2.4 GHz.

The sum of the coax cable losses at each end of a wireless link plays a role in determining the distance over which the link operates. See the link budget discussion in Chapter 2 for the link budget distance computation and the maximum loss that the coax can contribute. The most important consideration in selecting the proper coax for a particular installation is to avoid excessive loss at the same time you avoid excessive cost.

Size

Coax is available in a wide range of diameters from about 1/16 of an inch (1.58 mm) up to over 1 inch (2.54 cm). The larger the diameter, the lower the loss. Also, the larger the coax diameter, the heavier and more expensive the cost of the coax.

Type

In addition to standard coaxial cable, the following additional cable types are available:

- **Plenum**—Plenum cable is manufactured using material that meets building code standards for being placed into horizontal air plenums. Plenum-rated cable materials do not give off toxic fumes and can be safely placed into air ventilation plenums that carry breathable air.

- **Riser**—Riser cable is manufactured using material that meets building code standards for being placed into vertical riser systems that run between floors of a building. Riser-rated cable materials burn slowly and inhibit the spread of fire vertically from floor to floor in a building.

- **Direct burial**—Direct burial cable is manufactured using material that resists the spread of moisture through the cable. When water intrudes into standard cable, it typically spreads along the cable. When this occurs, cable losses rise significantly, and the only way to correct the problem is to replace the entire cable. In contrast, direct burial cable resists the intrusion and spread of moisture and can be directly buried without experiencing moisture problems.

- **Flexible**—Flexible cable is significantly more flexible than standard cable. Use flexible cable where cable needs to make sharp bends or where cable needs to flex, move, or rotate.

Power-Handling Capability

Coaxial cable has limits on the amount of power that it can handle before failing. Fortunately, all commonly used cable types handle many times more power than the maximum legal 1-watt (W) transmitter output power allowed in license-free systems.

Upper Frequency Limit

Although, in general, larger-diameter coax with lower loss is better than smaller diameter coax, there is a maximum cutoff frequency limit when the coax size becomes so large that the coax begins to behave like waveguide. If you deploy 5-GHz equipment, discuss this size limitation with the manufacturer or distributor of your wireless equipment. In general, at 5 GHz, use coax with a maximum diameter of 0.9 inch (2.3 cm). Larger diameter coax is not recommended.

Feed System Connector Locations and Types

Coaxial connectors perform many functions in wireless systems. Although many different connector types are available, in practice, only a few different types are used. The most commonly used connector is the N connector.

When you know the location of a connector, you can often predict the type of connector that is used. Coaxial connectors are used in the following locations:

- **Wireless equipment inputs and outputs**—This is the area with the largest variety of possible connectors. FCC rules specify that wireless equipment manufacturers must use connectors that are not generally available. The reason for this rule is to make it difficult to use the equipment with antenna systems (and amplifiers) that do not meet FCC certification requirements. The FCC is concerned that equipment operators will add amplifiers that transmit at illegally high power levels.

NOTE   Unfortunately, the FCC concern appears to be justified. A small number of license-free network operators do apparently transmit at power levels that exceed FCC regulations. Sometimes these operators have not taken the time to become familiar with the FCC rules. Other times, the violators know the rules but choose to ignore them in the belief that they will not be caught. These operators appear not to care about the interference that their overpower operation can cause to other wireless networks. At press time, it has been reported in the U.S. that the FCC has begun to enforce the power level rules more widely. Lawbreakers beware!

- **Pigtails**—Typically, short, small-diameter "pigtail" connecting cables are used to bridge from equipment connectors to the rest of the antenna system. These pigtails have an equipment-specific connector on one end and a standard larger-diameter connector on the other end. The larger diameter connector is typically an N connector.

- **Jumpers**—Jumpers are generally short, larger-diameter connecting cables. Jumpers are usually used between different peripheral devices as well as between large-diameter antenna cable runs and the antennas themselves. Jumpers generally use N connectors.

- **Peripherals**—Peripheral devices, such as lightning arresters, are placed between the wireless equipment and the antenna system. These devices generally use N connectors.

- **Antenna cable runs**—Coaxial cable runs from wireless peripherals up to antenna systems generally use N connectors, although some equipment manufacturers occasionally use other large-diameter connectors.

Antenna-Mounting Hardware

Although there are exceptions, most antennas are designed to mount around a vertical pipe, mast, or tower leg using a U-bolt, as shown in Figure 5-24.

Figure 5-24 *Antenna U-Bolt Mounting Hardware*

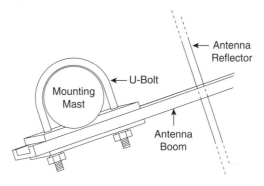

A U-bolt bracket typically mounts through two holes in the antenna boom or other antenna-support element. The U-bolt then clamps around the antenna support mast or tower leg. When the U-bolt is tightened, it grips the mast and holds the antenna firmly in position.

Antenna Coverings

Many antennas operate for years outdoors, uncovered and exposed to the weather. In some harsh environments, antenna coverings are used to either minimize damage to the antenna from the weather or reduce the wind resistance of the antenna system.

When antenna coverings are used, the coverings are called radomes. Radomes are made out of nonconducting material (such as fiberglass) to prevent the radome from altering the radiation pattern of the antenna. Some radome advantages are:

- Preventing moisture and precipitation from corroding the metallic parts of the antenna and degrading antenna performance
- Covering the antenna to reduce snow and ice buildup
- Covering the antenna to reduce wind loading on the antenna, the antenna mast, and the tower

Review Questions

1   When comparing light energy to wireless energy, a light bulb can be compared to what antenna element?

2   The orientation of an antenna's E-field determines what characteristic of the antenna's operation?

3   Relative to each other, the E-field of a vertically polarized antenna and the E-field of a horizontally polarized antenna are what?

4   Omnidirectional antennas are available with either vertical or horizontal polarization. True or false?

5   A diversity receiving system can automatically select the best signal from one of two antennas. True or false?

6   When using a diversity system, the two antennas must always be the same type and point in the same direction. True or false?

7   Anyone who deploys an outdoor license-free wireless system can provide reliable wireless service. True or false?

8   A strong signal arriving at your receiver from another wireless network increases your network throughput. True or false?

9   How much is the typical cross-polarization isolation between a horizontally polarized and a vertically polarized antenna?

10   A sectorized antenna system does not allow you to serve more end users. True or false?

11   In a sectorized antenna system, all the sector antennas should be identical. True or false?

12   Sector antennas in a sectorized antenna system should always be mounted perfectly vertical. True or false?

CHAPTER 6

Evaluating and Selecting Wireless Equipment

The equipment that you select for your broadband wireless wide-area network (WAN) plays a major role in the reliability, scalability, and profitability of your network. This chapter helps you evaluate and select your wireless network equipment.

This chapter does not list feature information vendor by vendor. The quantity of information would be overwhelming and the listing would quickly become outdated. Instead, this chapter aims to help you understand the features and characteristics that are available on wireless equipment. When you understand the features and their significance, you will be in a position to select the equipment that best meets your network needs.

Any New Features This Week?

Wireless equipment is evolving rapidly. Wireless hardware and software features change each week. I have attempted to describe all the significant wireless hardware and software features that were offered (by at least one equipment manufacturer) at the time I wrote this chapter in 2002. Because of rapid equipment evolution, I suggest that you supplement the information presented here with your own feature research.

This chapter contains the following major sections:

- A description of the equipment selection process.

- A brief explanation of the International Organization for Standardization (ISO) Open Systems Interconnection (OSI) seven-layer reference model. An understanding of this model helps you understand how various wireless features fit into your network.

- A list of equipment features, arranged by OSI layer. Following each feature is an explanation of the feature.

- A summary of the features that are the most desirable for wireless backbone equipment, access points (APs), customer premises equipment (CPE), wireless network cards, mesh network nodes, and amplifiers.

- A discussion of compatibility issues that can cause problems when mixing wireless equipment from different vendors.

- Suggestions about evaluating and receiving vendor support.

Overview of the Equipment Selection Process

Your equipment purchase can involve spending only a few hundred dollars, or it can involve spending hundreds of thousands of dollars. The more money that you plan to spend, the more important it is that you include all of the following steps in your selection process.

Reviewing Your Wireless Network Needs

Before you select your wireless equipment, take the time to review your wireless network needs:

- How many wireless end users do you want to serve?
- What network architectural elements do you want your wireless network to include?
- Do you need only point-to-point links or will you deploy point-to-multipoint APs?
- Do you need wireless backbone bandwidth?
- Do you need mesh network nodes or repeaters?
- What features will your wireless network need so that it can connect to your wired network?
- Will you need routing or only bridging?

After you have reviewed both the wireless network features and the wired features that you need, you are ready to begin researching specific wireless equipment features.

Researching Equipment Features

Now that you know your network needs, you can begin listing wireless equipment that matches your needs. The most difficult part of the research process is not learning what features a particular brand of equipment offers. The most difficult part is learning what features are *not* offered or which features do not work the way you expect them to work.

If you have not worked with wireless equipment before, it can be difficult to get an accurate picture by looking only at press releases and advertising flyers. Press releases are typically loaded with attractive buzzwords that promise wireless performance and wireless benefits that are sometimes exaggerated or theoretical. Advertising flyers and spec sheets do not lie about equipment performance, but they sometimes omit information that would reveal performance shortcomings.

Evaluate equipment that offers the specific features that you need, such as distance and bandwidth capabilities, but before you decide to buy, visit a network where that particular vendor's equipment is deployed.

Visiting Deployment Sites

After you have researched equipment features, you will have one or more equipment vendors who can provide equipment that appears (at least on paper) to meet your wireless needs. It is appropriate and proper for you to ask the vendors to recommend one or two existing wireless networks that have deployed their equipment. Visit these sites and talk with the network operators who have deployed the equipment.

Your visit will allow you to learn what features work especially well and what features do not work as expected. You will learn which expectations were exceeded (the good news) and which expectations were not met (the not-so-good news). You will learn if the equipment is easy or difficult to manage. You will also learn if vendor support is poor, good, or outstanding. This is information that you cannot obtain from a spec sheet or an advertising flyer. With the benefit of this information, can make an accurate and informed decision about which equipment to purchase.

Testing Wireless Equipment in the Lab

When you have completed your site visits, there will probably be one or two vendors that you think would be good equipment providers. At this point, consider making a small equipment purchase consisting of either a pair of wireless units or one AP and one CPE unit.

Set up these units indoors and become familiar with them. Configure the units and measure their throughput in both directions. Learn to use the diagnostics.

TIP

Practice safety when you are working near wireless equipment. High amounts of microwave energy can cause damage to the human body, so minimize your exposure to this type of energy. Do not point a directional antenna at yourself or at any other nearby person. Turn the wireless equipment off any time you are not testing it. Remember: When you double the distance between yourself and a wireless antenna, you reduce the amount of radiation reaching you to one-fourth the previous level. Whenever possible, maintain as much distance as possible between yourself and a wireless antenna.

When your indoor testing is complete and you are comfortable with the units, proceed to outdoor testing.

Testing Wireless Equipment Outdoors

Testing wireless equipment outdoors allows you to test the range, throughput, and reliability of the equipment in the presence of real-world noise, interference, and weather.

For your outdoor testing, perform the following steps:

Step 1   Pick two locations that are as far apart as the maximum link distance that you expect the equipment to cover. For example, if you plan to build a wireless cell with a 4-mile (6.4 km) radius, pick an AP location that is high enough to have at least two line-of-sight (LOS) paths that are at least 4 miles long.

Step 2   Test using an AP antenna system similar to the one that you expect to use in your actual network deployment.

Step 3   Temporarily set up the CPE at first one and then the other of your two test locations.

Step 4   Test during the busiest part of the day and repeat the throughput tests that you performed indoors. It is important that you test the throughput from the CPE to the AP. This is an important test of the AP's capability to receive in the presence of noise and interference. For more details about throughput testing, see the description in Chapter 7, "Installing Outdoor Wireless Systems."

Step 5   If possible, repeat your performance testing several times over a period of several days or weeks. The equipment performance should remain constant throughout the entire test period.

Your outdoor testing will not tell you how many customers the AP will handle at full load, but it will give you a good preliminary performance indication. If all your test results are good, proceed to the following purchase decision step.

Making Purchase Decisions

Your testing should bring you to the point where you are most comfortable with the performance of one or two brands of wireless equipment. You can now make your purchase decision and be fairly confident that the equipment you buy will meet your performance expectations.

OSI and TCP/IP Reference Models

Several different but similar layered data architectures have been developed to allow reliable data transfer between different computer systems and between different networks. When you understand a little about the service layers and the protocols that these architectures use, you will be in a good position to understand the similarities and the differences between different brands of wireless equipment.

The seven-layer ISO OSI reference model was first proposed around 1983 to allow connectivity (or interworking) between different computer systems. Prior to the OSI reference

model, computer systems made by one manufacturer could not easily communicate with computer systems made by other manufacturers. The intent of the OSI reference model was to allow computer systems to successfully communicate with each other even though different vendors manufactured them. Figure 6-1 shows the OSI reference model alongside the
TCP/IP architecture.

Figure 6-1   *OSI and TCP/IP*

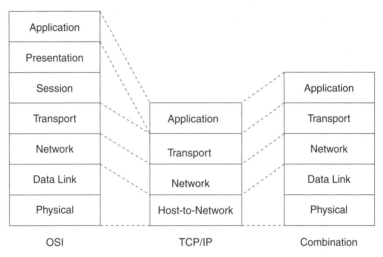

Beginning in the 1970s, the United States Department of Defense began promoting computer networking between university research departments and government installations. One of the primary goals of this internetworking effort was to develop a survivable network—one that would be able to continue communicating even if some of the network nodes or some of the communications links were destroyed. This new networking effort was based on two primary protocols: the Transmission Control Protocol (TCP) and the Internet Protocol (IP). TCP performed transport layer functions equivalent to the transport layer in the OSI model. IP performed network layer functions that were equivalent to the network layer (Layer 3) in the OSI model. When application layer (Layer 7) protocols (Telnet, FTP, SMTP, and so on) and physical (Layer 1) and data link layer (Layer 2) protocols were added, the result was an architecture that effectively contained five layers. Figure 6-1 shows the TCP/IP model alongside the OSI reference model for comparison.

The TCP/IP architecture is functionally equivalent to the OSI reference model. The major similarities and differences are as follows:

- Both models have an application, a transport, and a network/Internet layer.
- The TCP/IP model does not have a session layer (Layer 5 of the OSI reference model) or a presentation layer (Layer 6 of the OSI reference model).

- Both models have a lower layer that connects the upper layers to the actual physical network. In the OSI reference model, the lower layer (Layer 1) is called the physical layer. In the original TCP/IP model, the lower layer was called the host-to-network layer. In present-day use, TCP/IP networks use the combination of a Layer 2 sublayer called the medium access control (MAC) sublayer along with Layer 1 to provide connectivity over the wireless link.

Virtually all the wireless equipment features that you evaluate operate at the physical, data link, and network layers of the OSI and TCP/IP reference models. The wireless features and functionality (modulation type, data rate, and so on) take place at the physical layer. Access to (and sharing of) the wireless medium takes place at the data link layer. Routing takes place at the network layer.

Peer Protocols

Peer protocols run across the Internet but provide communication only between same-layer processes. One example of this same-layer communication process is a Hypertext Transfer Protocol (HTTP) web browser running on the application layer of one network. The HTTP browser retrieves information from its peer web server running on the application layer of another network. Although the HTTP communication is application-layer-to-application layer (peer-to-peer), both networks communicate downward through their lower network layers.

Services

Information is passed from the top (application) layer of one network down through the lower layers. Each layer provides a set of services for the layer just above it and utilizes the services provided by the layer just below it. The set of services between two layers is referred to as the *interface* between the two layers. For example, Layer 6 provides services for Layer 7; Layer 5 provides services for Layer 6; and so on. In this way, Layer 7 (the application layer) can communicate all the way down to Layer 1 (the physical layer).

The following list illustrates how services and protocols operate. When your web browser uses HTTP over a wireless network, the information flow is as follows:

1 The HTTP information request originates at the application layer on the originating network.

2 The HTTP request travels downward from the application layer (using the services provided by all the intermediate layers) to the physical layer on the originating network. The physical layer uses the appropriate wireless *protocol* (for example, the appropriate direct sequence spread spectrum modulation or DSSS) to communicate the request over the air wirelessly to the physical layer on the other network.

3 The physical layer on the other network uses the DSSS protocol to receive the request from the originating network. The physical layer then passes the information up through its interface to the data link layer. Using higher and higher layer services, the request passes upward until it eventually reaches the application layer. There, the HTTP protocol processes the request and replies with a response.

4 Using services of lower and lower layers, the response travels downward to the physical layer. Using the Layer 1 DSSS protocol, the response is transmitted over the air back to the physical layer of the originating network.

5 Using services, the originating network passes the response upward to the application layer where the HTTP protocol receives the response to its original request.

Basic Packet Structure and Frame Types

Packet switching store-and-forward techniques underlie the operation of layered architectures. Packet switching uses an underlying data structure, called a *packet*. A packet is like a hamburger on a bun. Although the exact packet structure varies from layer to layer and protocol to protocol, most packets contain a data payload section. The data payload is the hamburger in the middle of the bun. Other fields encapsulate (surround) the data payload and make up the bun. The bun typically provides the following:

- Source and destination address information
- Packet numbering information
- Packet acknowledgment information
- Error detection and correction information

Figure 6-2 shows this general packet structure.

Figure 6-2   *General Packet Structure*

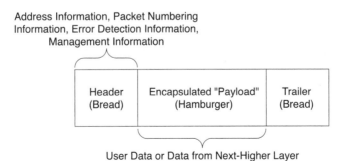

Packets prepared by Layer 2 (the data link layer) are called *frames*. Not all frames contain payload data. Wireless APs and wireless stations exchange three types of frames, each with the following functions:

- Data frames carry user payload data (the hamburger) between different wireless network nodes.

- Control frames carry information such as request-to-send (RTS) and clear-to-send (CTS) messages as well as frame acknowledgments (ACK).

- Management frames carry association and authentication requests and responses in addition to beacon information.

Application Layer Functions and Protocols

The application layer is where the end user programs run. Telnet, Simple Mail Transfer Protocol (SMTP), File Transfer Protocol (FTP), and HTTP are examples of application layer protocols. Wireless equipment that you evaluate will likely have network management software that operates at the application layer level.

Transport Layer Functions and Protocols

The transport layer's job is to provide reliable communications from application to application regardless of the lower-layer protocols and communications links. The transport layer encapsulates data from the application layer (and the session layer, if used) and passes it down to the network layer.

Typical transport layer protocols are TCP and User Datagram Protocol (UDP). Wireless equipment that you evaluate does not usually have features that operate at the transport layer level.

Network Layer Functions and Protocols

The essential network layer protocol is IP. In addition to IP, the network layer often utilizes other routing protocols such as Routing Information Protocol (RIP) and Border Gateway Protocol (BGP).

The network layer encapsulates data (the hamburger) from the transport layer between IP source, IP destination, and IP routing information. Packet routing typically goes from intermediate network to intermediate network before the packets finally arrive at their destination network.

Data Link Layer Functions and Protocols

The data link layer includes the logical link control (LLC) sublayer and the MAC sublayer. The data link layer normally performs a wide variety of functions, including segmenting the bit stream into frames, error handling, flow control, and access control.

Examples of data link layer protocols include Point-to-Point Protocol (PPP) and Spanning Tree Protocol.

LLC Sublayer Functions and Protocols

The LLC sublayer makes up the top half of the data link layer and interfaces to the network layer (above) and the MAC sublayer (below). The LLC Sublayer encapsulates the Layer 3 data by adding sequence and acknowledgment numbers. The LLC Sublayer might provide different service options, depending on the network software.

MAC Sublayer Functions and Protocols

The MAC sublayer makes up the bottom half of the data link layer. The MAC sublayer interfaces to the physical (wireless) layer and provides the following functions:

- **Reliable delivery**—The MAC sublayer provides a reliable delivery mechanism that looks for an acknowledgment for every frame that is sent. If an acknowledgment is not received, the MAC sublayer retransmits the frame.

- **Access control**—The MAC sublayer controls access to the wireless channel. The two basic types of access control are carrier sense multiple access with collision avoidance (CSMA/CA) and polling. CSMA/CA is a distributed coordination function (DCF) because the decision about when to transmit is distributed to all wireless stations. Each wireless station listens before transmitting. If a station hears that the frequency is busy, it backs off (waits) a random amount of time and tries again. When the frequency is clear, the station proceeds to transmit. In addition, a request-to-send/clear-to-send (RTS/CTS) mechanism can be enabled. Large packets are more likely to collide; therefore, stations that have packets larger than the RTS/CTS threshold must request and receive clearance from the AP MAC before they can transmit their packets. Finally, in networks that have heavy traffic and many end users, a point coordination function (PCF) can be used. One single point (the MAC in the AP) coordinates transmissions from all stations. The PCF polls each wireless station and then tells each end user when it can transmit.

NOTE   You might have heard of wireless networks with a hidden node problem. This problem can occur in a network that uses DCF. In most wireless networks, certain wireless stations cannot hear all the other wireless stations. Under heavy traffic loads, several stations might try to transmit at the same time. This can happen even when the stations are using RTS/CTS. When stations transmit at the same time, collisions occur and network throughput drops drastically. The solution to hidden-node problems is to use wireless equipment that can support PCF.

- **Encryption**—The MAC also provides encryption. The most frequently used encryption method is wired equivalent privacy (WEP).

MAC control frame subtypes include RTS, CTS, and ACK. Examples of management frame subtypes include Beacon, Probe Request, Authentication, and Association Request.

Physical Layer Functions and Protocols

The physical layer transports encapsulated data from the data link layer and transmits it wirelessly to the distant network. There are several physical layer wireless standards. There are also many proprietary physical layer wireless protocols. In addition to your wireless feature evaluation, you will evaluate physical layer wired-interface features such as Ethernet and serial port features.

Physical Layer Wired-Interface Features

This section describes the wired-interface feature options that you will encounter when you begin to research and select your wireless equipment.

NOTE   No wireless equipment vendor offers all the listed features in any model of their wireless equipment—nor should they. Each wireless network is built to serve a specific set of end user needs. These end user needs dictate the best set of wired and wireless features for that particular network. Each feature listed in the following sections is offered on at least one brand and model of wireless equipment. It is important that, as you consider the available features, you keep your wireless network needs in mind. Your equipment research involves finding the best match between your network needs and the wireless equipment feature set offered on a particular model of wireless equipment.

Your physical layer wired-interface feature evaluation includes some or all of the following:

- Low-speed data ports
- Ethernet ports
- High-speed data ports
- Voice interfaces

Low-Speed Data Ports

Most wireless equipment contains at least one low-speed port, such as the following:

- **Low-speed serial data ports**—On some equipment, a low-speed serial data port is used for initial system configuration. The serial port speed generally ranges between 4800 bits per second (bps) and 19.2 kilobits per second (kbps).

- **Low-speed user data ports**—Early wireless modems were frequently designed to transport only low-speed serial data over the wireless link. Port speeds range from 4800 bps to 128 kbps.

- **Dialup telco interfaces**—Dialup telco interfaces provide low-speed dial backup connectivity for times when a higher-speed primary link, such as a T1 or digital subscriber line (DSL) link, is unavailable.

Ethernet Ports

Ethernet interfaces allow network data to access the wireless network. Wireless equipment can include one or more of the following Ethernet interfaces:

- **10Base-T**—This is the most common Ethernet interface.
- **100Base-TX**—This interface is found on higher-speed wireless equipment.
- **Ethernet hubs or switches**—This interface is found on some wireless APs.

High-Speed Data Ports

In addition to Ethernet interfaces, it is often desirable to use wireless bridges or routers to transport other high-speed non-Ethernet data streams. To transport these streams, wireless equipment can include the following interfaces:

- **Digital subscriber line (DSL) interfaces**—DSL interfaces enable a wireless bridge or router to extend or share a DSL connection.

- **Cable interfaces**—Cable interfaces enable wireless equipment to extend or share a cable Internet connection.

- **Asynchronous Transfer Mode (ATM) interfaces**—ATM interfaces enable wireless equipment to connect to and from an ATM network.

- **T1/E1 interfaces**—T1/E1 interfaces enable wireless equipment to extend a 1.544 megabit per second (Mbps) T1 line or a 2.048 Mbps E1 line from point A to point B, for example, between two private automatic branch exchanges (PABXs). Some models of wireless equipment provide T1/E1 connectivity only. Other wireless equipment models provide simultaneous wireless Ethernet and T1/E1 connectivity.

TIP	Telecommunications managers who want to provide both Ethernet and voice-PABX connectivity between buildings find wireless equipment that simultaneously provides both Ethernet and T1 connectivity to be especially useful.

- **T3/E3 interfaces**—45-Mbps T3 interfaces enable full-duplex wireless equipment to provide T3 connectivity between two points.

- **Optical Carrier 3 (OC-3) interfaces**—155-Mbps OC-3 interfaces enable full-duplex wireless equipment to provide OC-3 connectivity between two points. Wireless OC-3 equipment usually has the capability to carry several T1 or E1 circuits in addition to the OC-3 circuit.

- **Optical Carrier 12 (OC-12) interface**s—622-Mbps OC-12 interfaces allow full-duplex wireless equipment to provide OC-12 connectivity between two points.

TIP	Remember that, in general, there is an inverse relationship between wireless bandwidth and wireless distance; as bandwidth goes up, distance goes down. OC-12 wireless equipment typically operates only over distances up to approximately 1312 ft. (400 m).

Voice Interfaces

Voice interfaces enable wireless equipment to carry voice in addition to data. The following types of voice interfaces are possible:

- **Voice over Internet Protocol (VoIP) interfaces**—VoIP interfaces allow IP telephones to connect directly to the wireless equipment and to make on-network voice calls. Making calls to the public switched telephone network (PSTN) requires the use of an external telephone gateway.

- **Talkback/orderwire interfaces**—A talkback interface (sometimes called an *order wire*) provides a two-way voice circuit. Maintenance personnel normally use this circuit for end-to-end voice communication over the wireless link while servicing the wireless equipment.

Wired-Interface Security Features

Physical layer wired-interface security features limit user access to the system administration console via a serial port or an Ethernet port. Successful entry of a password is required before gaining access to system administration functions. Additionally, some equipment allows a management station IP address to be configured. Attempts to access the system administration console from other IP addresses are refused.

Physical Layer Wireless-Interface Features

Wireless features operate at the physical layer; therefore, your wireless-interface feature evaluation covers a broad range of features. The following sections cover these feature categories:

- **NLOS**—Non line-of-sight and near line-of-sight equipment capabilities
- **Wireless frequency bands**—Propagation characteristics and equipment availability for each of the license-free bands
- **Modulation types**—Various types of modulation used by license-free equipment
- **Bandwidth and throughput**—Tradeoffs between data rate, data throughput, and link distance
- **Noise and interference-reduction features**—Receiver and antenna features that improve signal reception abilities
- **Security**—Physical layer wireless security features
- **Miscellaneous wireless features**—Transmit and receive features that can play a significant role in the performance of your wireless network operation

Non Line-of-Sight Features

In the broadband wireless industry, there is no agreement about the exact meaning of the term *NLOS*. Here are two common ways that NLOS is used:

- **Near line-of-sight**—When equipment vendors state that their equipment has *near*-LOS capabilities, they are claiming that it operates satisfactorily even when there is a partially obstructed line-of-sight path, as long as there are not too many obstacles to the line-of-sight path. For example, perhaps a few trees are intruding into the Fresnel zone.
- **Non line-of sight**—When equipment vendors state that their equipment has *non*-LOS capabilities, they are claiming that it operates satisfactorily even when there is an obstructed line-of-sight path. For example, perhaps buildings, trees, and hills are completely blocking the path.

Because there is no standard definition of NLOS, the process of evaluating NLOS performance claims is a challenging one. Almost all vendors of NLOS equipment (either accidentally or intentionally) exclude information about the range of their NLOS equipment. The impression is left with the customer (you) that the NLOS equipment has the same communications range as LOS wireless equipment. This is never the case; the range of NLOS equipment is always substantially less than the range of equipment that is operating over a true, unobstructed LOS path.

Now, you will learn about features that actually improve performance in NLOS environments. Two significant challenges that an NLOS environment presents for wireless equipment are as follows:

- **Multipath**—Any equipment feature that improves performance in a multipath environment also improves performance in an NLOS environment. These features are as follows:
  - Diversity antennas
  - Circularly polarized antennas
  - Smart antennas that constantly adjust their beamwidth to receive and transmit energy directly to and from each individual end user antenna
  - Adaptive equalization
  - Multicarrier modulation, such as OFDM

  Whenever possible, always try to design your wireless WANs to use LOS paths. You will achieve more reliable coverage at longer distances.

- **Attenuation**—Attenuation losses in a non-LOS environment are the reason that the communications range in an NLOS environment is less than in a LOS environment. The following equipment and network features reduce attention and improve NLOS performance:
  - Receiver sensitivity
  - 900 MHz frequency band
  - Mesh networks

Wireless Frequency Bands

The following sections describe the license-free frequency bands, including the propagation characteristics and the power levels of each band.

900 MHz

900 MHz is the lowest-frequency industrial, scientific, and medical (ISM) band. The total width of the band is 26 MHz. Signals in this band have a wavelength of approximately 12 inches (30 cm). These signals have the capability to pass through some obstructions without being completely lost. For example, they can pass through light trees and diffract

over one low hill and still be strong enough to be received several miles away. 900 MHz is the best band to use when there are just a few obstacles to the LOS path. Table 6-1 shows 900-MHz power levels.

Table 6-1   *Power Levels for the 900-MHz Band*

Band	Maximum Transmitter Power	Maximum Antenna Gain	EIRP (Equivalent Isotropic Radiated Power)
902 to 928 MHz	+30 dBm (1 Watt)	+6 dBi	+36 dBi (4 Watts, relative to an isotropic antenna)

2.4 GHz

2.4 GHz is the middle ISM band. The total width of the band is 83 MHz. Signals in this band have a wavelength of approximately 4.8 inches (12 cm). These signals have little capability to pass through obstructions without being lost. Passing through one wall can result in 10 to 12 dB of attenuation. Attenuation from trees varies depending on the presence of leaves and whether the leaves are wet or dry but, on average, the attenuation from trees is approximately .5 dB per meter. One 30-ft (10-meter) diameter tree (the tree canopy/leaves are 30 feet across, not the tree trunk) results in about 5 dB of attenuation; 6 dB of attenuation reduces the length of a wireless link to 1/2 of its previous length. You can see that passing a 2.4-GHz signal through a few trees can easily reduce the usable length of the wireless path to a few hundred feet. Table 6-2 shows 2.4-GHz power levels.

Table 6-2   *Power Levels for the 2.4 GHz Band*

Band	Maximum Transmitter Power	Maximum Antenna Gain	Maximum EIRP
2403 to 2483 MHz (Point-to-Multipoint)	+30 dBm (1 Watt)	+6 dBi	+36 dBi (4 Watts).
2403 to 2483 MHz (Point-to-Point only)	+30 dBm (1 Watt)	(3-to-1 Rule) For every 3 dBi (above +6 dBi) of antenna gain, reduce the transmitter power by 1 dB. (For example, for a +9 dBi antenna, reduce transmitter power to +29 dBm.)	Depends on antenna size. With a +24 dBi antenna and +24 dBm of transmitter power, +48 dBi (64 Watts) is possible in a Point-to-Point (only) link.
2403 to 2483 MHz Wideband frequency hopping spread spectrum using from 15 to 74 hopping frequencies	+21 dBm (125 mW)	+6 dBi	+27 dBi (500 mW).

3.5 GHz

The 3.5-GHz band is not available for use in the United States; however, some frequency subbands between 3.3 and 4.0 GHz are available for use (usually on a licensed basis) in a number of other countries. This band is mentioned here because equipment for this band is, in many cases, similar to equipment for the 2.4-GHz band. Signals in this band have a wavelength of approximately 9 cm (3.4 in). The propagation characteristics are somewhat similar to the 2.4-GHz band, although attenuation from trees and other obstructions is higher.

5 GHz

There are four license-free subbands at 5 GHz, although two of these bands overlap each other. There is one ISM band from 5725 to 5850 MHz (5.725 to 5.850 GHz), and there are three Unlicensed National Information Infrastructure (U-NII) bands: 5150 to 5250 MHz, 5250 to 5350 MHz, and 5725 to 5825 MHz. The ISM band is 125 MHz wide, and each U-NII band is 100 MHz wide. Signals in the 5-GHz subbands have a wavelength of approximately 2 inches (5 cm). Each 5 GHz subband is wider than the entire 2.4-GHz band; therefore, it is possible to build 5-GHz wireless equipment that provides more bandwidth and more throughput than equipment for any other license-free band. The attenuation from trees at 5 GHz is about 1.2 dB per meter; therefore, each 30-ft (10-meter) diameter tree (crown) that blocks an LOS path reduces the length of a wireless link by approximately 75 percent. Table 6-3 shows 5-GHz power levels.

Table 6-3 *Power Levels for the 5-GHz Band*

Band	Maximum Transmitter Power	Maximum Antenna Gain	EIRP
ISM 5725 to 5850 MHz	+30 dBm (1 Watt)	+6 dBi	+36 dBi (4 Watts). Note that point-to-point systems can use an antenna with more than +6 dBi gain with no transmitter power reduction.
U-NII 5150 to 5250 MHz	+17 dBm (50 mW)	+6 dBi	+23 dBi (500 mW; indoor use only per FCC regulations.)
U-NII 5250 to 5350 MHz	+24 dBm (250 mW)	+6 dBi	+30 dBi. (1 Watt).
U-NII 5725 to 5825 MHz	+30 dBm (1 Watt)	+6 dBi	+36 dBi (4 Watts) Note that point-to-point systems can use an antenna with up to +23 dBi gain with no transmitter power reduction.

60 GHz

The 59 to 64-GHz ISM band was approved for use in the United States in 1999. The total width of this band is almost 5 GHz. Signals in this band have a wavelength of about 2/10 of an inch (1/2 cm). Signals at this frequency are attenuated by the presence of oxygen in the air; therefore, the maximum wireless link distance is approximately half a mile (800 m), assuming that a LOS path is available. Obstructions completely block the signal. The advantage of this band is that equipment is available that provides point-to-point raw data rates up to 622 Mbps. In addition, the oxygen absorption means that the likelihood of interference from other networks is low.

Modulation Types

This section covers the following information:

- A quick review of the modulation process
- A direct sequence spread spectrum (DSSS) description
- A frequency hopping spread spectrum (FHSS) description
- An orthogonal frequency division multiplexing (OFDM) description
- A brief mention of other spread spectrum and non-spread types of modulation

Understanding the Modulation Process

Chapter 1, "An Introduction to Broadband License-Free Wireless Wide-Area Networking," defined *modulation* as the process of adding intelligence to the signal. The modulation process creates a change in some combination of the amplitude, the frequency, or the phase of a signal. Many types of modulation exist, including amplitude modulation used by commercial AM broadcast stations and frequency modulation (FM) used by police departments and fire departments, for example.

Spread spectrum modulation was originally designed for use by the military to camouflage the existence of and the content of military communications. Descriptions of the two types of spread spectrum modulation follow.

Direct Sequence Spread Spectrum (DSSS) Modulation

DSSS modulation simultaneously widens (spreads) a data signal out and reduces the amplitude (technically, it reduces the power density) of the signal. The resulting modulated signal resembles a low-level noise signal that is widely dispersed around a single frequency. The modulated DSSS signal is wider than the bandwidth of the original data. For example, an 11-Mbps raw data rate signal becomes a 22-MHz-wide DSSS signal. In the 2.4-GHz frequency band, there is enough room for three nonoverlapping 11 Mbps-wide signal channels. Each time a DSSS signal is transmitted, the wireless energy is centered around only one frequency; therefore, DSSS modulation is a *single-carrier* modulation scheme.

Frequency Hopping Spread Spectrum Modulation

Frequency Hopping Spread Spectrum (FHSS) modulation does not spread its signal energy out, but it rapidly shifts the energy from frequency to frequency. A narrowband FHSS signal is transmitted first on one narrow (1-MHz) channel and then quickly shifted to another channel, then another, and another, and so on. The rapid frequency hopping gives this type of modulation its name. The two following types of FHSS are now allowed in the 2.4-GHz band:

- **Narrowband frequency hopping**—Narrowband FHSS signals are 1 MHz wide. They hop using a total of 79 different frequencies. The signal can hop between these frequencies in 78 unique hopping patterns or hopping sequences. 802.11 standards define narrowband frequency hopping.

NOTE   Hopping sequences are sometimes different in different countries. Check with your national telecommunications authority for the regulations in your country.

- **Wideband frequency hopping**—Wideband FHSS signals can be up to 5 MHz wide and can hop using a total of less than 75 different frequencies. Typical wideband FHSS systems use far less than 75 frequencies; one such system uses 43 frequencies with a signal that is 1.7 MHz wide. Wideband frequency hopping systems are relatively new and are just beginning to be deployed in outdoor wireless WANs.

FHSS equipment changes its center frequency each time it hops; however, each time it transmits, the wireless energy is still centered on only one frequency. FHSS is, therefore, a single-carrier modulation scheme.

Orthogonal Frequency Division Multiplexing Modulation

Orthogonal Frequency Division Multiplexing (OFDM) modulation transmits bursts that use more than one carrier frequency simultaneously. Compared to a DSSS signal, an OFDM signal has the following characteristics:

- Occupies the same amount of bandwidth
- Uses 52 carriers instead of one carrier
- Carries more information with each transmitted burst
- Is more resistant to multipath fading

802.11a equipment uses OFDM modulation and operates on the 5-GHz band; 802.11g uses OFDM on the 2.4-GHz band. OFDM is a *multicarrier* modulation scheme because it transmits using more than one carrier simultaneously.

Other Spread Spectrum Modulation Types

Other types of spread spectrum modulation are now legal to use. These versions are proprietary to particular manufacturers and do not interoperate with 802.11b, 802.11a, or 802.11g systems.

One example of a proprietary spread spectrum modulation type is multicarrier DSSS. Rather than using just one DSSS carrier, multicarrier DSSS uses several simultaneous carrier frequencies to transport data. This multicarrier approach is a hybrid combination of single-carrier and multicarrier modulation.

Other Nonspread Spectrum Modulation Types

In the ISM bands, the FCC originally required that spread spectrum modulation be used. Recent rule changes now allow additional modulation types. In the U-NII bands, nonspread spectrum modulation types are permitted, and equipment manufacturers use proprietary digital modulation schemes to offer a variety of high-bandwidth point-to-point and point-to-multipoint systems.

Bandwidth and Throughput

It is important for you to understand wireless throughput so that you can meet (or exceed) the expectations of your wireless end users. This section describes the following:

* The difference between the wireless data rate and the wireless throughput
* The tradeoff between throughput and distance
* Examples of low, medium, and high throughput equipment

Comparison Between Data Rate and Throughput (Including Simplex Versus Duplex Throughput)

There is a common misunderstanding regarding the bandwidth, the data rate, and the throughput of a wireless device:

* Bandwidth refers to the raw data rate of the device.
* Throughput refers to the actual amount of end user data that the device can transfer in a given time interval.

The result of this misunderstanding is that wireless network users are frequently disappointed in the wireless throughput (data transfer speeds) that they experience.

Understandably, wireless equipment manufacturers want their equipment to look as attractive as possible to potential buyers. For this reason, they usually use the raw data rate in their sales and advertising material. An 802.11b AP, for example, provides a raw data rate of 11 Mbps.

Wireless users have a different expectation; they are interested in how fast a web page or a file downloads. They are interested in the capability of the wireless device to deliver their data. When the wireless users' 802.11b AP delivers just 5.5 Mbps of data throughput, they feel that there must be a problem with the equipment.

Most frequently, the real data throughput potential of a half-duplex wireless network is approximately 50 percent of the raw data rate. An 802.11b AP operating at the maximum 11-Mbps raw data rate has a maximum throughput potential of about 5.5 Mbps. This difference between raw data rate and actual throughput has several causes, including these:

- The framing and signaling overhead
- The half-duplex turnaround time between transmit and receive
- The lower efficiency inherent in the transmission of small packets

Collisions between wireless users and interference from other networks can reduce the throughput below 50 percent. Chapter 8, "Solving Noise and Interference Problems," discusses this issue in more detail.

Remember that your end users rely on you to set their throughput expectations realistically. When they measure their throughput and discover that it meets or slightly exceeds the throughput that you told them to expect, they will judge your wireless network performance to be good.

Tradeoff Between Data Rate and Distance

As you evaluate wireless equipment, you will invariably compare different equipment brands based on how long of a link they can support. Link distance is important; however, during your comparison, it is important that you compare apples to apples. When you compare two brands of wireless equipment side by side, you must compare their link distances at the same data rate. Other factors being equal, the higher the throughput (or the higher the raw data rate), the shorter the communications range. Table 6-4 lists the typical outdoor link distances from an 802.11b AP (using a standard low-gain omnidirectional antenna).

Table 6-4   *Examples of 802.11b Data Rates Versus Distances*

Data Rate	Distance in Ft. (m)
11 Mbps	500 (152)
5.5 Mbps	885 (270)
2 Mbps	1300 (396)
1 Mbps	1500 (457)

As the data rate increases, the maximum AP link distance decreases. AP data rates automatically fall back to the next lower level when the AP detects the signal quality decreasing as the link distance increases.

Sub-1 Mbps Data Rates

Two types of wireless systems operate at sub-1 Mbps data rates:

- Low-speed (such as 4800 bps to 128 kbps) wireless modems that provide a point-to-point wireless extension for an RS-232 serial data system.

- 128 kbps to 1 Mbps point-to-point or point-to-multipoint wireless Ethernet bridges or AP systems. These systems are useful for Internet access.

1-Mbps to 11-Mbps Data Rates

Most point-to-multipoint wireless WAN systems are in this category. This category also includes both 802.11 (2 Mbps) and 802.11b (11 Mbps) systems.

12-Mbps to 60-Mbps Data Rates

This category includes both high-bandwidth point-to-point backbone equipment and point-to-multipoint equipment. Here are some examples:

- Point-to-point equipment is available with bandwidths of 12 Mbps, 20 Mbps, 24 Mbps, and 45 Mbps.

- Point-to-multipoint equipment is available with shared, aggregate bandwidths of 20 Mbps, 40 Mbps, 54 Mbps, and 60 Mbps.

- 802.11a WLAN equipment is becoming available. However, as this book was being written, this equipment was not yet appropriate for use in outdoor wireless networks. The power level was too low, and there is no connector to attach an outdoor antenna.

Over 60-Mbps Data Rates

The higher in frequency wireless equipment operates, the more bandwidth that is available. Products that provide more than 60 Mbps of bandwidth operate almost exclusively in the 5.3- and 5.8-GHz U-NII bands, although a few short-range products operate in the 60-GHz band. Products that operate in these bands have aggregate bandwidths of 90 Mbps, 100 Mbps, 155 Mbps (OC-3), 200 Mbps, 480 Mbps, 622 Mbps (OC-12), and 872 Mbps. All these are full-duplex products.

Noise and Interference Reduction Features

Noise is defined as anything and everything other than the desired signal. Interference reduces the throughput of a wireless network. Interference has many sources, so it is important that you consider and utilize all possible noise-reduction features.

NOTE   Chapter 8 is devoted completely to the topic of understanding and minimizing the effects of noise and interference. Refer to Chapter 8 for additional information as you read about the following interference-reduction features.

In the outdoor wireless environment, many potential interference sources exist. You can use a few equipment characteristics to provide some help in minimizing the effects of interference.

The following interference-reduction features operate at the physical layer to help reduce the effects that interference can have on both AP and CPE throughput.

Receiver Selectivity

Selectivity is the capability of a receiver to reject signals that are not exactly on the desired receiving frequency. No receiver is perfectly selective; no receiver has the capability to completely reject all off-frequency signals; therefore, all receivers are susceptible to being overloaded by nearby, strong off-frequency signals. These off-frequency signals can be within the license-free band (in-band interference), or they can be outside the band (out-of-band interference).

Overloading causes a receiver to become desensitized (to experience a reduced sensitivity) to the desired signals. The symptom of a desensitized receiver is a reduction in the receiving distance. Some receivers allow you to configure a higher receive threshold level. This feature enables you to intentionally reduce the sensitivity and therefore reduce the intensity of the overloading. This feature is similar to a "squelch" control on an FM two-way radio.

It can be difficult for you to compare receiver selectivity and to predict overload resistance because most manufacturers do not publish overload specifications. Keep the following general guidelines in mind as you evaluate wireless equipment:

- Wireless equipment that is designed for outdoor WAN use should be less susceptible to being overloaded when compared to indoor wireless LAN equipment.

- Wireless equipment that is designed for indoor LAN use is likely to be more susceptible to being overloaded when used outdoors.

- All wireless equipment might need to have an external bandpass filter added when there are one or more strong, nearby transmitters such as FM, AM, or television broadcast transmitters.

Multipath Resistance

Multipath fading is a fact of life at microwave frequencies. *Multipath* is caused when signal reflections cause several signals (echoes) to be received almost simultaneously. Equipment features that minimize the effects of multipath include the following:

- **Antenna diversity**—Antenna diversity helps minimize multipath by using two separate antennas. The antennas are separated from each other, and when the signal fades, one antenna receives a stronger signal than the other antenna. The receiver automatically selects the strongest antenna signal on each incoming packet, so fading is reduced.

- **Circular antenna polarization**—Circularly polarized antennas discriminate against multipath interference. Equipment that offers the option of using a circularly polarized antenna provides more protection against multipath compared to equipment without a circularly polarized antenna.

- **OFDM**—Equipment that uses orthogonal frequency division multiplexing modulation provides more immunity to multipath interference compared to non-OFDM equipment.

Multipath interference is worse in a physical environment where you find many obstacles that reflect wireless signals. The center of a city with many tall, flat, reflective metal building surfaces is a high multipath environment. If you plan to deploy wireless service in a high-multipath environment, use as many multipath-reduction features and techniques as possible.

Miscellaneous Interference Reduction Techniques

There are many sources of noise and interference besides multipath. The following miscellaneous features help reduce the distance-robbing effects of noise and interference:

- **Selectable antenna polarization**—Interference from other wireless systems is usually either vertically polarized or horizontally polarized. Equipment that allows you to select either vertical or horizontal polarization allows you to minimize interference from other systems by selecting polarization opposite to other, interfering networks.

- **Smart antenna technology**—Smart antennas enable the antenna pattern beamwidth to be automatically adjusted under software control. In this way, the antenna pattern can be automatically steered to minimize or avoid interference. Smart antenna technology is a relatively new technology that is just beginning to appear in license-free wireless WAN equipment.

- **Smart radio features**—Smart radio features include the radio's capability to automatically scan the available frequencies and to choose the frequency with the least amount of interference. Automatic power adjustment is another smart radio feature. The wireless equipment measures the strength and the quality of the received signal and adjusts the transmit power level up or down to maintain the desired link quality. Using only the amount of power needed minimizes the interference to other wireless systems.

Physical Layer Wireless Security Features

There are a number of physical layer wireless security features as well as many higher-layer security features. The following sections describe the main physical layer security features.

Antenna Pattern/Signal Strength

Although not immediately obvious, antenna directivity provides a certain measure of security. Unauthorized wireless users must physically position themselves in an area where a usable signal exists. This is another reason to carefully consider where you radiate your signal. Rather than broadcasting it everywhere, use directional antennas to radiate only into the areas where your end users are located.

Modulation Type

Like antenna directivity, modulation type is a not-so-obvious security feature. If a wireless network uses DSSS, a hacker must use the same DSSS modulation type. Likewise, if a network uses FHSS, a hacker must use FHSS. If a network uses another proprietary modulation type, an unauthorized user must use the same proprietary modulation type. Therefore, proprietary modulation types provide a higher level of physical layer security than 802.11b, for example.

Network ID (SSID, ESSID)

Several different logical networks can exist in the same physical space. Wireless packets contain a service set identifier (SSID), extended service set identifier (ESSID), or network ID to specify the logical network that a wireless station belongs to. The ESSID is a basic network security feature. If a wireless station does not possess the correct ESSID (or network ID), it cannot connect to a wireless network.

Miscellaneous Wireless Features

This section describes miscellaneous transmit and receive features. Although these features cannot be neatly classified into a specific section, their presence or absence can play a significant role in the performance of your wireless network operation; evaluate them carefully.

Miscellaneous Transmit Features

The following miscellaneous transmitter features can affect the design and performance of your wireless WAN:

- **Transmitter output power**—Most license-free wireless equipment is limited by Federal Communications Commission (FCC) regulations to one watt (+30 dBm) of transmitter output power. Available transmitter output power levels typically vary from 1 watt (1W) down to 200 mW, 100mW, 50 mW, and 30 mW.

TIP   The role of transmitter power in the successful operation of a wireless network is often misunderstood. Many people believe that more power is always better; however, this is not true in many cases. Your best approach is to transmit with only the amount of power that you need to cover your desired service area. Transmitting with too much power results in a transmitting range that is larger than your receiving range. This causes unnecessary interference to other networks. The owner of the other networks might then feel the need to retaliate with excessive transmitter power, which can lead to a cycle of escalation in which everyone loses.

- **Configurable transmitter power control**—A few models of wireless equipment allow you to configure the transmitter output power; however, for most wireless equipment, the power output is not configurable. Only one or two equipment models exist where the AP automatically configures the transmitter power of the end user nodes. The purpose of automatic power control is to use only the power needed for a reliable link. Avoiding the use of excessive power minimizes interference between the end user nodes.

Miscellaneous Receive Features

The following receive features affect the performance of your wireless WAN in many ways:

- **Receiver threshold**—A receiver starts working (receiving and decoding an incoming signal) when the signal reaches the receiver threshold level. Signals below the threshold are either not received or are received with numerous errors. Signals above the threshold are received with a low error rate. The low error rate allows the wireless link to deliver maximum throughput. If you are comparing two different receiver thresholds, the receiver with the lower threshold receives over a longer distance. For example, a receiver with a –85 dBm threshold is better than a receiver with a –80 dBm threshold.

NOTE   When comparing receiver thresholds, compare the threshold values at the same data rate. Comparisons at different data rates are invalid because as the data rate goes up, a receiver's threshold goes up. Stated another way, as the data rate goes up, the receiver becomes less sensitive.

- **Noise figure**—Receivers create noise in their circuitry. *Noise figure* refers to internal noise or the relative lack of internal noise created by the receiver. The lower the internal noise, the better a weak signal is received. A 3-dB noise figure is better than a 6-dB noise figure, for example.

Miscellaneous Transmit/Receive Features

The following features, when present, apply on both transmit and receive:

- **AP and bridge**—Some wireless APs can be used either as an AP (connecting to many end users) or as a bridge. An AP with bridging capability provides you with more network flexibility than an AP without the capability to work as a bridge.

- **AP and repeater**—Most APs can serve both as an AP and as a repeater at the same time.

- **Number of wireless ports**—Most wireless equipment has one wireless port. Some equipment has more than one wireless port. Multiport equipment can operate simultaneously on more than one frequency or more than one band. One example is an AP that has one 2.4-GHz and one 5-GHz wireless port.

- **External antenna connector**—Wireless WAN equipment must always be connected to an antenna that has LOS paths to the end users. Except in the case of CPE that has the radio integrated with the antenna, this means that the wireless equipment must have a connector for an external antenna. Equipment that is designed to be used indoors often lacks a connector for an external antenna.

- **Split (indoor/outdoor) hardware architecture**—Indoor/outdoor architecture splits the wireless hardware. The microwave part of the equipment is placed outdoors, near the antenna. The low-frequency part of the equipment is placed indoors. The two halves of the radio are connected with either coax or fiber. With a split architecture, coax cable losses between the microwave section and the antenna are almost eliminated, consequently improving the wireless performance.

- **Integrated antenna/radio**—With increasing frequency, wireless equipment (especially 802.11b) equipment is becoming available with the radio physically located inside the antenna. Integrated equipment has the same advantage as split-architecture equipment—eliminating transmission line losses to improve wireless performance. The connection from the antenna/radio to the end user network is made with Ethernet cable. Power-over-Ethernet (PoE) to the antenna and radio is provided using the nondata conductors in the Ethernet cable.

- **Multifrequency management commonality**—A few equipment vendors now offer a wireless equipment family that operates on different frequency bands but can be managed from a common management platform. This equipment provides management economies for those wireless ISPs that need to deploy wireless systems on different bands.

- **Antenna alignment aids**—Some equipment, especially split architecture or integrated antenna and radio equipment, provides visual or aural antenna alignment aids. These aids, typically a series of LEDs or an audible tone, help the installer align the antenna for the highest signal level without leaving the antenna location.

- **Availability of FCC-certified antenna systems**—Most equipment vendors provide at least one antenna system that is FCC-certified for use with the equipment. Some vendors provide a number of certified antenna systems. The more vendor-certified antenna systems are available, the more flexibility you have to use an antenna system that provides the service-area coverage that you need.

Data Link Layer Features

The sections that follow describe features that operate at the data link layer.

Bridging Features

Bridging takes place at the data link layer and is based on the MAC addresses of the end user equipment. The typical wireless bridge contains a table of MAC addresses and bridge ports. Packets are forwarded to the correct bridge port based on the MAC address table information. Your data link layer feature evaluation includes the following features.

MAC Address Table Size

The MAC address table of a wireless bridge is finite in size. The table might be large enough to contain one or two thousand MAC addresses or small enough to contain only one. In most cases, the MAC address table size is larger than the number of simultaneous end user connections.

Number of Simultaneous Connections

Each wireless AP or bridge is designed to connect to only a specific number of end users at the same time. In general, the more simultaneous users it supports, the higher the cost of the wireless bridge or AP.

TIP   Sometimes, an equipment vendor's advertising confuses the MAC address table size with the number of simultaneous end user connections. For example, an advertisement might state that one AP can support up to 1000 users. The ad might fail to mention that only 128 of the users can be connected at the same time. This type of error can be caused by an error on the part of the person preparing the advertisement. This person might be unclear about MAC address table size versus the number of simultaneous connections. If you see claims like this that appear to be excessive or too good to be true, ask the vendor to confirm that the advertised information is correct.

A wireless bridge is designed to support many wireless users, typically from 50 to several hundred. One special type of wireless bridge is called an *Ethernet converter*. Originally, an Ethernet converter was designed to bridge between one Ethernet port (on one computer) and a wireless WAN. Currently, Ethernet converters are available that support bridging between up to eight computers and the wireless WAN. This expanded Ethernet converter is called a *super Ethernet converter (SEC)*.

Spanning Tree Protocol

Most wireless point-to-point bridges implement the 802.3 Spanning Tree Protocol. In bridged networks, it is important to avoid routing loops (more than one simultaneous path). The 802.3 Spanning Tree Protocol senses the presence of routing loops and disables one route to avoid looping.

Switching

Wireless APs occasionally contain a built-in switch. The switch allows Ethernet connectivity from the AP to a number of Ethernet devices without needing to purchase an external switch.

Support for VLAN Tagging

Virtual LAN (VLAN) tagging allows the definition of a VLAN, as opposed to a geographically located LAN. Support for VLAN tagging allows the wireless device to support the operation of a VLAN.

MAC Sublayer Features

The MAC layer is a sublayer of the data link layer (Layer 2) in the OSI reference model. MAC features can be either standards-based or proprietary. In all cases, the primary purpose of the MAC sublayer is to provide reliable data delivery over the inherently noisy and collision-prone wireless medium. The MAC sublayer performs the following general functions:

- **Error control**—The MAC sublayer implements a frame-exchange protocol with an acknowledgment procedure. This procedure maximizes the chance that every packet is delivered error free across the wireless link.

- **Congestion management**—The MAC sublayer works to minimize congestion on the wireless medium. The MAC sublayer utilizes several methods to determine which station is allowed to gain access to the wireless medium. The 802.11b MAC specifications contain both a CSMA/CA contention-based access scheme and a polling-based access scheme. Most 802.11b equipment does not implement the polling feature.

- **Packet aggregation**— The MAC sublayer can maximize throughput by aggregating several small packets together into one larger packet. This reduces the number of times the wireless equipment must switch back and forth between receive and transmit (the switching time is also called the *turnaround time*), thereby making more time available to pass data traffic.

- **Data protection**—Encryption (in general) can take place at several different layers; however, WEP encryption takes place at the MAC level. 64-bit and 128-bit WEP encryption schemes are in common use.

Data Link Layer Security Features

The following sections analyze data link layer security features that might be offered by the equipment that you are evaluating.

MAC Address Access Control Lists

When providing wireless Internet access, it is desirable to deny access to any end user whose account is not current or who is not authorized to use your network. Most APs allow you to configure an access control list (ACL). Unless the ACL contains the specific MAC address of an end user, that end user will not be allowed to connect to the AP.

Protocol Filtering

Protocol filtering permits you to deny bridging based on the Layer 2 packet protocol. Protocols such as IPX, NetBEUI, DECNet, or AppleTalk can be denied.

MAC Address Pair Filtering

In bridged networks, it is occasionally desirable to provide filtering for specific address pairs. The filtering can either allow a connection between two specific MAC addresses, or it can deny a connection between two specific MAC addresses.

Authentication

Authentication is the process that a network uses to determine if an end user is allowed to connect to the network. Authentication schemes require an exchange of management frames between the authenticator (the network) and the end user who is requesting network access. Simple authentication schemes provide minimal security, whereas more complex schemes provide higher levels of security.

Several network layers are typically involved in the authentication process; however, because Layer 2 plays a prominent role, authentication is outlined here.

Open-system authentication is the least secure; it simply requires a station to identify itself to an AP and request that it be granted authentication.

A more secure authentication system is shared-key authentication using WEP. The shared key is distributed to all stations that are authorized to use the network. The stations use the shared key to respond to challenge text sent to them by the AP. If a station responds to the challenge text correctly, the AP grants network access.

A more secure authentication system is based on one of the 802.1x authentication types defined in the Extensible Authentication Protocol (EAP). EAP is defined in RFC 2284 and includes a number of different authentication methods. 802.1x requires using three entities:

- A supplicant (the station requesting authentication)
- The authenticator (typically the AP)
- The authentication server (such as a Remote Authentication Dial-In User Service [RADIUS] server)

EAP implementations typically allocate a new encryption key each time a wireless user begins a new session. A number of wireless vendors provide proprietary authentication features that are based on EAP and 802.1x. In the future, 802.11i wireless standards will likely evolve out of the current 802.1x standards.

Encryption

Sending an unencrypted packet over the air increases the chances that an unauthorized person could intercept and decode the packet. A variety of encryption schemes make it harder for this to occur. In addition to WEP encryption (already described), other available encryption schemes include the following:

- **Data Encryption Standard (DES)** — A 64-bit encryption standard with a user-selected encryption key.

- **Triple DES (3DES)** — Uses three 64-bit keys. The first key encrypts the data, the second key decrypts the data, and the third key re-encrypts the data.

- **Advanced Encryption Standard (AES)** — The most current U.S. Government-approved encryption standard. It uses a Rijndael (pronounced "rain-doll") algorithm with either a 128-bit, 192-bit, or 256-bit encryption key. AES requires a math coprocessor; therefore, it might not be compatible with existing 802.11b hardware. The upcoming 802.11i standard includes AES.

Data Link Layer Proprietary Security Features

Some currently available wireless products contain a combination of proprietary Layer 2 security features and industry-standard security. It is beyond the scope of this chapter to list these product combinations here; however, they include combinations of encryption, per-session key exchange, and frame authentication to provide high levels of security.

Network Layer Features

Routing takes place at the network layer. All wireless equipment currently available performs bridging; however, some models of wireless equipment also perform routing. Just as there is a wide range of routing features available with conventional (wired) routers, there is also a wide range of features available with wireless routers.

NOTE   Later in this chapter, there is an additional discussion of the advantages and disadvantages of selecting wireless equipment that includes routing.

Routing Features

The following sections contain descriptions of some of the routing protocols and features that are often available in wireless routers.

Static IP Routing

Every wireless router includes static IP routing. Static routing enables you to configure permanent IP routes.

Dynamic IP Routing

Some wireless routers include dynamic IP routing. These routers support one or more dynamic routing protocols. The most common of these supported protocols include the following:

- **Routing Information Protocol (RIP) v1 and v2**—RIP is an interior routing protocol. It is a distance-vector metric protocol that routes packets based on the number of routing hops needed to reach the destination. RIP is relatively easy to implement, but it does not take into account the bandwidth of each hop.

- **Open Shortest Path First (OSPF)**—OSPF is also an interior routing protocol. It is a link-state metric protocol. OSPF routes packets based on the shortest distance, the least delay, and the most bandwidth available to reach the destination.

Dynamic Host Configuration Protocol Server

A Dynamic Host Configuration Protocol (DHCP) server allows the allocation and reuse of IP addresses as end users need them. The DHCP server allocates an address when a DHCP client logs on. When the client logs off, the IP address is returned to the address pool, ready to be reused when another client logs on.

Network Address Translation

Like DHCP, Network Address Translation (NAT) expands the pool of usable IP addresses. NAT allows the use of a pool of private nonroutable IP addresses within a network. When IP traffic needs to be routed over the Internet, NAT translates the nonroutable addresses to an Internet-routable address.

Point-to-Point Protocol over Ethernet

Point-to-Point Protocol over Ethernet (PPPoE) allows an ISP to authenticate end users. Some wireless routers support PPPoE by passing PPPoE packets to the PPPoE server.

Bandwidth Management

Wireless equipment occasionally includes bandwidth management features. This allows the bandwidth available to and from each MAC or IP address to be throttled or limited to a specified level. This feature allows you to manage your total available bandwidth, to offer different service levels to different groups of end users, and to serve more end users. Some equipment allows end user bandwidth to be throttled at different speeds in different (downstream and upstream) directions.

NOTE   Some wireless routers allow you to allocate bandwidth based on either the IP address of the end user or the MAC address of the end user.

Quality of Service (QoS)

Quality of service functionality is not one, but a set of features that work together to prioritize different service levels for different users. One use, for example, is to prioritize the handling and thereby reduce the latency for voice over IP (VoIP) packets.

Roaming

Roaming is the ability of an end user to move from AP to AP within the same subnet while maintaining a network connection. 802.11b APs usually include roaming capabilities. The vast majority of wireless WANs provide service to fixed end user locations; therefore, roaming is not used. If you need to design or deploy a wireless WAN that includes roaming, you should evaluate the following:

- **Reassociation speed**—The length of time it takes for an end user to be switched from one AP to another.
- **Tunable parameters**—Any other AP parameters that are designed specifically to enable smooth roaming.
- **Compatibility issues**—AP-to-AP communication standards are not specified in 802.11b. If you anticipate building a network that supports roaming, you should plan to buy all of your APs from the same vendor.

Network Layer Security Features

The following network layer security features are often available on wireless routers.

IP Address Access Control Lists

Some wireless routers allow specific IP addresses to be included in an ACL. Addresses in the list can either be denied or allowed network access.

Firewalls

Wireless routers sometimes contain firewall features. These features allow traffic to flow outward from a local network to the Internet. Traffic flowing inward from the Internet to the local network is filtered or blocked.

Virtual Private Networks

Virtual private network (VPN) features include IP Security (IPSec) encryption capabilities and tunneling capabilities, such as the Point-to-Point Tunneling Protocol (PPTP).

Application Layer Features

Application layer features play a significant role in the network design, configuration, management, monitoring, and security of your wireless network.

Network Design

Many factors of network design, including terrain, distance, buildings, trees, and the presence of other networks, influence the design of your network. Sometimes, relatively expensive tools (such as spectrum analyzers) are needed to assist during the network design process. Sometimes, however, inexpensive tools are available to help you with network design.

Some wireless LAN equipment vendors include site survey utility software along with their wireless equipment. These usually display signal strength, noise level, signal-to-noise ratio (SNR), and signal quality information. Although these utilities are often designed for indoor use, they are useful to show you how well a signal from your AP is being received at different locations within your desired outdoor coverage area. These utilities are also useful for antenna alignment. Sometimes, low-cost (or free) hardware-specific utilities are available that function like a low-cost spectrum analyzer. Although these low-cost utilities do not have the full range of regular spectrum analyzer features, they do cover the entire 2.4-GHz band and show which channels are in use by other networks.

Network Management

Network management system (NMS) capabilities vary widely between different models of wireless equipment. Look for some of the following features:

- **Access method**—Methods used to access the NMS include serial port access, telnet access, generic Windows browser access, and proprietary Windows-based software. Generic browser access is probably the easiest method to use.

- **Wireless link statistics**—An NMS that provides statistics for each individual wireless link in a point-to-multipoint system is important to allow effective network monitoring. At a minimum, the following statistics should be available for each end user link and each AP: signal strength, noise level, and percentage of packets that need to be retransmitted.

- **Graphical usage statistics**—Make network management easier. You can identify light or heavy traffic patterns, perform usage-based billing based on either IP or MAC address, and see when bandwidth usage peaks.

- **Simple Network Management Protocol (SNMP)**—SNMP-based NMSs are fairly standard today. Some wireless equipment uses proprietary management software; however, many third-party management programs can manage SNMP-based systems.

- **Antenna-alignment utilities**—Generate wireless link traffic and allow the system administrator to see real-time statistics while turning the antenna to receive the highest signal.

- **Flood ping capability**—Floods a network with ping packet traffic. This test allows the system administrator to test the wireless link while simulating a traffic load.

Application Layer Security Features

The capability to interface with Remote Authentication Dial-In User Service (RADIUS) servers is possibly the most important Layer 7 security feature for wireless equipment.

Major Network Feature Decisions

Your network feature decisions have a major impact on the equipment that you choose to purchase and on the success and profitability of your wireless WAN. The following sections describe those decisions.

Market Versus Equipment Cost

The market that you choose to serve—commercial, residential, or some mixture of the two—largely determines the price range for the wireless equipment that you purchase, install, and resell. If you serve primarily residential users, you need to purchase lower-cost equipment. If you provide higher-value service by providing more bandwidth and additional value-added services to businesses, you can select higher-cost equipment with a larger feature set.

802.11b Compatibility—Yes or No?

If you choose to use 802.11b equipment for your wireless WAN, you gain some significant advantages and, at the same time, you face several disadvantages. The following sections discuss these advantages and disadvantages.

Advantages of 802.11b Compatibility

The advantages of using 802.11b equipment include the following:

- **Cost**—802.11b equipment is available at the lowest cost of any wireless equipment.
- **Availability**—802.11b equipment is widely available.

NOTE   At the time of this writing, 802.11a equipment that is operating in the 5-GHz U-NII bands (with bandwidths up to 54 Mbps) is beginning to become available. This equipment is currently designed for use in indoor LANs and not in outdoor WANs. Further product development might make outdoor versions available in the future.

Disadvantages of 802.11 Compatibility

The disadvantages of using 802.11b equipment outdoors include the following:

- **Security**—Although newer security mechanisms are being developed to supplement the current wired equivalent privacy (WEP) security, there is a somewhat greater chance of security being compromised because many people are familiar with 802.11b technology and more hacking tools are available.
- **Interference**—As more 802.11b APs are deployed, spectrum congestion and interference between wireless networks become more of an issue.
- **Support**—Most 802.11b equipment sold today is designed for low-cost in-home use. The level of vendor support for this equipment is likely to be low, especially when the equipment is used in an outdoor WAN environment. Vendors focus on supporting the equipment in its intended (indoor LAN) use and not in the outdoor WAN environment.

Bridged Versus Routed WANs

Every wireless WAN is interconnected with a wired network that includes routing. During the design phase of your wireless WAN, you need to determine how your WAN will inter-operate with your wired network. Based on your determinations, you will select wireless equipment that either performs bridging only or that performs both bridging and routing. The following questions can help you decide whether to purchase wireless equipment with built-in routing or whether to use external routers (or perhaps, no routers):

- **IP-based network services**—What advanced IP-based network services are already provided in your existing wired network? What IP-based network services will you need to provide immediately over your wireless network when it is first placed into service? What additional IP-based services (such as voice-over-IP) will you want to offer later to your wireless network users?

- **Edge routing**—Relative to your existing core routers, where do you need edge routing? If edge routing is (or will soon be) needed, is it better to select wireless equipment that includes this routing functionality initially, or is it better to select wireless bridges and add external routers later between a customer's wireless bridge and their LAN?

- **Multiple wireless backbone links**—If you anticipate using multiple wireless backbone links to provide extended wireless area coverage, you are more likely to deploy routing within the wireless backbone. You might decide that selecting wireless equipment with built-in routing is more practical or economical than using external routers.

Backbone Feature Decisions

Your backbone supplies the bandwidth that your APs distribute wirelessly to your end users. The following sections describe some key decisions that you will make as you select backbone equipment.

Backbone Capacity

Your first backbone decision is to determine how much throughput you need. This throughput decision is affected by the following factors:

- **Market needs**—How much throughput do your markets require? A backbone link that serves businesses located in several cities needs to provide more throughput than a link that serves only one or two small residential areas.

- **Number of users**—The number of wireless end users and the nature of their needs determine the amount of throughput that your backbone needs to provide.

- **Simplex versus duplex backbone**—Backbone equipment can be either simplex or duplex. A duplex backbone can provide up to 50 percent more throughput than a simplex backbone. Duplex backbone costs are generally higher because a duplex link contains two complete transmitting systems and two complete receiving systems.

- **Overselling ratio**—Internet usage is bursty. Most Internet users use bandwidth intermittently; therefore, ISPs can oversell bandwidth knowing that not all users will be on all the time. The number of times that you resell the same bandwidth (your overselling ratio) affects the amount of backbone bandwidth that you need. Your ISP experience combined with your observation of the usage patterns on your network help you determine your best overselling ratio and your backbone bandwidth needs.

Wired Versus Wireless Backbone

If economical wired backbone connectivity is available at your wireless AP location, it makes sense for you to use that wired connectivity. If wired backbone connectivity is not available or if the cost is too high, a wireless distribution system is the logical choice.

License-Free Versus Licensed Backbone

After you choose to use a wireless backbone, it is important for you to evaluate and compare the cost and the bandwidth of licensed wireless backbone equipment with the cost and the bandwidth of license-free wireless backbone equipment.

The advantages of using a license-free wireless backbone are

- **Cost**—The cost is generally lower.
- **Availability**—Equipment is generally available more rapidly.
- **Licensing**—There is no licensing cost, licensing paperwork, or licensing delay.

The disadvantage of using a license-free wireless backbone is that interference from other license-free networks is a possibility, and it is your responsibility to ensure that license-free equipment does not interfere with licensed equipment.

Given these advantages and disadvantages, it makes sense to use a license-free wireless backbone if you are reasonably certain that interference levels (both from other networks and from your own network) will remain reasonably low.

Dedicated Versus Shared Backbone Bandwidth

Wireless backbone links can be either of the following:

- Dedicated to providing only backbone bandwidth.
- Shared between backbone bandwidth and last-mile bandwidth. Examples of shared bandwidth include mesh networks and 802.11b repeaters that both connect end users and provide backbone connectivity for other APs.

Heavy bandwidth demands at one AP can cause slow performance at other APs. If possible, try to avoid sharing wireless link bandwidth between backbone use and last-mile access use. If you choose to share backbone bandwidth, you might find it necessary to use additional routers throughout the backbone to allocate and manage the bandwidth demands.

AP Feature Decisions

The list that follows describes some of the key decisions that you need to make as you select your AP equipment:

- **Frequency band**—Your choice of frequency band is probably the most important equipment decision that you will make. The difference in wireless propagation characteristics and interference levels between the license-free bands means that a poor decision here might result in an unusable network. Before making this decision, you should review the propagation characteristics of each band (discussed earlier in this chapter). You should also perform a wireless site survey (see Chapter 4, "Performing Site Surveys") to determine potential interference levels on a frequency band before you select equipment for that band. The information in Chapter 8 can help you if you find high levels of interference.

- **NLOS environment**—If you are considering buying equipment that operates in an NLOS environment, you need to either rule out or verify the range claims that the equipment manufacturer has made. You can do this by visiting an ISP that has the equipment deployed in an NLOS environment that is similar (such as the same density of trees and the same type of obstructions) to yours.

- **Modulation type**—Your choice of modulation type (DSSS, FHSS, or proprietary) is an important factor in the ultimate success of your network. Choose a modulation type that is compatible with the level and the type of interference in your coverage area.

- **802.11b or proprietary**—Every organization needs to match its budget to its mission. If your budget is modest, the lowest-cost indoor 802.11b equipment might be your only choice. A somewhat larger budget allows you to choose higher-cost 802.11b equipment with expanded feature and management capabilities. An even larger budget allows you to choose from the full range of wireless equipment.

- **Hot spot use**—802.11b APs deployed for hot spot use should be 802.1x-capable to implement improved security and to interface to external authentication and accounting servers.

- **End user polling**—Some APs implement end user polling as an option to the 802.11b CSMA/CA and RTS/CTS collision-avoidance mechanisms. If you plan to serve more than about 25 busy end users from one AP, polling increases your network reliability and performance.

- **Bandwidth management**—A few APs contain a bandwidth management capability that allows you to set bandwidth for each end user link. If the AP that you choose does not include this feature, consider adding this capability with an external bandwidth manager.

- **Support**—Vendor support is important when your wireless customers are looking to you to provide reliable Internet service. Talk with other wireless network operators to assess the availability of driver and firmware upgrades, as well as the response time and quality of support from their equipment vendors.

CPE Feature Decisions

Price is often the top consideration in the selection of CPE. The competition between broadband DSL and cable Internet access providers has driven the cost of broadband service down. It can be difficult for broadband wireless companies to compete at these low price points. For this reason, wireless providers constantly seek to lower the cost of CPE. Business users usually understand that they need to pay for value received; in contrast, residential users often seek to pay little (or nothing) for their CPE. Try not to cut too many corners in seeking and deploying low-cost CPE. Although cost is important, it is more important to deploy reliable, supportable, and manageable networks. The following discussion can help you make these cost-benefit decisions:

- **Wireless card versus external radio-based CPE**—Traditionally, license-free broadband wireless equipment is mounted indoors with a coaxial cable running to the outdoor antenna. In the drive to minimize CPE costs, wireless IPSs often choose to install wireless network interface cards (NICs) in their customers' computers, rather than purchase full-size (and higher priced) wireless bridges or routers. If you choose to deploy NICs in customer computers as CPE, recognize that some customers might expect you to provide no-cost PC support indefinitely, and this can be a costly situation for you. Also, be aware that the software tools needed to adequately monitor the quality of the customers' connection might not be available. This, too, can increase your customer support costs and raise your costs above the level where you can make a reasonable profit.

- **Separate versus integrated radio and antenna**—An alternative to the traditional wireless model is the integrated radio and antenna model. To reduce CPE costs and installation costs, wireless ISPs are now using (wherever possible) integrated radio and antenna equipment. These integrated units combine the radio and the antenna into one plastic or fiberglass enclosure that is mounted outdoors in a location with an LOS path to the AP. The integrated unit connects to the end user PC or network through either an Ethernet cable or, in a few cases, through a universal serial bus (USB) connection. The wireless performance is better because there is no coaxial cable loss between the antenna and the radio.

- **Split radio architecture**—There is one additional equipment configuration for you to evaluate: the split architecture. Split architecture actually divides the wireless unit into two physical pieces: an indoor section and an outdoor section. The indoor section contains the lower-power, lower-frequency circuits. The outdoor section contains the higher-power, higher-frequency circuits and mounts just below the antenna. Split architecture provides the benefits of the integrated radio and antenna architecture but also allows a greater choice of antennas because the antenna and radio are not built into one unit. Split architecture is often the most expensive configuration; however, it might be the best in terms of both performance and flexibility.

Wireless Network Card Decisions

If you decide to deploy wireless 802.11b cards as the customer CPE or if wireless cards plug into the AP that you are using, you must evaluate the following wireless card characteristics:

- **Transmitter**—Outlined earlier in this chapter; wireless cards share these same characteristics. The key characteristic is transmitter power output. The ideal transmitter would have a power output of 100 to 200 mW with a software-configurable power level.

- **Receiver characteristics**—Also outlined earlier, the better the receiver sensitivity (when combined with good selectivity), the better your wireless system performance will be.

- **External antenna connector**—An antenna is the key element in any wireless system. A wireless card needs to have a connector that allows an external antenna to be attached.

- **Form factor**—The most frequently used wireless card form factor is PCMCIA; however, other form factors are sometimes used. These other form factors include industry-standard architecture (ISA), peripheral component interconnect (PCI), and Compact Flash (CF).

Mesh Network Feature Decisions

You can evaluate mesh network equipment using the same considerations that you do for all other wireless equipment. Keep the following differences in mind, however:

- **Network deployment process**—Deploying a mesh network is different from deploying a point-to-multipoint network. Every mesh network node serves as a repeater and relay point for other network nodes. Nodes that are located farther away from the Internet connection must be relayed through closer network nodes. Before distant nodes can be deployed, nodes must be deployed closer to the Internet node. To provide coverage to an entire geographical area, the area must be *seeded*. Some nodes must be installed initially even if no end user is available to pay for the cost of the node.

- **Bandwidth and throughput limitations**—Mesh networks share backbone bandwidth with last mile bandwidth, which can reduce the amount of bandwidth to each end user. Be sure to factor this throughput limitation into your evaluation process and into your business plans.

- **Maximum hop limitations**—The multihop nature of mesh networks increases network latency and reduces network throughput. You will be limited to a maximum number of hops, so be sure to factor this limitation into your business plan.

Wireless Equipment Environmental Decisions

Remember environmental considerations when evaluating wireless equipment:

- **Operating temperature range**—All wireless equipment is designed to operate correctly between certain specified temperatures. Indoor equipment is designed to operate within a narrower temperature range than outdoor equipment. If you choose to use indoor equipment outdoors, be sure to provide cooling for it in the summer. In severe winter climates, it might also be necessary to add a heat source to keep the equipment warm.

- **Radio frequency (RF) immunity**—Many models of broadband wireless equipment are not designed to be used in a high-level RF environment. For example, locating a wireless LAN AP designed for home use in the equipment vault of a mountaintop transmitter site can lead to operating failures. The high-power transmitter energy can either come down the antenna cable and overload the AP receiver, or the energy can pass through the plastic case of the AP and disrupt the AP operation. If you plan to deploy equipment like this, plan to use an external bandpass filter in the antenna system. Also plan to mount the AP in a shielded and grounded metal equipment case. As an alternative, you can select equipment designed for high-RF environments. This equipment is usually designed for mounting in a standard 19-inch metal equipment rack.

Wireless Amplifier Feature Decisions

Wireless network operators often add external bidirectional amplifiers to their wireless systems. *External* means that the amplifier is external to the wireless equipment. Bidirectional amplifiers actually contain two amplifiers: one to amplify the transmitter signal and one to amplify the incoming received signals.

In the United States, FCC regulations require that external power amplifiers be marketed and sold only as part of a complete legally certified radio-cable-amplifier-antenna combination. The purpose of this regulation is to minimize the use of illegal overpowered equipment. Excess transmitter power raises the noise level, increases interference, and makes it harder for other, legal networks to operate correctly. Unfortunately, some wireless WAN operators ignore this regulation and intentionally use external power amplifiers in violation of FCC regulations. This behavior can result in heavy fines and equipment confiscation and also decreases the usability of the license-free bands for everyone.

NOTE	Illegal amplifier use is not the answer to making your WAN operate over longer distances. Often, a power amplifier actually decreases the receiving range of your WAN. In addition, using illegally high transmitter power causes substantial interference to other network operators who are operating legally. Finally, if illegal amplifier use increases, the FCC might be forced to step in with new, more restrictive regulations that could reduce license-free operating privileges for everyone. Resist the urge to amplify. Proper wireless network design and proper antenna system design provides you with the best network performance.

The following sections explain how external amplifiers work and how to use these amplifiers properly.

Transmit Amplification

On transmit, an external amplifier increases the transmitter power that reaches the antenna. This is useful when the power output of the transmitter is low and the cable length between the wireless equipment and the antenna system is long. Without an amplifier placed at the antenna, the high cable loss results in little signal reaching the antenna.

Here is an example of the correct way to use an amplifier. Start with a transmitter that has an output of 50 mW (+17 dBm). If the antenna cable has a loss of –14 dBm, the power reaching the antenna system is (+17 dBm – 14 dBm) = 3 dBm (2 mW). This is a low level of transmit power. If an amplifier with +14 dB of gain is added at the antenna, the +3 dBm that reaches the amplifier is amplified by +14 dB, resulting in a total of (3 dBm + 14 dB) +17 dBm (50 mW) reaching the antenna. The amplifier has added back the power that was lost in the antenna cable.

Receiver Amplification

On receive, an external amplifier mounted at the antenna performs two functions:

- It helps to overcome the signal loss that occurs in the antenna cable.
- It sets the SNR of the receiving system.

These two functions can lead to a small improvement in receiver performance if the amplifier has a good, low-noise design. In addition, a properly designed antenna should be used with the amplifier. If the antenna system design is poor, the amplifier can actually reduce the receiving range of the system.

Up/Down Converters

Up/down converters translate wireless signals from one frequency band to another. If the 2.4-GHz band is crowded in your area and the 5.8-GHz band is less crowded, you might want to use a 2.4-to-5.8 converter. Here is how this works. Each AP and end user station is equipped with a converter. Then, the following occurs:

- During transmit, each 2.4-GHz transmit signal is upconverted (translated up in frequency) to the 5.8-GHz band.

- During receive, the 5.8-GHz signal from the other station is downconverted to the 2.4-GHz band.

Using lower-cost 2.4-GHz equipment, communication actually takes place on the less crowded 5.8-GHz band. The advantage of this approach is that it usually costs less than buying more expensive equipment for 5.8 GHz. The disadvantage of this approach is that only a few manufacturers supply frequency converters, so your choice is limited. Converters need to be mounted at the antenna.

Compatibility Issues

Several compatibility issues can reduce the reliability of your network and consume troubleshooting time. If you are deploying an 802.11b network, never assume that different brands of wireless cards and wireless APs will work reliably together. Even hardware that is wireless fidelity (WiFi)-certified sometimes has firmware, software, operating system, and feature differences that can result in certain equipment combinations that do not work together. In most cases, equipment manufacturers do not cause these issues intentionally. There have, however, been a few instances in which large equipment vendors have intentionally created incompatibilities to boost the sales of their equipment and hinder the sale of lower-cost competitive equipment.

Watch for the folowing incompatibility issues:

- **Operating system software**—New features might not work with older software versions, or older features might not work in newer software versions. This situation can require that you upgrade all your wireless equipment software simultaneously.

- **NIC firmware**—Upgrades might have features that do not work even though they did work in earlier versions. NIC firmware might work when matched with older versions of AP software but not with upgraded AP software versions.

- **MAC incompatibilities**—Different brands of equipment that should work together do not work together or some of the features do not work.

- **NIC drivers**—Drivers might not be available for your OS or, if available, they might not be upgraded to work with newer versions of your OS.

- **USB**—There might be incompatibilities between wireless USB devices and certain PC operating systems.

- **Network management**—Network management software and diagnostics software can be unavailable or can be limited in their capability to manage mixed-equipment networks.

- **Timing**—Equipment that has timing designed for indoor (several hundred foot) distances might not work outdoors at longer (several mile) distances.

Here are some of the things that you can do to minimize the loss of time and money caused by these incompatibilities:

- **Standardize**—As much as possible, standardize on one brand of equipment for your APs and your CPE. Minimize the mixing and matching of different wireless equipment brands that talk to the same AP. Using a different brand of equipment is fine for wireless backhaul links; however, the fewer types of AP/CPE equipment that you use, the more efficiently you will be able to support that equipment and the more reliable your service will be.

- **Test time**—Be sure to plan for enough test time between the time that you build an AP and the time that you begin service from that AP. The more dissimilar your equipment, the more test time you need.

Wireless Support Issues

The quality of support from wireless vendors varies widely and ranges from excellent to none. In addition, technology changes rapidly; new software, new hardware, new firmware, and new drivers constantly become available. To maximize your chances of receiving effective support, do the following:

- **Research**—During your equipment research process, be sure to visit other organizations that have deployed the equipment you are considering. Ask the organizations to comment about the quality of vendor support they are receiving, including warranty support.

- **Realistic approach**—There still is no free lunch. Be realistic with your support expectations. You deserve to be notified by your vendor when equipment problems are discovered. You should rightfully expect that your vendor would not discontinue support for equipment that you have purchased; however, after your warranty period has expired, it is not unreasonable for a vendor to charge for software upgrades or new and improved hardware. Expect to pay a reasonable amount to receive a high level of continuing vendor support. You need your equipment vendor to make a profit so that it will continue to be there when you need it.

- **Support groups**—A number of online support groups are available for specific brands of wireless equipment. Find a discussion group for your equipment and join it, if possible, even before you purchase your equipment. You, your end users, and the entire industry will benefit from this helpful and friendly sharing of information.

Review Questions

1 Why is it important to visit an actual deployment site before you purchase wireless equipment?

2 The electromagnetic waves that we call wireless exist at what layer of the seven-layer OSI reference model?

3 How is a packet like a hamburger sandwich?

4 Why does a wireless network need a big MAC?

5 Wireless bandwidth and wireless throughput are the same thing. True or false?

6 The communications range under NLOS conditions is about the same as the communications range under LOS conditions. True or false?

7 DSSS equipment hops from frequency to frequency. True or false?

8 Other things being equal, the higher the data rate, the shorter the communications distance. True or false?

9 If you start receiving interference from another network, the best thing to do is to get an amplifier. True or false?

10 Any 802.11b equipment works with any other 802.11b equipment. True or false?

CHAPTER 7

Installing Outdoor Wireless Systems

The correct installation of outdoor wireless systems is vital to reliable network operation. In broad terms, the three stages of successful installation are as follows:

- Planning and preparation
- Installation
- Testing and verification

This chapter provides information and guidance for you as you plan and install your outdoor wireless equipment and antenna systems.

Preparing for Outdoor Wireless Installations

Successfully installing outdoor wireless equipment requires, more than anything, a consistent and efficient installation process. That process includes the following components.

Planning

Plan your installation process to be as consistent as possible from installation site to installation site. Installations should be as similar to each other as possible. Try to use the same:

- **Wireless equipment**—Have one or two basic customer premises equipment (CPE) packages (such as one package for a single-PC end user and one package for a multiple-PC end user). The fewer end user packages, the lower your inventory and support costs.

- **Cable**—Use only a few types of cable. One type could be 0.4-inch (1 cm) diameter coax and the second type could be outdoor Category 5 (Cat5) Ethernet cable. Using fewer cable types reduces your inventory, tool, training, and connector costs.

- **Antennas**—Use only a few CPE antenna packages. Package 1 might be a +8-dBi panel antenna for end users within 1 mile (1.6 km) of your access point, package 2 might be a +14-dBi panel antenna for users within two miles (3.2 km) of your access point, and package 3 might be a +21-dBi parabolic antenna for end users located between 2 miles (3.2 km) and 5 miles (8 km) from your access point.

- **Test techniques**—Use one test technique to verify the performance of your point-to-point links. Repeat the same basic test at various locations throughout the coverage area of each point-to-multipoint sector that you install. Several suggested tests are described at the end of this chapter.

- **Documentation**—Use the same access-point documentation process (and documentation paperwork) for each access-point sector that you install. Use the same CPE documentation process for each customer installation.

Collaboration

In a perfect world, 100 percent of the installation details would be decided during the site survey process, well in advance of the actual installation. The actual world is still a few percentage points short of being perfect (quite a few points short, actually); therefore, installers often find that they need to make some installation decisions during the actual installation process. The installer must become a collaborator with the person who performed the site survey (perhaps you are one and the same person) and constructively contribute to fill in the details that the person performing the site survey did not address.

Safety Training

Safety training is required for all installation personnel. The training should cover all the following:

- **Height awareness**—This includes heights and the possibility of being injured or disabled by working above the ground.

- **Tower safety**—If your company expects you to do tower work, it should train you in tower climbing techniques and tower rescue techniques.

- **Government regulations**—These are Federal and State Occupational Safety and Health Administration (OSHA) rules and regulations.

- **Personal protection equipment**—Hats, boots, eye protection, gloves, sunscreen, radiation monitors, and other personal protection equipment are all essential.

- **Hoisting techniques**—This involves using ladders, ropes, and pulleys safely.

- **Microwave safety techniques**—This involves avoiding the injury caused by excessive exposure to microwave radiation from antenna systems.

- **Weather restrictions**—The weather conditions should cause you to stop working and take shelter. You should stop work and go inside when it is raining, snowing, lightning, and when there are high winds.

Availability and Use of Proper Tools

The proper tools (portable drills, hand tools, ladders, ropes, buckets, safety equipment, and so on) need to be available to all installation personnel. In addition, training needs to be provided in the safe and skillful use of all tools. Managers are responsible for both providing the necessary tools and verifying that training has been completed.

Professional Work Attitude

A professional installer does more than just collaborate with the person who performed the site survey. He interacts with many people and needs to possess and to express the following:

- **Positive attitude**—A constructive, positive, can-do approach to solving the problems that can occur during installation

- **Personal interaction skills**—The ability and willingness to work in a respectful, helpful, and friendly fashion with customers, facility managers, installation crewmembers, other trades people, city employees, and others who are involved in various aspects of the installation process

- **Responsibility**—A willingness to accept responsibility for the successful completion of each installation job

- **Attentiveness**—The ability to remain focused on the details of the job, the dynamics of personal interaction, and the adherence to safe work practices and habits

Verifying the Installation Documentation

A site survey, properly performed in advance of installation, should supply you with all the information shown in Table 4-2 of Chapter 4, "Performing Site Surveys." This information is summarized here:

- **Equipment location**—The location where the main wireless equipment will be located.

- **Antenna mounting location**—The location and the mounting method for the antenna system.

- **Antenna alignment information**—The antenna direction and the uptilt or downtilt angle, if any.

- **Cabling details**—The cable type, route, and building entry point.

- **Grounding location**—The grounding wire type, route, and ground connection point location.

- **Equivalent Isotropic Radiated Power (EIRP) calculation**—The equivalent power that will be radiated from the antenna. You need to recalculate this level and verify that the Federal Communications Commission (FCC) power limits will not be exceeded. See Tables 6-1, 6-2, and 6-3 in Chapter 6, "Evaluating and Selecting Wireless Equipment," for a summary of the legal power levels. Table 7-1 provides several examples of EIRP calculations for point-to-multipoint systems.

Table 7-1   *Equivalent Isotropic Radiated Power Examples*

Transmitter Output Power Level	Power Gain or Loss	Resulting Power Level	Antenna Gain	Resulting EIRP	Legal? (Yes or No)
1 Watt (+30 dBm)	3 ft (1 m) of small diameter coax with a total of −1 dB of loss	+29 dBm	Antenna with a gain of +6 dBi	+35 dBi	Yes
100 mW (+20 dBm)	Amplifier with a gain of +14 dB	+34 dBm	Antenna with a gain of +8 dBi	+42 dBi	No
25 mW (+14 dBm)	Amplifier with a gain of +14 dB	+28 dBm	Antenna with a gain of +8 dBi	+36 dBi	Yes

Installing Tower-Mounted Antenna Systems

Only properly trained personnel should perform tower work. If your company chooses not to train its employees to perform this work, it needs to contract this work to properly trained and properly insured antenna installers. The contracted installers should use proper climbing and hoisting tools to safely install, repair, or modify your tower-mounted antennas. If your company chooses to obtain tower training for you, your training needs to teach you the proper tools, techniques, and practices to use when you install tower-mounted antenna systems.

The goal of antenna system installation is to safely install the proper antenna (the antenna with the correct directivity, gain, wind-loading, and appearance) high enough off the ground to provide a reliable line-of-sight (LOS) signal path. The antenna must remain in the air, weatherproofed, and pointed in the proper direction indefinitely. The wireless equipment, all other connected equipment, and all nearby people and buildings must also be protected from lightning damage, physical damage, and injury.

Working in High-RF Environments

Installers who do antenna installation work on pre-existing towers have one advantage and one disadvantage when compared to installers who do only nontower antenna installation work. The advantage is that tower antenna installers do not usually have to worry about installing the tower. Tower installation includes designing the tower, digging a hole for the base, installing the base and the guy-wire anchors, erecting the tower sections, installing the guy wires, and installing the tower grounding system.

The disadvantage that tower antenna installers have to face is that they often must work in high-intensity radio-frequency (RF) environments. High RF environments include commercial AM, FM, and television broadcast station transmitting sites. In environments like this, it is necessary to protect both the wireless equipment and the installation personnel.

Microwave Radiation Won't Kill You...Immediately

Sometimes, you might need to work in high RF environments such as building rooftops with transmitting antennas for five or ten different wireless services. When you work in these environments, you need to take the same precautions to protect yourself that tower personnel must take.

Protecting Your Personal Safety

The long-term health effects of exposure to high and low levels of microwave radiation are not fully known or understood. Controversy will probably continue for a number of years until we (human guinea pigs) can say conclusively that exposure to microwave radiation is (or is not) harmful to our health. Until more is known, you should practice prudent avoidance. This means that you should act to be aware of sources of RF radiation and intentionally limit any and all unnecessary exposure to RF energy. Following are some ways to do this:

- Use external antennas on wireless devices (such as wireless cards in your laptop or your customer's laptop) whenever possible.

- Keep as much distance as possible between yourself and transmitting antennas. Do not get in front of a directional transmitting antenna when the transmitter is on.

- Turn off all transmitters when you are not using them. (This includes cell phones; they transmit even when you are not making a call.)

- If you work in a wireless lab, use a nonradiating "dummy load" whenever possible during the testing of wireless transmitting equipment.

- Use a headset on your cell phone; then place the cell phone as far as possible away from your body.

- Avoid making fun of people (like me) who tell you that exposure to wireless energy can cause health risks. Sure, health nuts like me could turn out to be wrong, but on the other hand, are you willing to bet the health of your unborn children on it? Now, please... Turn off your pocket or belt-carried cell phone when it doesn't absolutely need to be on. (The world won't end if you pick up your cell phone messages from voicemail every 30 minutes.) Play it safe.

Monitor and limit your exposure to high RF levels. Personal RF monitors are available that can be worn on your belt. These monitors provide an audible warning when RF levels exceed safety thresholds. Some products also continuously log RF exposure levels.

If your job responsibilities require you to work regularly in high-RF environments, your safety tools should include a personal RF monitor, and your company's safety program should include both RF safety training and RF exposure-level monitoring.

If your personal monitor indicates that your RF exposure is too high, you might need to request that one or more transmitters be scheduled to be turned off long enough for you to complete your installation work.

Protecting the Wireless Equipment

Just as humans might be injured by exposure to high levels of wireless energy, wireless equipment can also be damaged, either temporarily or permanently. Wireless equipment that is installed in high-RF locations needs to be protected with bandpass filtering. Bandpass filtering attenuates (reduces) the level of out-of-band RF energy and protects wireless receivers from being overloaded and desensitized, with a corresponding decrease in their ability to receive weak signals.

Tower Equipment-Mounting Scenarios

Most of the time when you need to do a tower-mounted antenna and equipment installation, you are installing access point (AP) equipment rather than CPE equipment. Figure 7-1 illustrates the three typical AP equipment-mounting configurations, which are as follows:

- Mounting the wireless equipment inside and the antenna system outside (Figure 7-1a).
- Mounting the wireless equipment outside, below the antenna, on the tower (Figure 7-1b).
- Mounting the wireless equipment inside of the antenna itself. This configuration is coming into wider use, especially for CPE (Figure 7-1c).

Figure 7-1   *Inside/Outside Equipment-Mounting Configurations*

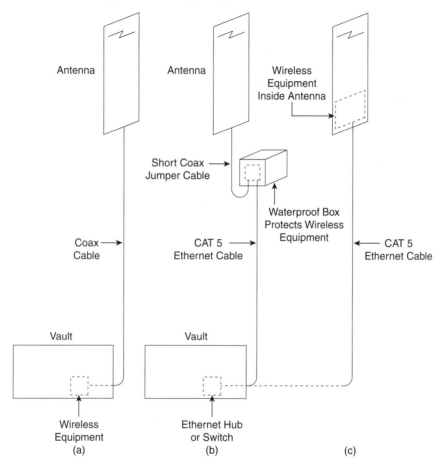

Mounting Wireless Equipment Inside

At submicrowave frequencies (below 1000 MHz), wireless equipment is traditionally mounted inside the building or inside a special equipment shelter (vault or hut). Coax cable then runs outside, up the tower, and to the antenna. The wireless equipment is inside, protected from the weather, and accessible for maintenance and servicing. The only disadvantage of mounting the equipment inside is the transmit signal that is lost in the coax cable running from the equipment to the antenna and the receive signal that is lost in the coax running from the antenna to the equipment. At submicrowave frequencies, this is not a serious problem; however, in the license-free microwave frequency bands, this signal loss becomes high.

Mounting Wireless Equipment on the Tower

In the 2.4 GHz and 5 GHz license-free bands, wireless equipment is often mounted outside to overcome the high coaxial cable signal loss. The wireless equipment is mounted as close to the antenna system as possible—normally on the tower, just below the antenna. The equipment is connected to the antenna with a short (3 ft or 1 m) jumper cable. A variation of this configuration is to mount the wireless equipment inside the wireless antenna. The nonwireless equipment port is connected to the network equipment (inside, on the ground) with outdoor-rated CAT5 Ethernet cable.

Installing Rooftop-Mounted Antenna Systems

Most of your installation work consists of installing rooftop-mounted antenna systems at customer locations, both businesses and residences. The installation includes the following steps:

1   Building a base on the roof for the antenna mast

2   Installing and waterproofing the antenna

3   Attaching the cable and weatherproofing the connection

4   Raising the mast and aiming the antenna

5   Running the cabling to the equipment

6   Installing lightning protection, including grounding the mast and cable

7   Testing the completed installation

8   Documenting both the installation and the testing results

The following sections provide more detail in each of these areas.

Building the Roof-Mounted Antenna Base

All roof-mounted antenna masts need a base that holds them in place. Ideally, the mast base should be a nonpenetrating type; no holes should be drilled in the roof to mount or secure the base. A nonpenetrating base prevents leaks in the roof caused by imperfectly sealed nails or screws.

NOTE   If you use a wall-mounted mast or a small dish-type antenna mount, you can disregard this antenna-base section. Use the appropriate wall-mounting hardware to attach your antenna mount to the wall.

Several commercial mast bases are available; however, most installations can be done using a base that you can build yourself. This lowers the overall cost of the installation. To build your own flat-roof base, use two 5-ft lengths of pressure-treated 4 × 4 lumber and do the following:

1 Raise the two 4 × 4 pieces of lumber individually to the roof and place them in a T shape. Connect them using one T-shaped bracket and two right angle brackets, as shown in Figure 7-2. Align the stem of the T to point toward the edge of the roof and toward the far end of the wireless link.

Figure 7-2 *Building a Flat-Roof Mast Base*

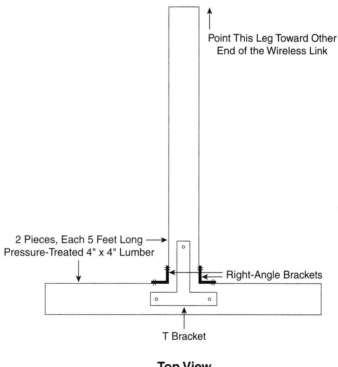

Top View

TIP   If you need to mount an antenna base over the peak of a roof instead of on a flat roof, you can still use the wooden T base. Cut the leg of the T and position the cut over the peak of the roof. Use a right-angle bracket (hammer it slightly flat to match the angle of the peak) to connect the two cut pieces.

---

2   Place a 5-ft tall tripod on top of the center of the base. Move it around until each of the three legs of the tripod is centered on top of one of the three legs of the base. Use one or two 1.5-inch (4 cm) large-diameter hex head screws to attach each of the tripod feet to the wood base.

3   Remove the screw holding the tripod leg that points toward the other end of the wireless link. Hinge the tripod down until it is horizontal on the roof.

4   Insert the mast completely into the tripod, and then place a tool bucket (or other object) underneath the mast to support it in a position raised approximately 15 degrees from horizontal.

Installing the Antenna

When your mast base is prepared and your mast installed, you are ready to attach and connect your antenna. Do this as follows:

1   Lightly tighten the tripod screws so that they keep the mast from rotating inside the tripod.

2   Extend the top section of the mast just enough to make room to attach the antenna onto the top section of the mast. Attach the antenna to the mast and tighten the antenna hardware well so that the antenna will not turn on the mast in a strong wind.

3   Install any mast-mounted equipment such as amplifiers or frequency converters on the mast, just below the antenna. If you need to mount nonwaterproof equipment on the mast (such as indoor CPE or a bandpass filter) you can use an appropriate National Electrical Manufacturer's Association (NEMA) box. NEMA boxes are waterproof and prevent moisture from rain or snow from damaging the equipment. Larger hardware stores should have several sizes available.

4   Attach the cable to the antenna. If you are using mast-mounted equipment, connect the cable to the equipment and connect a short coax jumper between the equipment and the antenna.

Waterproofing the Connections and the Equipment

Because water runs downward, you should, whenever possible, mount the equipment in a position that places the connectors on the bottom. This reduces their exposure to rain and snow. The suggestions in the sections that follow will be helpful as you complete your waterproofing.

Using Drip Loops

Make a drip loop just before the point where each cable connector attaches to an antenna and to any piece of mast-mounted equipment. A drip loop extends below the connector/equipment junction and prevents water from running down the cable and into the equipment. Figure 7-3 shows a drip loop.

Figure 7-3   *Drip Loop*

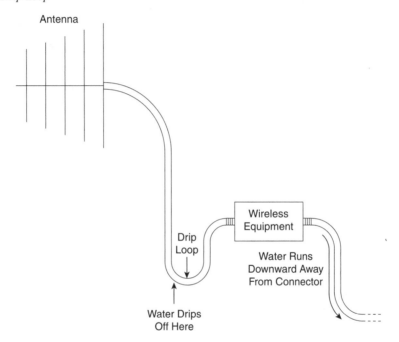

Applying Waterproofing

Several products and product combinations can effectively seal outdoor cable connectors. Regardless of which product you standardize on, to use it effectively, you must "think like water." This means that you must be extremely observant and notice every method by which water could enter your antenna system. Water can find the tiniest pinhole in your cable, connectors, outdoor amplifiers, frequency converters, lightning arrestors, and filters. Water can also enter any antenna that is not correctly designed or sealed. You can use any of the following products to make your connections watertight:

- **Cold-shrink tubing**—Cold-shrink tubing is placed around the connector joint. The cold-shrink tube string is pulled and the tube shrinks around the joint, sealing it.

- **Heat-shrink tubing**—Heat-shrink tubing is placed around the joint and shrinks around the joint when it is heated with a heat gun or a propane torch.

- **Self-galvanizing tape**—Self-galvanizing tape is wrapped around the joint and stretched as it is wrapped. It chemically bonds to itself, forming a waterproof layer. Wrap the tape in the direction that tightens the connector, not in the direction that loosens it.

- **Coax-seal**—Coax-seal is not a tube or a tape; it is semisticky, like a ball of tar. It is formed all around the joint, covering it and keeping out moisture. It remains semisoft so that the connection can be checked or changed in the future.

Cold-shrink, heat-shrink, self-galvanizing tape, and coax-seal all generally seal a joint without the use of additional tape or sealer; however, one or more layers of high-quality black electrical tape is often used as a final outer wrap over the top as an additional moisture-barrier. Black electrical tape is sometimes placed underneath the other products to make it easier to remove the other tape or tube if the joint ever needs to be reworked. See Appendix B, "Wireless Hardware, Software, and Service Provider Organizations," for information about suppliers of these products.

Outdoor wireless equipment and outdoor antennas are designed to be weatherproof. Does this mean that they are always perfectly waterproof? Usually they are, but it is wise to examine them closely and to add a light coat of a liquid sealer over any area where it appears that water could enter. Be especially careful to seal around case-mounted ground lugs and along the edge of any equipment case that lacks obvious gaskets. One liquid sealant that is often used is Scotchcoat, which is available in the electrical department of most large hardware stores.

TIP	Scotchcoat can seep out through the threads around the top of its own can. If you use Scotchcoat, carry the can vertically inside a slightly larger, empty metal can. The larger can will contain any Scotchcoat that seeps out of the original can. Carry both cans vertically because if either can falls over on its side, the Scotchcoat will seep out.

Although outdoor antennas are designed to be waterproof, there are occasional reports of antennas that have design or material flaws that allow water to enter the antenna and degrade performance. Apply sealant around any antenna seam that appears to have less than a 100 percent waterproof factory seal.

Antennas frequently have a drain hole that is designed to face downward and to allow any moisture that condenses inside the antenna to drain out. Be especially careful *not* to seal this drain hole. Mount the antenna in a position that allows any drain hole to face downward. To prevent antenna failure due to water, restrict yourself to using only antennas that you have successfully tested outdoors over a period of time. After you have used an antenna in varying weather conditions, you will have first-hand knowledge about the antenna's reliability. You can stop using models that prove to be unreliable.

Attaching the Guy Wires

Any pushup mast with an antenna that extends more than 5 ft (1.5 m) above the top of the tripod (or other mast attachment point) should have at least one set of guy wires installed. The guy wires

- Keep the antenna from moving in the wind and causing the signal to fade
- Keep the wind from blowing the mast over and possibly causing damage or injury

Guy wires attach to the mast with guy wire rings that come with the mast. Guy wires attach to the building with anchor hooks arranged every 120 degrees around the mast. The distance from the mast base to each anchor hook should be a minimum of 80 percent of the height of the mast. For example, the anchor hooks for a 30-ft (9 m) mast should be at least 24 ft (7.3 m) from the base of the mast. Place one turnbuckle in each guy wire. The turnbuckle allows you to adjust the tension on each guy wire. A 30-ft pushup mast might need up to three sets of guy wires, depending on the extended height of the mast. Use the following guidelines to determine how many sets of guy wires your mast needs:

- If the extended height is 10 ft (3 m) to 13 ft (4 m), use one set of three guy wires attached to the mast 9 ft (2.7 m) above the base.

- If the extended height is 16 ft (5 m) to 20 ft (6 m), use one set of guy wires attached 10 ft (3 m) above the base and a second set attached 2 ft (61 cm) below the antenna.

- If the extended height is from 25 ft (7.6 m) to 30 ft (9 m), use one set of guy wires 10 ft (3 m) above the base, a second set at 20 ft (6 m), and a third set attached 2 ft (61 cm) below the antenna.

Precut the guy wires to the approximate length needed and attach all of them to the mast while the mast is still horizontal on the roof. Run the lower end of each guy wire loosely through its corresponding guy wire anchor. This way, the guy wire is already in place when it is time to fasten it permanently through the guy anchor and tighten the turnbuckle.

Raising the Antenna and Mast

Raising the antenna mast with the antenna already installed and the cable running down the mast can be a physical challenge.

WARNING   The only way to raise a 20 or 30-ft (6 - 9m) mast safely is by using at least a two-person crew. Do not attempt to raise a mast working alone.

Safety awareness must be everyone's highest priority in the installation crew. An antenna mast that falls on a person can cause a serious, painful, crippling injury. The following section describes how to raise a 30-ft (9 m), three-section pushup mast from 10 ft (3 m) up to the full height of 30 ft (9 m). Raise the mast and antenna by doing the following:

1 With the mast extended just 10 ft (3 m), both installers should raise the tripod and mast to the vertical position. Insert a screw through the third leg of the tripod and attach this screw into the wood base. Refer to the antenna alignment information in your site survey documentation and note the direction that the antenna needs to point. Rotate the mast until the antenna points in the correct direction; then fully tighten the tripod screws that hold the mast into the tripod. Now, the base and the tripod are supporting the mast in a vertical position.

2 One installer should place a 5-ft (1.5 m) or a 6-ft (2 m) stepladder alongside the mast. Position the ladder so that the person on the ladder can easily reach the 10-ft (3 m) point on the mast.

3 Attach and tighten the lower set of three guy wires. The mast is now firmly held in position by this set of guy wires. The site survey documentation might specify an elevation angle for the antenna, for example, up two degrees or down one degree. If needed, loosen the antenna-mounting hardware, adjust the antenna elevation angle, and retighten the hardware. The mast is now ready to be extended up to final height.

4 The installer on the top of the ladder pushes the mast up and secures the cable to the mast as he raises the mast. The other installer is at the bottom of the ladder and is the safety person who holds the ladder firmly in place throughout the mast-raising procedure.

NOTE   Remember: The person on the bottom needs to be wearing a hard hat in case a tool falls from above. The person on the ladder should be wearing gloves to protect his hands from possible injury by any sharp metal edges on the mast.

---

5 Double-check again and confirm that the antenna is pointing in the proper direction. The top section of the mast is pushed up first and the middle section of the mast is pushed up last. The person on the ladder pushes the top section of the mast up approximately 3 ft (1 m) at a time. Stop every 3 ft (1 m) by tightening the clamp between the top section and the second section and secure the cable to the mast using black zip-tie straps. As the mast is extended, keep the antenna pointed in the proper direction and keep the cable running down along the same side of the mast.

6 When the top section is fully extended, tighten the clamp that secures the top section to the middle section. Now, push the middle section up 3 ft (1 m) at a time, stopping to fasten the cable to the mast. When the mast is fully extended, tighten the clamp that secures the middle section to the bottom section.

7   Tighten the middle set and the upper set of guy wires. Adjust the guy wire turnbuckles while observing the mast from two different directions until the mast is vertical when observed from each direction. You can also use a level and place it against two sides of the mast to confirm that the mast is vertical. Cut off the excess guy wire and twist a short piece of guy wire in a figure-eight shape from end-to-end through each of the turnbuckles. These safety wires prevent the wind from loosening the turnbuckle and also help to keep the guy wire from separating completely if the turnbuckle should ever break.

8   After the entire installation has been completed, put the new system on the air. Ask one person to look at the signal strength reading while you loosen the mast hardware and rotate the mast and antenna back and forth. Rotate the antenna several times through the compass heading that you obtained from the site survey documentation. Leave the antenna pointed in the direction of the highest signal strength and tighten the mast hardware firmly.

TIP   It is easiest to peak the signal strength if you use a pair of cell phones or two-way radios to communicate between the person turning the antenna and the person watching the receive signal strength indicator.

CAUTION   If you do not feel confident and safe performing the mast/antenna procedure, have the antenna system installed by a professional antenna installation crew.

Running the Cabling

Running the cabling is one of the harder parts of installing a wireless system. It can sometimes be dusty, dirty, and even dangerous. You might be installing either coax cable or Category 5 Ethernet cable. Ethernet cable is easier to install because it is smaller and more flexible than coax.

You can install the cable from inside the building up to the antenna location or from the outside antenna location down to the equipment location. Neither installation direction (up or down) is better than the other. The actual route that the cable takes should have been determined at the time of the site survey, and that information should be supplied to you as part of the installation documentation. The following steps describe the process of installing the cable from the outside antenna down to the wireless equipment:

1 Unroll or unspool enough cable on the roof of the building to extend from the antenna down to the equipment location. The installation documentation should provide you with this information. Include approximately 20 ft (6 m) of extra cable. It is better to have too much cable and have to cut off the extra than to have too little cable and have to splice more on.

2 Run the cable before you install a connector on the far end of the cable. Install the connector as the last step after the cable is completely run. Refer to the installation documentation and run the cable along the described route. Run the cable and attach it as neatly as possible to the building. Along vertical walls, use a correctly sized cable staple hammered into the wall to hold the cable firmly in place. Using the correct staple (designed to fit the cable) is important to avoid flattening the cable. Avoid making kinks and sharp bends in coax because they will cause impedance "bumps" in the cable with increased signal loss. Use an electrician's snake and electrician's pulling lubricant if you need to pull the cable through electrical conduit.

3 Install the lightning arrestor at the location specified in the installation documentation. Ideally, the lightning arrestor should be installed at the point just before the cable enters the building. Waterproof the lightning arrestor connectors if the lightning arrestor is exposed to the weather. Connect the lightning arrestor to a good ground (see the following section).

4 Use a pre-existing entry hole to route the cable from the outside to the inside of the building, whenever possible. If you need to drill a hole through the building, drill the hole on a vertical surface, not on a horizontal surface. If you drill a hole through concrete, you will likely need to use a rotary hammer drill and a special concrete drill bit. These can often be rented at a tool rental shop. Be sure to use a drip loop and some silicone sealant to prevent water from entering the cable-entry hole.

Grounding and Lightning Protection

It is necessary to provide a good low-resistance, low-impedance ground connection for every antenna mast and every lightning arrestor. Why is it necessary to provide lightning protection? The typical lightning strike produces a peak current of approximately 18,000 Amps (18 kA). A lightning strike generates a voltage differential of approximately 243,000 volts (243 kV) across an unguyed tower and 108,000 volts (108 kV) across a guyed tower. As a lightning bolt passes through the air, it raises the temperature of the air to 60,000 degrees and causes the air to glow brighter than the surface of the sun. You must shunt as much of this energy as possible directly to the ground to minimize damage to the wireless equipment, to the building, and to any people who might be nearby.

Don't Worry—It's Only a Quarter of a Million Volts

Sermon Mode = ON

It is essential that you install a lightning protector (a lightning arrestor) on every wireless installation that you do. The risks from installing unprotected antenna systems are just too great. Even if you are located in an area that has little lighting, don't take a chance. Install lightning protection on every outdoor antenna system installation.

Sermon Mode = OFF

Types of Lightning Arrestors

You can install any or all of the following three types of lightning arrestors, depending on the configuration of the wireless equipment:

- **Coaxial arrestors that pass direct current (DC)**—Used where DC-powered equipment, such as mast-mounted amplifiers or frequency converters, is mounted near the antenna. DC power is carried on the center conductor of the coax cable.

- **Coaxial arrestors that do not pass DC**—Used where no equipment is near the antenna that needs DC power.

- **Category 5 arrestors that carry DC power over Ethernet (PoE)**—Used where the wireless equipment is located near the antenna or inside the antenna housing and receives power over the Category 5 Ethernet cable. This type of arrestor provides protection for all of the wire conductors—the Ethernet wires and the power wires.

Ground Connections

Finding a good ground connection point near the coax or Category 5 cable run is one of the most challenging parts of a wireless installation. The ground wire route and the ground connection point is another one of the tasks that should be performed during the site survey before the installation crew is dispatched. The following grounding information should prove useful to you during installation when you verify the site survey grounding information:

- **Grounding tower-mounted antenna systems**—Grounding a lightning arrestor for a tower-mounted antenna is relatively easy. First, the coax shield should be grounded both at the antenna and at the base of the tower using coax-grounding kits. The coax shield should also be grounded to the tower every 75 ft (23 m) using a coax grounding kit. (See Appendix B for vendor information.) There should be a grounded bulkhead panel at the point where the coax enters the equipment vault or the building. A lightning arrestor should be mounted on the bulkhead panel; this grounds the lightning arrestor. The bulkhead panel serves as a single-point ground system. Ground wires from all the equipment come together and connect to the ground system here.

- **Grounding commercial-building mast-mounted antenna systems**—Finding a good ground connection for a mast-mounted antenna system on the roof of a commercial building can be difficult. Both the mast and the lightning arrestor need to be grounded. Here are some single-point ground location options:
  - The structural steel framing of the building is the best lightning-protection ground.
  - A connection to the building's concrete-encased steel rebar also provides a good ground connection.
  - If a ground bus bar is already installed inside of a rooftop penthouse, it can be used as the ground connection point.
  - The least effective ground is a ground wire that runs over the edge of the roof and down to an 8-ft (2.5 m) ground rod in the earth.

CAUTION   Do *not* use electrical conduit for a ground connection. Building rooftops often have exposed conduit, but there is no guarantee that the conduit runs straight down to the building single-point ground system. Using conduit as a ground point might not provide protection against lightning injury and damage.

- **Grounding residence-mounted antenna systems**—Grounding an antenna system that is mounted on a residence usually requires that you drive a ground rod directly into the ground below the point where the lightning arrestor is installed as the cable enters the building. Sometimes, you might get lucky and be able to attach your ground wire to an existing ground rod where the electrical power distribution panel is grounded.

The required size and insulation color of your ground wire can vary from city to city (depending on your local building code); however, the minimum wire size is usually number 8. If you are in doubt, check with your local building department or a competent local electrician. You can usually find ground wire and ground-wire clamps of various sizes at large hardware stores.

Installing the Wireless Equipment

The site survey information should indicate where to install the wireless equipment. The equipment location should have the following characteristics:

- **Power**—Alternating current (AC) or, in a few cases, direct current (DC) power must be available. If operation of the equipment is important during commercial power outages, a source of backup power, such as an uninterruptible power system (UPS), should be available.

- **Space and accessibility**—There should be enough space both for the equipment and for service personnel to work on the equipment. The space should be locked so that the equipment is protected against unauthorized access.

- **Temperature**—The temperature of the equipment location should be controlled so that the temperature specifications of the equipment are not exceeded. Often, this requires that the equipment be mounted in a room with air conditioning for summer cooling and heating for winter warmth.

- **Dryness and cleanliness**—The equipment should be installed in an area that is free from exposure to moisture and free from dust and dirt.

- **Short cable run**—If coax is used, the equipment should be placed as close as possible to the antenna location. If Category 5 Ethernet cable is used, the length of the Category 5 cable should not exceed 300 ft (91 m).

- **Grounding**—A single-point ground system should be available or installable.

- **Seismic protection**—The equipment should be braced to prevent damage or injury in the event of an earthquake.

Testing Wireless Systems

The need to perform proper testing of a newly installed wireless system is frequently overlooked. Further, the time needed to perform this testing is often underestimated. The sections that follow describe why it is necessary to test wireless systems and what the proper test methods are to use.

Testing Point-to-Point Wireless Links

Always test each newly installed point-to-point wireless link by measuring the throughput, the fade margin, and the applications that the end user will use. The following sections describe these tests.

Measuring the Throughput

A wireless link that has been correctly installed should work immediately. It should be capable of delivering the full amount of data that it is rated to carry. The actual data throughput that the link delivers can be measured by transferring a large file and calculating the transfer speed.

TIP   You are measuring the speed of the wireless link, not the speed of the link and the speed of the Internet. To measure only the link speed, copy (download) a large file from a lightly loaded machine at your network operating center (NOC) to your laptop at the newly installed end user location. Then, upload the same file from your laptop to your NOC. You avoid going out on the Internet, so you avoid having variable Internet traffic levels change the results of your test.

For example, if a new wireless link requires 90 seconds to transfer a 10-megabyte (MB) file (with 8 bits per byte; the file contains 80,000,000 bits), the link speed is (80,000,000 bits divided by 90 seconds) 889 kilobits per second (kbps). If the same file transfer requires 125 seconds, the link speed is 640 kbps. Repeat the test several times; the results should be similar each time.

Some links might be configured for different uplink and downlink speeds, so be sure to test the throughput in each direction. Also, be sure that your test computers are fast enough to operate at the full link speed; otherwise, they might not be able to fill the link to capacity. In this case, you might be able to use two pairs of computers to transfer two files simultaneously. If using two computers on each end is not practical, do one file transfer and compare the indicated speed to the speeds that you have previously seen on well-operating links with the same amount of bandwidth.

Measuring the Fade Margin

Chapter 2, "Understanding Wireless Fundamentals," described fade margin, which is the amount of extra signal that a microwave link needs to overcome the fading that occurs normally. If the wireless equipment is *not* contained inside the antenna housing (a and b but not c in Figure 7-1), you can use a variable attenuator to measure the fade margin on the link. A variable attenuator does just what it sounds like: It adds an adjustable amount of attenuation (loss) into the signal path. The amount of loss can be adjusted, usually in 1 dB steps, from –1 dB up to approximately –70 dB. A normal length (less than 10 miles or 16 km) link usually needs at least 10 dB of fade margin to operate reliably. The higher the fade margin, the more reliable the link will be.

To measure the actual fade margin on a newly installed link, do the following:

1 Measure and record the throughput on the new link, as described in the previous section.

2 Insert a variable attenuator between the antenna and the wireless equipment. If the equipment is located inside, insert the variable attenuator at the bottom end of the coax. If the equipment is located outside, near the antenna, insert the attenuator in the coax between the equipment and the antenna.

3 Repeat the throughput test and add attenuation −1 dB at a time. Watch to see when the throughput starts to drop significantly. At that point, record the setting of the variable attenuator. The attenuator setting is equal to the fade margin of the wireless link.

4 To confirm that the fade margin reading is correct, reduce the attenuator by −1 dB (use 1 dB less attenuation—for example, reduce the attenuator from −11 dB to −10 dB) and repeat the throughput test. The throughput should go up again and return to the level before the attenuator was added.

5 Record the measured fade margin in your installation documentation.

Testing Applications over the Link

After you measure the throughput and record the fade margin, test one or two of the applications that the new wireless end user is going to use over the link. Many times, this application is web browsing. Select a few web pages and confirm that the link is working well as it downloads these web pages. After you verify that the applications are working, demonstrate the operation of the new wireless link to the end user.

Testing Point-to-Multipoint Wireless Links

Testing the performance of a point-to-multipoint wireless access point is similar to testing a point-to-point link except that you need to repeat the testing from a number of locations inside the access point coverage area.

Choose several points that are located in various parts of the coverage area. Some of these points should be at the far edge of the area, and some points should be close to the access point. When you have successfully verified that the access point is actually covering the proper area and that the throughput is correct (in both directions) at each end point, your testing is complete. Be sure to document the throughput and the fade margin for each point that you test.

Documenting the Test Results

Double-check to be sure that you have made a complete written record of the entire installation process as well as all the over-the-air link-testing results. When you return to your office, file the documentation so that it will be available if the link ever needs to be serviced in the future.

Review Questions

1 A site survey is normally performed immediately after a wireless installation is completed. True or false?

2 Anyone can install wireless antennas on radio towers as long as they are not afraid of heights. True or false?

3 At microwave frequencies, the signal loss in coax cable is relatively high. True or false?

4 A typical lightning strike produces a peak current of approximately how many amps?

5 Fading is normal for microwave signals. What term is used to describe the extra signal power that every microwave link needs to overcome this fading?

6 What should you do immediately after you test the throughput on a newly installed wireless link?

7 Name one advantage of standardizing on only a few customer premise equipment packages.

8 If your job responsibilities require you to work regularly in high-RF environments, you should use what piece of personal protective equipment?

CHAPTER 8

Solving Noise and Interference Problems

One challenge that you will eventually face when operating your outdoor license-free network is how to minimize the throughput-reducing effects of interference and noise. Although noise has many potential causes, there are also many techniques that you can use to minimize the impact of noise on your network. This chapter summarizes the following topics:

- The importance of understanding signal-to-noise ratio (SNR)
- How to maximize the desired signal strength
- How to minimize the noise from your own network
- How to minimize the noise from other networks
- How to minimize the noise from out-of-band transmitters
- How to monitor network performance and detect emerging noise problems
- How to use direction-finding techniques to pinpoint the location of noise sources

You need to become familiar with noise-reduction techniques before you need to use them. Noise problems can either develop slowly or they can appear suddenly. By becoming familiar with noise-reduction techniques now, you will know how to respond and what to do when a noise problem appears.

The noise-reduction techniques discussed in this chapter apply to all broadband wireless networks. It does not matter if you operate a direct-sequence spread spectrum (DSSS) network, a frequency-hopping spread spectrum (FHSS) network, a point-to-point wireless link, or some other type of broadband microwave network.

Understanding SNR

A strong signal alone is not enough for a broadband wireless receiver to work reliably. To work well, the level of the received signal must be consistently higher than the level of the received noise; in other words, the SNR must be high. A high SNR requires that both of the following conditions be met simultaneously:

- **The receiver must receive a signal that is at or above the receiver threshold level**— The threshold is the level where the receiver wakes up, detects that a signal is present, and begins to successfully decode the signal. Part A of Figure 8-1 uses a decibel (dB) scale to show the relationship of the receiver threshold to the level of the incoming signal.

- **The noise level at the receiver input must be lower than the desired incoming signal**—If the noise is high, the signal strength of the signal must be higher than the incoming noise level. Part B of Figure 8-1 shows the relationship between the receiver threshold, a high noise level, and two incoming signals. One incoming signal is lower than the noise level and will not be successfully decoded. The other signal is higher than the noise level and will be successfully decoded.

Figure 8-1   *Relationship Between Receiver Threshold, Signal Level, and Noise Level*

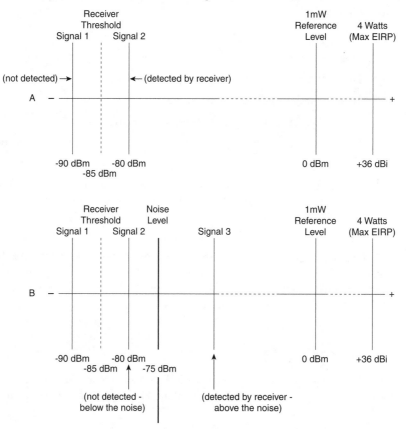

To summarize, for reliable receiver operation, there must be a good SNR at the receiver antenna input. The SNR allows the receiver to separate the signal from the noise. To design and operate a reliable wireless network, you need to be able to simultaneously maximize the desired signal level and to minimize the existing (and future) noise and interference level.

Maximizing the Signal Level

You have direct control over maximizing the signal strengths of received signals. The procedures for doing this have been discussed throughout this book and include the following:

- **Link budget**—Make sure that each link is designed with enough transmit power, receive sensitivity, fade margin, and antenna gain to overcome the free-space path loss and the coax loss.

- **Line-of-sight (LOS) paths**—Make sure that each wireless link has an LOS path with an unobstructed view from end to end.

- **Fresnel zone**—Make sure that each link has a clear Fresnel zone and that there is enough clearance above and between path obstacles to avoid additional signal loss.

- **Installation**—Make sure during installation that each antenna system is mounted securely, aligned correctly, and waterproofed completely.

When it comes to noise and interference, the situation is different. You have only indirect control over the noise level.

Minimizing the Noise and Interference Level

You do not have direct control over most noise and interference sources. Remember: Noise is defined as "everything other than the desired signal." Therefore, noise includes all the following:

- **Natural noise**—Atmospheric and galactic noise.

- **Manmade noise**—Noise that is present in the radio-frequency (RF) environment and that is picked up by your antenna. This includes noise from microwave ovens, cordless telephones, and indoor wireless LANs.

- **Receiver noise**—Noise generated inside the receiver circuitry.

- **Interference from other networks**—Interference caused by other signals in the same band coming from other nearby wireless networks.

- **Interference from your network**—Interference caused by signals coming from your own network. This interference occurs when you are using the same frequency more than once, using channels that do not have enough space between them, or selecting incorrect frequency-hopping sequences.

- **Interference from out-of-band signals**—Interference caused by strong, nearby signals outside of the frequency band that you are using.

It is important for you to use a combination of all the possible noise-reduction techniques to receive as little noise as possible and thereby maximize your SNR. This is true both during the initial system design as well as throughout the life of your network.

NOTE   Noise levels in each area are different. In a city, noise levels are usually higher than in a rural area. The more people who live in an area, the more wireless devices are present, and the higher the noise level. If you are located in a rural area, do not automatically assume that there are no sources of noise. There is less noise than in a city, but it is likely that your network is not the only network in use. Use a spectrum analyzer or wireless site survey utility to look for other networks and sources of noise in your area.

Table 8-1 summarizes the noise-reduction techniques that you can use as you are designing your network. If you fail to design a noise-resistant network or if other noise sources appear after you deploy your network, you can use the solutions in the two right columns to reduce the impact that the noise has on your throughput.

Table 8-1   *Noise Sources and Solutions*

Source of Noise	Location of Original Noise Solution Description	Symptom	Solution (Before Beginning Wireless Service)	Solution (After Beginning Wireless Service)
Antenna directional patterns ignored. (Antenna pattern is too broad.)	Chapter 4, "Antenna Radiation Patterns" section.	Reduced throughput caused by picking up noise from unwanted directions.	Choose a more directional antenna for your access point (AP) with a coverage pattern that covers only the desired service area.	Research, design, purchase, install, and test a new, more directional antenna system.
High noise level from other transmitters near your AP location. These transmitters might be out-of-band (AM, FM, or TV broadcasting, paging, or two-way radio) or in-band (other networks in the same license-free band)	Chapter 4, "RF Site Survey" section; Chapter 5, "Cross Polarization" and "Sector Antenna Systems" sections.	Reduced throughput caused by picking up noise from nearby transmitters.	Perform an RF site survey using a spectrum analyzer.	Review Table 4-3 in Chapter 4. Then do one of the following: *For in-band noise:* Temporarily shut down all the transmitters on your network and use a spectrum analyzer to attempt to locate the source of interference. If the noise cannot be reduced, it might be necessary for you to move your AP to a new location. If you locate the interference source, reconfigure your antenna system polarization, directivity, or downtilt to reduce the noise. *For out-of-band noise:* Temporarily add a bandpass filter between the antenna and the radio to see if the throughput improves.

Table 8-1   *Noise Sources and Solutions (Continued)*

Source of Noise	Location of Original Noise Solution Description	Symptom	Solution (Before Beginning Wireless Service)	Solution (After Beginning Wireless Service)
Interference from another network that is on the same DSSS frequency channel.	Chapter 4 (Table 4-3).	Reduced throughput.	Choose a DSSS channel with as little use as possible, as determined by a spectrum analyzer.	Change DSSS channels; choose one with the least amount of use, as determined by a spectrum analyzer.
Interference from other networks using the same FHSS hopping sequence or using another hopping set.	Chapter 4 (Table 4-3).	Reduced throughput.	Coordinate your choice of hopping set and hopping sequence. Use the same hopping set as the other FHSS networks in your area but a different hopping sequence within that set.	Change your choice of hopping set and hopping sequence. Use the same hopping set as the other FHSS networks in your area but a different hopping sequence within that set.
Interference from another radio or from another AP in your network.	Chapter 5, "Isolating Antenna Systems" and "Sector Antenna Systems" sections.	Reduced throughput on both your APs.	Prepare a frequency plan. (See the "Minimizing Noise from Your DSSS Network" section following this table). Design your network to ensure adequate isolation between your antenna systems that operate on the same frequency. Use a combination of antenna directivity, cross polarization, antenna downtilting, vertical separation, horizontal separation, and obstruction isolation between your antennas.	Temporarily shut down one of your networks while you add isolation between your antenna systems by using a combination of the techniques listed at the left.

continues

Table 8-1   *Noise Sources and Solutions (Continued)*

Source of Noise	Location of Original Noise Solution Description	Symptom	Solution (Before Beginning Wireless Service)	Solution (After Beginning Wireless Service)
Wireless packet collisions between end users on your own network.	Chapter 6, "Access Point Feature Decisions" section.	Reduced throughput under moderate and heavy traffic levels.	Select equipment that is capable of polling end users rather than using the standard carrier sense multiple access with collision avoidance (CSMA/CA) protocol that allows hidden-node end users to collide with each other.	Upgrade both AP and user software to a version that provides end user polling. If this is not possible, install a bandwidth manager that can throttle (limit) each end user to a predetermined bandwidth level. If necessary, throttle end user upload speeds at a level less than their download speeds.
Multipath	Chapter 2, "Multipath" section; Chapter 5, "Polarization Selection Examples" and "Diversity Antenna System" sections. Chapter 6, "Multipath Resistance" section.	High error rates with reduced throughput.	Avoid placing wireless APs in reflection-prone locations. Use circularly polarized antennas whenever possible if you must operate in an area with reflective buildings, standing bodies of water, or large sections of concrete parking lots.	Move your APs to less reflective areas; temporarily substitute a circularly polarized antenna system on your AP and test to see if the throughput under load is improved.

Minimizing Noise from Your DSSS Network

After you successfully deploy your network, it is likely that the demand for service on your network will increase. This means that you will add more users to your existing AP and you might also add new APs. As you add APs, your risk of self-interference increases because the number of nonoverlapping channels that you can use in any geographical area is limited. For example, on the 2.4 GHz band in the United States, you can use a maximum of three nonoverlapping channels: channels 1, 6, and 11.

To eliminate self-interference between your AP sectors, make a frequency plan before you deploy your network. The frequency plan should show all of the following information:

- Location of each AP
- Geographic area covered by each AP sector
- Frequency used in each sector
- Antenna polarization used in each sector
- Equivalent isotropic radiated power (EIRP) used in each sector

If your plan uses more than three frequencies at the same AP location or if two or more of your AP sectors are within wireless range of each other, you need to reuse (share) one or more channels. To reuse channels, design your antenna systems so that there is at least 121 dB of isolation (wireless signal loss) between them. When you have this much isolation, the receiver in one sector can no longer hear the transmitter from the other sector. Now, you can use the same frequency on both sectors (or one sector and one wireless backhaul link) without causing self-interference.

Figure 8-2 provides an example of a frequency plan that requires one frequency to be reused.

Figure 8-2   *Example of a Frequency Plan*

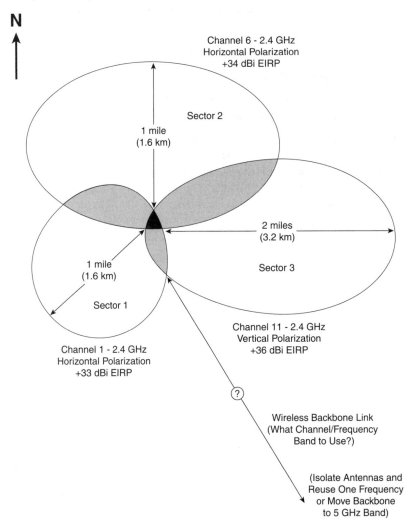

Figure 8-2 shows one AP with three point-to-multipoint sectors and one point-to-point wireless backbone link. This AP requires a total of four frequencies; however, at 2.4 GHz, there are only three non-overlapping frequencies (channels 1, 6, and 11). You can use either one of the following two solutions for this problem:

- **Antenna system isolation**—Isolate two of the antenna systems to allow the same frequency to be reused simultaneously for two different purposes; for example, one point-to-multipoint sector and the backhaul might be isolated and on the same frequency. Use the techniques summarized in the "Interference from another radio or from another AP in your network" row of Table 8-1. These techniques are described in more detail in the "Noise Reduction from Your Network" section of Chapter 5.

- **Different frequency bands**—Move one sector (or move the backbone link) to a different frequency band. For example, you could move the backbone link to the 5-GHz band. Now all three non-overlapping 2.4-GHz frequencies are available for use, one per sector, with no interference and no throughput loss from the backbone link.

Minimizing Noise from Your FHSS Network

If you operate a FHSS network, each sector has a lower throughput compared to a DSSS network; however, you can still deploy more sectors on the same tower or rooftop before you generate a significant level of self-interference. To minimize self-interference, do the following:

- Be sure to choose hopping sequences from the same hopping set for all sectors located in the same geographical area. For example, if you deploy six sectors on the same rooftop, the six different hopping sequences must be in the same hopping set. If another network is in the same area (your network or someone else's network), both your network and the other network should choose unique hopping sequences from the same hopping set.

- Avoid locating (collocating) more than 10 sectors on the same tower or rooftop or in the same geographical area where the sector antenna patterns can overlap.

Wow! 10,000 Sectors and No Self-Interference!

Some equipment vendors claim that up to 15 FHSS sectors can be collocated (placed on the same tower or rooftop) without significant self-interference. Personally, I will believe this claim when I actually see an FHSS system that can run fully loaded with traffic without a significant reduction in throughput (in other words, without self-interference). Until I see such a system, I would advise running no more than 10 collocated sectors unless you use effective antenna-isolation techniques. If you isolate some of the sector antennas completely from each other, you can run more collocated sectors without self-interference.

Minimizing Noise from Other Networks

The more people who live in a specific area, the more likely it is that there will be more than one broadband wireless network. The more networks, the more likely you are to experience noise from the other networks.

The best way to minimize noise from other networks is to do a wireless site survey before you commit to placing your AP in a specific location. If your AP is already in place and cannot be moved, you can use any or all of the techniques outlined in the "High noise level from other transmitters near your AP location" row of Table 8-1 to minimize your reception of signals from the other networks.

Minimizing Noise from Out-of-Band Transmitters

When your receiver is located close to high-power transmitters, the signals from those transmitters can overload (overpower) your receiver and act like noise to reduce your SNR. This effect is called de-*sensitization*, or *desense*. Out-of-band sources of desense can include AM, FM, paging, television broadcast, and terrestrial satellite radio transmitters. Performing a wireless site survey before selecting an AP location normally prevents desense problems from occurring; however, many times an AP location is chosen without performing a wireless site survey.

You can solve an out-of-band transmitter noise problem in two ways:

- **Move your access point**—Moving your AP to another location reduces the signal strength of the other transmitter at the input of your receiver and allows your receiver to operate at full sensitivity. Moving an AP that has already been placed in service can be difficult because end users are already connected to it.

- **Use a bandpass filter**—Placing a bandpass filter between your antenna and your wireless equipment attenuates all signals below and above the license-free band and allows your receiver to hear the incoming signals from your end users. The filter does not significantly attenuate signals within the license-free band.

Signal-to-Noise Variations over Time

Noise problems might occur at different times and noise might increase at different rates or last for different lengths of time. You need to be prepared to deal with all of the noise conditions mentioned in the following sections.

High Noise Level Before Installation

Noise levels might already be high before you begin to design and install your network. For example, other networks might already be operating in the same area. The high noise level from these networks will cause your SNR to be low. If a wireless site survey indicates a high noise level, you should find another location for your AP.

Slowly Increasing Noise Level

After you install your network, it is likely that the noise level will slowly increase over time. This increase occurs because more people will use more wireless devices as time goes on. The result will be that your SNR will decrease slowly over time. Be sure to monitor your network performance statistics. Be ready to redesign your network or your antenna systems to improve your SNR, if needed.

Suddenly Increasing Noise Level

Normally, noise increases slowly over a period of time; however, it is also possible for noise to increase suddenly. Noise that suddenly increases can be of the following two types:

- **Steady**—This is noise that increases suddenly and is present constantly or almost all the time. This noise is likely coming from a new network that has been deployed in the same general area as your network. This noise decreases your SNR and reduces your network throughput. It is important for you to locate the other network, contact the network operator, and ask that person to coordinate their frequency, antenna polarization, or antenna pattern with you. Most people understand the need to cooperate. Occasionally, you might meet someone who refuses to cooperate. In this case, you might need to redesign your antenna system to reject more of the noise from that system.

- **Intermittent**—This is noise that increases suddenly and that comes and goes. It might be present for only a few hours a day or a few weeks of the year. Temporary noise sources include network testing on other networks, military exercises using wireless equipment, cell phone traffic peaks, the operation of industrial equipment, and other sources, which might be difficult to identify. When this noise occurs, your network throughput slows down or stops. Patient, careful investigation with a spectrum analyzer can lead you to the source of this noise. After you identify the source, you might need to redesign your antenna system to reject more of the noise.

Using Direction-Finding Techniques to Locate Noise Sources

The following direction-finding tools and techniques allow you to find the location of a transmitter or other noise source that is interfering with your AP and reducing your network throughput.

Direction-Finding Tools

The following tools allow you to detect and locate interfering signals:

- **Spectrum analyzer**—A spectrum analyzer (SA) allows you to see other signals both inside and outside the frequency band that you are using. See Chapter 4, "Performing Site Surveys," for an explanation of how to use a spectrum analyzer and how to determine interference levels.

- **Directional antenna**—A directional antenna attached to the spectrum analyzer indicates the direction that an interfering signal is coming from as well as the signal polarization. A panel antenna with approximately 30 degrees of horizontal and vertical beamwidth is recommended.

- **Compass** — A compass allows you to read the direction that your directional antenna is pointing when the interference level is highest.

- **Map** — A map allows you to draw a line from the location where you take each of your spectrum analyzer readings to the location where the interfering signal is coming from.

- **Attenuator** — An attenuator (either a variable attenuator or a series of fixed attenuators) allows you to reduce the level of the incoming interference when you get close to it. Reducing this level prevents your spectrum analyzer from becoming overloaded and giving distorted readings.

Triangulation

Triangulation is a technique that allows you to pinpoint the location of the antenna that is connected to an interfering transmitter. Triangulation requires you to take a series of at least three directional readings from different locations. The spot where the readings cross is the location of the transmitter. Figure 8-3 shows an example of using triangulation to find the location of an interfering transmitter.

Figure 8-3   *Example of Triangulation*

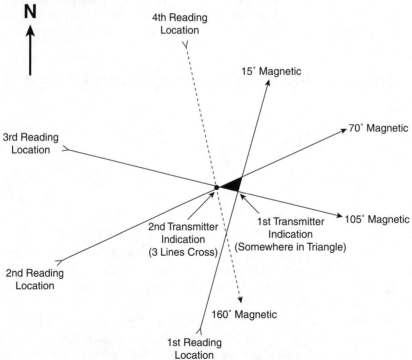

The triangulation steps are as follows:

Step 1   Identify the signal on the SA that you believe is causing the interference. Rotate your panel antenna to both the horizontal and the vertical polarization positions to determine the polarization of the signal.

NOTE   Review the radio frequency (RF) site survey principles in Chapter 4. Interference is relative, not absolute. There is no absolute indication that one particular transmitter is the only cause of the noise that you are receiving; it is possible that several, simultaneous noise sources exist. For this reason, it is good to practice direction finding before you use it to track down real interference.

Step 2   Use the directional antenna and the compass to determine the direction that the interfering signal appears to be coming from. Draw a line on the map that starts at your present location and extends in the compass direction of the interfering signal.

Step 3   Move to a different location (not on the first map line) a mile or two away. Take a second directional reading and draw another line on the map. The second line should start at your current location and extend in the direction of the interfering signal.

Step 4   Move to a third location, take a third reading, and draw a third line on the map. The three lines should either cross at one point or form a small triangle. If the lines cross at one point, go to that point. If the three lines form a triangle, move to a fourth location, take a reading, and draw a fourth line. Go to the location where at least three of the lines cross.

Step 5   As you get closer to the transmitter, the signal becomes stronger. Insert the attenuator(s) between your directional antenna and the spectrum analyzer to reduce the signal strength and prevent the spectrum analyzer from becoming overloaded.

Step 6   Finally, good eyesight is an asset when you are hunting a noise source. The better you are at spotting antennas visually, the easier it will be for you to quickly identify the exact rooftop or tower where the interfering transmitter's antenna system is located. Carry a pair of binoculars so that you can get a close-up look at the antennas that you locate.

Step 7   Confirm the polarization of the interfering signal and save an SA file showing the signal details. Record all the relevant additional information: the antenna system location and description, the signal strength, the polarization, and the network operator.

Monitoring Network Performance

You need to be familiar with all the noise-reduction techniques described in earlier chapters and summarized in this chapter so that you can respond immediately if noise problems do occur.

It is important for you to continually monitor your network performance so that you can detect SNR deterioration before it slows down your network and causes your end user's throughput to decrease. You can use a combination of the following techniques to detect SNR deterioration:

- **Monitoring SNR directly**—Some wireless equipment allows you to read signal strength, noise level, and SNR directly at each end user and at each AP location. Monitor and log or graph these SNR values each week. If you notice deterioration at one end user, the problem is probably at that location only. Perhaps the end user's antenna has turned in the wind or a neighbor has set up a new AP with an outdoor antenna. If you notice SNR deterioration at your AP, service to all users on that AP is slowed down. Perhaps water has gotten into your AP antenna or maybe another wireless network has started operating nearby or from the same tower that you are on.

- **Monitoring retransmission percentage**—If your equipment does not monitor SNR directly, you must monitor your network performance indirectly to detect problems. Most wireless equipment allows you to access management statistics that show the percentage of wireless packets that were retransmitted. The higher this percentage, the slower the network operates. A retransmit percentage of no more than 10 percent is desirable. Monitor and graph this information from each AP sector and each end user each week. If you see that this percentage is increasing over time, look for and correct the cause of the deterioration before your end users become unhappy with the slower network performance.

- **Monitoring ping latency**—If your equipment does not allow you to monitor SNR or packet retransmission percentage, you can monitor the average time needed for a large ping packet to be sent and returned over each link. Send a string of large (1400 byte) ping packets to each end user and note the pattern of the return times. If return times are consistently low (25 ms or less), the link is operating well. If return times are consistently high (50 ms and above), the link is operating poorly. If return times fluctuate between low values and high values, the link is experiencing problems that are causing performance to suffer. Locate and correct the source of the problem as soon as possible.

Regardless of the monitoring method that you use, keep a running record of the monitored information so that you can detect any deterioration over time.

Documenting Noise-Reduction Results

In addition to saving performance-monitoring information, it is important to document or log the results of all the noise-reduction activities that you perform. This documentation should include the date, the problem symptoms, the actions that you took or the network changes that you made, and the result of the actions or changes. This log will save you time performing future noise-reduction work because you can look back and quickly see the activities that have already been done.

Minimizing Interference to Licensed Wireless Systems

Just as other transmitters can create noise problems for you, your transmitters can create noise for other wireless operators, both license-free and licensed.

The licensed users in several parts of the license-free bands include amateur radio operators. Amateur radio operators perform many public service activities as well as advancing wireless knowledge through experimentation. Amateur operators use parts of the 900-MHz, 2.4-GHz, and 5-GHz bands for amateur television, satellite communications, moonbounce, and other weak-signal work.

Try to make personal contact with the amateurs in your area so that you can coordinate your use of these shared microwave bands with their use. This way, you can minimize any interference that you might cause them and they can minimize interference that they might cause you.

Review Questions

1 For reliable network operation, signal strength is more important than SNR. True or false?

2 A reliable wireless link needs a line-of-sight path and an unobstructed Fresnel zone. True or false?

3 Will the noise level always be low in a rural area?

4 How many nonoverlapping 2.4 GHz channels are available for use in the United States?

5 The consequence of a low SNR is reduced network throughput. True or false?

6 Reusing a DSSS frequency at the same AP location requires how many decibels of antenna isolation?

7 To avoid interference, collocated FHSS sectors should use different hopping sequences and different hopping sets. True or false?

8 When is the SNR highest at an AP?

9 When the percentage of retransmitted packets reaches 20 percent, you should start looking for the cause of the network slowdown. True or false?

10 Explain why it is necessary to write down the results of your noise-reduction efforts.

CHAPTER 9

Providing Broadband Wireless Internet Access

This entire book deals with issues that wireless Internet service providers (WISPs) need to address. This chapter in particular expands on some of these issues and introduces additional issues that you, as a wireless ISP, need to consider.

Planning for WISP Success

The success of any business depends to a large extent on the presence of a successful business plan. The business plan must correctly anticipate the profitable delivery of a needed service. In this case, the service is broadband wireless Internet access. The following sections help you understand some of the critical planning issues that your business plan must address.

Obtaining ISP and WISP Experience

What is a wireless ISP? It can resemble one of the following or some combination of the following two models.

Small and Simple WISP Model

A small, simple WISP can be nothing more than a wireless hotspot at the corner coffee shop or a community network that provides Internet access in a public park. The wireless range is limited to a few hundred feet in the case of the coffee shop or to a block or two in the case of the park. The WISP provides no additional services, such as e-mail accounts or domain hosting. The WISP only connects users to the Internet. The small WISP might charge an hourly or a daily fee for the wireless service, or in the case of the community network, the service might be provided at no charge.

If you plan to run a small WISP, you will not need a lot of traditional ISP knowledge. You *will* need to know enough to answer simple questions from customers, such as how to log in and how to configure Dynamic Host Configuration Protocol (DHCP). You will not need to know how to configure a core router or how to set up a domain name server. You can probably get the answers you need from the wired ISP to which your wireless access point (AP) is connected.

Large and Complex WISP Model

A large, complex WISP can provide wireless services in many cities covering hundreds of square miles. It might have dozens of wireless sectors and connect customers who are up to 20 miles away from a wireless AP. This WISP might also offer a full spectrum of wired ISP services including traditional dialup, digital subscriber line (DSL), Frame Relay, Integrated Services Digital Network (ISDN), and T1 access. It will offer e-mail, domain hosting, server farms, networking, and other advanced services.

If you plan to run a large and complex WISP, you must either have extensive ISP experience or you must hire people who have advanced ISP experience. You might also want to consider forming a partnership with an existing wired ISP; they provide the wired infra-structure and you provide the wireless infrastructure. Being successful as a large WISP requires having experienced ISP help.

To run a large, complex WISP, you also need extensive wireless experience. You can gain this experience either by educating yourself and then working with wireless on the job or by hiring employees who have substantial wireless experience. Either way, the more quickly you obtain this wireless experience, the more quickly your WISP will be successful.

Gaining Wireless Knowledge

If you plan to deploy outdoor wireless links, you need to understand the basic wireless principles that successful wireless network operation is based on.

The cost of 802.11b local-area network (LAN) equipment is continuing to decrease, and many new WISPs are using this equipment in outdoor wide-area network (WAN) deploy-ments. You might believe that your wireless network deployment will be"plug and play," but nothing could be further from the truth. You must educate yourself about how wireless works and about how to deploy it successfully in an outdoor environment where there is noise and interference.

The wireless WISP world today is much larger than just 802.11b. Wireless WISPs have been around since about 1995—in other words, since long before 802.11b. Many WISPs have deployed and will continue to deploy non-802.11b equipment. Regardless of whether you have chosen to use 802.11b equipment or not, you need to be aware of these other equipment options. After your wireless signals leave the antenna, they will be sharing the "ether" with all the other signals in your area, 802.11b, non-802.11b, and other, non-WISP transmitters.

Following are some of the ways that you can gain the wireless knowledge that you need:

- **Read the advertising literature**—This is a good way to get an overall view of wireless principles, but be aware that this literature is designed to sell you equipment as well as to inform you. Always assume that there will be a few points that are either not mentioned or not completely accurate.

- **Join an e-mail list**—This is an excellent way to share your experience with others. You will learn and you will help others learn when you contribute to these lists. See Appendix B, "Wireless Hardware, Software, and Service Provider Organizations," for some of these lists.

- **Attend educational seminars**—Attending educational seminars is another good way to learn about wireless principles. Many times, these presentations give you a chance to ask questions. Keep in mind that most of these seminars are also designed to sell you equipment. This means that you have to focus on separating the educational material from the marketing material.

- **Visit existing WISPs**—This is one of the best ways to learn how real-world wireless equipment works. If you are fortunate enough to have an existing WISP nearby (one who doesn't see you as a competitive threat), visit it and observe its operation. Ask the WISP operators questions about the techniques that worked well for them. Ask them which of their initial expectations were met and which expectations needed to be changed.

- **Experiment with license-free wireless equipment**—If you are far enough along in your business planning to select one or two wireless equipment vendors, you can purchase a pair of radios and do your own testing and experimenting. If you have access to a pair of older radios, you can test with those. As you test the wireless equipment outdoors, you will feel your wireless understanding and knowledge grow.

- **Become a radio amateur**—If your interest in wireless is strong, you should consider obtaining your amateur radio license. Obtaining your entry-level license is easy and (in many countries) you no longer have to learn the Morse code. In many areas, amateur radio clubs teach free or low-cost licensing classes that run for a few weeks. At the end of the class, you take your licensing test and join the ranks of a select group of wireless experimenters. Then, you have the opportunity to experiment with licensed wireless equipment and vastly expand your wireless knowledge.

Serving Niche Markets

Broadband Internet access is advantageous to businesses, residences, and home office workers; however, wireless Internet access is not the best choice for all these potential customers. In many cities, low-cost broadband Internet access is already available in the form of digital subscriber line (DSL) service or broadband cable Internet service. Successful WISP business plans take this reality into account and focus on serving niche markets— those areas where broadband service does not already exist. It is difficult for a WISP to operate profitably while competing head to head with multimillion-dollar corporations such as the incumbent local telephone companies and the nationwide cable providers. A discussion of some of these niche markets follows:

- **Fixed business market**—Fast, reliable, wireless Internet access is valuable for many businesses. Businesses are willing to pay for value, but they expect prompt and efficient support from their ISP. Even when business customers have other broadband choices, WISPs that offer high-quality, fairly priced service can successfully compete for this business and make a profit.

- **Fixed residential market**—In cities where cable and DSL are available, customers in this market expect that price competition between the broadband carriers will provide them with fast service at low cost. This is not a good niche market for WISPs to compete in unless existing broadband service providers are not available. In that case, this is a good niche market where a WISP can supply service and price it to make a small profit.

- **Fixed SOHO market**—The small-office/home-office (SOHO) market is a cross between the business market and the residential market. If cable and DSL are not available, this is a good niche market where you can be profitable.

- **Portable market**—Portable wireless customers are nomadic. The customer first connects from one location (for example, a coffee shop) and then connects from another location (maybe an airport lounge), but he does not stay connected while traveling between the two locations. This is a difficult niche market to be profitable in. If you are interested in this market, see the discussion of wireless hotspots that appears later in this chapter.

- **Mobile market**—The mobile market, in which a customer connects and stays connected while driving or moving from AP to AP, is the most difficult market to be profitable in. Without pointing out all the reasons why profitability is difficult, you can look at the cell phone market that provides mobile voice connectivity. In spite of cell phone companies' large user base and billions of dollars of investment, most of them are losing money.

Differentiating Between Bandwidth and Throughput

This book differentiates between wireless throughput and wireless bandwidth. The throughput (data transfer speed) determines the experience that your customers have when using your network, not the theoretical bandwidth.

Your customers are not interested in paying for some theoretical bandwidth that they cannot perceive. They want to be charged for the throughput that they actually experience every time they load a new Web page or press the Enter key. Delivering throughput is the only thing that you can charge for. Because throughput is your only deliverable, you cannot afford to waste it. Plan to maximize, manage, and monitor your available wireless throughput.

Pricing Your Service Offerings

In the past, some WISP owners priced their services too low to make a profit in the hopes of quickly building up their installed base of customers and then selling their WISP at a big profit. In most cases, those owners ended up losing money, not making money.

Price your wireless services high enough so that you can make a profit. If low-cost carriers, such as telephone companies or cable companies, are already providing residential service in your area, you are probably better off looking for other niche markets to serve with wireless rather than trying to compete with these giants.

To operate most profitably with the throughput that you have available, you need to offer tiered levels of service. Customers pay for the throughput level they need today. When they need more throughput, you should charge them more for it.

Overselling Throughput

All ISPs—both wired and wireless—sell the same throughput to more than one customer. This overselling is possible because no ISP customer uses all his bandwidth (throughput) all the time. As a WISP, you will oversell (or share) your wireless throughput. If your customers ask if you are supplying dedicated or shared bandwidth, you can advise them that you are supplying shared bandwidth. You can also tell them that you manage your throughput carefully to be sure that the network is not overloaded and that they receive the throughput that they expect. You might even want to set up a test file on one of your servers that your customers can download to test their wireless throughput.

When you start wireless service on a new sector, it is best to use conservative overselling ratios, such as these:

- **Business customers**—A 6-to-1 ratio
- **SOHO customers**—An 8-to-1 ratio
- **Residential customers**—A 10-to-1 ratio

You can monitor your network performance, as described in the later section, "Determining Network Capacity," and adjust your overselling ratio upward when you see that your network performance is stable and reliable.

Committing to High-Reliability Service

Your customers will naturally wonder if their wireless service is going to be reliable. This concern stems from their experience with other wireless services such as cell phone services that occasionally drop their calls. When you first propose wireless service to customers, you need to be prepared to address these concerns. Then, you need to follow through on your promises by actually delivering reliable service.

Preplanning the Installation Process

Planning for a cost-effective installation process is critical to operating a profitable WISP. The installation process is important enough that you need to include it in your initial business plan. For more information, see the section "Deploying Stable Networks," later in this chapter.

Designing Reliable Networks

This entire book is about reliable wireless network design. This section reviews the most important wireless network design principles and provides some additional design techniques for you. The goal of successful network design is a stable, noise-resistant architecture that is easy to maintain and expand.

Selecting Low-Noise AP Locations

One of the most crucial decisions that affects your ability to deliver reliable throughput is your selection of low-noise locations for your APs. Please review the section "Access Point Vulnerability to Noise" in Chapter 4, "Performing Site Surveys," for the finer details.

Selecting low-noise AP locations requires more than just performing wireless site surveys. It is also important for you to think outside the box—to see beyond what looks like the obvious AP locations.

Avoiding Commonly Used High Spots

Try to avoid placing your APs on the highest mountain in the area or the tallest building downtown. These are the areas where many other transmitters are already clustered. If you locate your APs there, you expose your receivers to high noise levels. Unless you know how to protect your receivers against overload, they might be desensitized, have their signal-to-noise ratio (SNR) reduced, and be unable to receive very well.

My Building Is Taller Than Your Building!

Several times, I have seen WISPs proudly announce that they just obtained roof rights on the tallest building in town. Later, when they installed their APs, they experienced a short receiving range because of too much noise. Their pride in being on the tallest building in town did not translate into successful and profitable operation of their WISP.

Rather than locate on the highest building, it is better to use the second-highest or the third-highest building—whichever building *does not* have a lot of already-existing transmitters.

Your transmitting range will not be reduced much, but your receiving range will be noticeably improved.

The same principle (avoiding high-RF locations) holds true when you locate on a mountain. You do not need to be up on the top with all the FM, television, and two-way radio transmitters. Look for a site that is part way down on the side of the mountain. Your coverage area will be just as large; however, you will avoid receiving problems. The monthly site rental will probably also be lower.

To carry this principle further, you might not need to be on the mountain at all. Often, sites down in the foothills much closer to town will not only avoid receiver problems but will also increase the strength of the signal to and from your service area.

To summarize, do not blindly pick the highest location around. Pick the quietest available spot that is closest to your customers and just high enough to avoid line-of-sight (LOS) problems between you and your customers.

Avoiding Cell Sites

Locating your APs at cell sites presents three common problems:

- Receiver overloading (discussed earlier)
- In-band interference from 2.4-GHz and 5-GHz license-free T1 backhaul links used by the cell phone companies
- High site rent

You can avoid these problems by selecting your AP locations as far away as possible from cell sites.

Locating on the Periphery

Here is one more reason not to follow the herd and place your APs on the highest building in town. When your AP is near the center of your service area, all of your customers' antennas are going to be pointing toward the center of a circle. Their signals don't just stop when they reach your AP. Those signals keep going beyond the AP, and that means that they keep going toward your customers located on the other side of town. The collision potential is horrendous—basically, your customers are radiating toward each other. You can avoid this problem by placing your APs around the outside periphery of your coverage area. Now your customers are no longer radiating their signals toward each other and colliding with each other.

Planning for Emergencies

Fires, tornados, hurricanes, earthquakes, and other emergencies do happen. Think about the locations where you would need to place a temporary AP if something happened to an AP that you are using now. Which property owners would allow you to place a temporary AP on their property?

Planning for emergencies has another advantage. It can help you become aware of potential locations for new APs when you expand your network in the future.

Learning to Spell Decibels

If you drive a car, it is important for you to understand how many gallons (liters, litres) of fuel is in the fuel tank. The same goes when you use wireless; decibels (dBs) measure transmitter signal strength, receiver signal levels, antenna radiation patterns, interference levels, and so on. You need to understand how to use decibels and keep practicing until using them becomes easy.

In the two-way radio industry, there is an old joke that says, "It takes five years to learn how to spell dB." This means that it takes five years of practice before it becomes intuitively easy to work with decibels. This practice is needed because decibel measurement is not linear; it is logarithmic. Decibels are exponents, and they represent logarithmic power gains and losses.

Numbers that increase and decrease logarithmically get bigger (and smaller) much faster than normal. This is the same as wireless signal levels, which grow bigger and smaller much faster than normal (nonlogarithmic) numbers. Wireless signals become small quickly after they leave an antenna, and that is why logarithms are needed to represent their signal strength.

Table 9-1 shows how a simple one-number increase in the log of a number represents an increase of 10 times more than the previous value.

Table 9-1 *Examples of Log Values Increasing Logarithmically*

Number	Number of Times the Number Is Multiplied by Itself	Product (Total After Multiplying)	Log (Power of 10)
10	1 (10 to the first power)	10	1
10 * 10	2 (10 squared)	100	2
10 * 10 * 10	3 (10 cubed)	1000	3
10 * 10 * 10 * 10	4 (10 to the fourth power)	10,000	4

The first row of Table 9-1 says that 10 raised to the first power equals 10. The second row says that 10 raised to the second power (10 squared or 10×10) is 100. The exponent has changed from 1 to 2, but the product (the result of the multiplication) has changed from 10 to 100. That's a pretty big increase in the product when the exponent (the log) has only changed from a 1 to a 2. You can see that representing wireless power using a logarithmic notation (such as decibels) allows the easy representation of small amounts and large amounts of power. Decibels are covered in more detail in Chapter 2, "Understanding Wireless Fundamentals." It would be good for you to review the explanation in Chapter 2 and practice using decibel values as often as possible. To become good at wireless design, you need to be able to spell dB.

Using Licensed Backhauls

Remember that there are a limited number of license-free frequencies and that reusing these frequencies can be done; however, it is technically challenging and requires a lot of antenna isolation. If you run out of frequencies or if you need a high-throughput backbone link, consider using high-bandwidth licensed wireless equipment. The cost for a pair of licensed 18-GHz, 45-Mbps radios is not much more than the cost of high-bandwidth license-free equipment.

Licensed radios also enjoy protection from interference that license-free radios do not enjoy. Licensed radios are available in the 6-GHz, 11-GHz, 18-GHz, and 23-GHz ranges. The cost of obtaining a Federal Communications Commission (FCC) license is typically around $2000 per licensed link, and the license is good for 10 years. Except in the 23-GHz band, you can begin operation about 45 days after you start the FCC licensing procedure.

Deploying Stable Networks

Many important techniques contribute to the deployment of stable wireless networks. Most of these techniques were covered in earlier chapters; however, for those readers who opened the book directly to this chapter and have not yet read the earlier chapters, the sections that follow review these topics briefly.

Wireless Site Surveys

Perform a wireless site survey before you finalize the selection of a wireless AP location. The site survey confirms that the noise and interference are low enough to allow the AP to receive well. Please review the information in Chapter 4 that describes how to do a wireless site survey.

Standardizing Customer Premises Equipment (CPE)

Use only a few, standard combinations of customer premises equipment (CPE), cables, and antennas. This simplifies the installation process and minimizes inventory cost, as explained in Chapter 7, "Installing Outdoor Wireless Systems."

Avoiding Needless Equipment Mixing

Use a minimum of different brands of wireless APs and wireless cards. For example, a Brand A AP with a Brand B wireless card linking to a Brand C wireless card in a Brand D radio can be unreliable and difficult to maintain. Please (re)read the section "Compatibility Issues" in Chapter 6, "Evaluating and Selecting Wireless Equipment."

Meeting the Customer at the Ethernet

Most non-802.11b equipment connects to the customer's computer (or network) with an Ethernet interface. If you use 802.11b equipment in your wireless network, try to avoid the temptation to provide wireless service by just inserting a wireless card into your customer's computer. On the surface, this might appear to be the lowest-cost method of providing service; however, it might actually increase your costs and reduce your profits for the following reasons:

- **Long-term support costs**—After you open or insert a wireless card into a customer's computer, it is difficult to refuse to correct each problem that the customer experiences with that computer. For example, the customer might expect you to fix power supply failures and hard disk crashes. These problems, in most cases, are unrelated to the actual wireless card installation but, in the user's mind, the wireless card might be perceived as the cause of each problem. The cost of responding to and fixing these problems can result in a net loss for you.

- **Network management deficiencies**—The client software that goes with most wireless cards does not usually possess a full set of network management and monitoring capabilities. For example, you might not be able to remotely view signal strength or link performance statistics. In addition, you might not be able to perform remote throughput management tasks such as throttling throughput to that end user.

A better, more cost-effective approach than using wireless cards in customers' computers is interfacing with the customer's computer at the Ethernet level. You can provide wireless equipment that is external to the customer's computer and that connects via Ethernet to the customer's computer (or network). If the customer does not already have an Ethernet card installed, you can refer him to a company that provides computer-networking support.

Some WISPs have deployed wireless USB adapters (modified to accept an external antenna) in an attempt to provide low-cost CPE equipment and avoid opening the customer's computer. This approach works in some cases; however, sometimes USB/ motherboard/software compatibility issues occur. In addition, some virtual private networking (VPN) features might not work with the USB adapter.

The price of wireless CPE that provides an Ethernet interface to customers' networks keeps decreasing. It is becoming more feasible to deploy such equipment. As a bonus, low-cost CPE equipment is available in a weatherproof housing and with power-over-Ethernet. Mounting such equipment outside, at the antenna, eliminates coax cable loss and increases link reliability.

Measuring Fade Margin

Use a standard throughput test and measure the fade margin for every newly installed end user. This confirms that the installation was done correctly and that service will be reliable. See Chapter 7 for details about measuring the fade margin.

Allowing AP Test Time

Do not assume that every new AP will perform perfectly when it is first turned on. Allow plenty of test time so that you can adjust, correct, and verify the performance of the new AP before you start using it to provide service. Chapter 7 covers the AP testing procedures.

Managing Network Throughput

Network throughput is your most important asset because that is what your customers pay you to deliver to them. The consequences of failing to manage throughput do not show up until your network becomes heavily loaded; then your network throughput deteriorates rapidly. If you are in the WISP business to make a profit, you need to manage your network's throughput; the next few sections help you perform this management function.

Minimizing Lost Throughput

The less network throughput that you lose, the more throughput remains for you to sell. Do your best to lose as little throughput as possible from the following causes:

- **Misunderstanding**—Do not confuse bandwidth (the raw data rate on a link) with throughput (the actual amount of data that the link carries). To avoid this misunderstanding, reread the section "Comparison Between Data Rate and Throughput (Including Simplex Versus Duplex Throughput)" in Chapter 6.

- **Wireless collisions**—Every collision between wireless users results in a loss of that time slot and a loss of throughput. You can minimize collisions by using software that polls your users. If your software does not include polling, the next-best thing you can do is fine-tune the RTS/CTS threshold to help minimize the packet collisions between users.

- **Interference and noise**—Every packet that needs to be repeated before it is successfully received causes lost time slots and lost throughput. The more you can reduce noise and interference in your network, the more throughput you can retain to sell to your customers.

Reusing Frequencies Successfully

Unless you are located in a small town, you need to reuse frequencies. Unless your antenna systems are completely isolated from each other, reusing frequencies causes you to lose throughput. The section "Benefiting from Antenna System Isolation" in Chapter 5, "Selecting Antenna Systems," explains how to isolate antennas so that you can reuse frequencies without losing throughput. The section "Minimizing Noise from Your DSSS Network" in Chapter 8, "Solving Noise and Interference Problems," provides an example of making a frequency reuse plan. Review these sections now so that you can successfully re-use frequencies and still obtain full throughput on each frequency.

Allocating Throughput Per Customer

In life, the same size of shoe doesn't fit all feet. In wireless networks, one size of throughput doesn't fit all wireless users. To manage your network throughput profitably, you need to sell customers only the amount of throughput that they need or want. Offer your customers a tiered service plan that allows them to buy only as much throughput as they need. Practice throughput management so that your customers get the throughput they pay for.

Some wireless equipment includes throughput management features such as the following:

- **Maximum rate throttling**—This feature allows you to set the maximum throughput that each customer will have, such as 128 kbps or 512 kbps, for example.

- **MIR/CIR**—This feature allows you to set both a maximum information rate (MIR) and a committed information rate (CIR) for each customer. The equipment always reserves at least the CIR for the customer; however, when the network isn't busy, the equipment allows the customer to obtain (up to) the MIR.

- **Asymmetrical throughput rates**—Some equipment allows you to assign throughput asymmetrically to each customer. In other words, you can set customers' bandwidth to be different depending on whether they are downloading or uploading. By configuring the upload speed to be slower than the download speed, you can serve more customers on your network.

If your wireless equipment does not already include these features, you can gain per-customer control by adding an external throughput control router. See Appendix B for vendor information.

Determining Network Capacity

You need to know how your network is performing and when your network reaches maximum capacity. The following tools and techniques can help you evaluate your network performance:

- **Ping latency**—Pinging across a wireless link with a string of 1400 byte packets is a real-time test that you can run to get a quick view of network performance. Interpreting these test results is described in the section "Monitoring Network Performance" in Chapter 8.

- **Retransmit percentage**—The percentage of packets that need to be retransmitted before they are successfully received is another meaningful indication of network performance. The section "Monitoring Network Performance" in Chapter 8 provides a detailed explanation.

- **MRTG**—Many WISPs use the Multi Router Traffic Grapher (MRTG) tool to monitor traffic levels and network traffic loading over time. Appendix B contains a link to more information about this tool.

Keeping Some Throughput in Reserve

Your network can provide up to a maximum throughput level; however, this level is affected by several factors that you cannot control. These uncontrollable factors include noise, interference, equipment deterioration, and the sudden appearance of nearby networks. It is important for you to keep some of your throughput unsold, in reserve, to provide a cushion of protection for your wireless customers. As you gain experience monitoring the performance of your network, you'll be able to estimate how much additional throughput you can sell. Always plan to leave some potential throughput unsold.

How Much Throughput Headroom Is Enough?

Based on my personal observations (and my play-it-safe nature), I would suggest that you leave 25 to 30 percent of your throughput unsold. It is more important to ensure your customers' satisfaction than to attempt to squeeze out every last penny of profit. Without a throughput reserve, all your customers will become instantly unhappy when another network suddenly appears and their throughput drops to zero.

Enhancing Network Security

As a wireless network operator, you want to do everything possible to help your customers feel comfortable using your network. Your customers want to be reassured that their data will remain confidential and that their network will not be attacked or hacked. The more information that you give your customers about your security procedures, the more comfortable they will feel.

There are many steps that you need to take to maintain and preserve the confidentiality and integrity of your customer's data. At the same time, you want to prevent unauthorized users from stealing service on your network.

First, as you already know, security is relative, not absolute. Although no network can be made 100 percent secure 100 percent of the time, every step you take reduces the likelihood of a security problem. Explain this to your customers and advise them of the security precautions that you have taken at each layer of your network. Here are some of those precautions:

- **Practice wired network security**—Secure your wired network. Stay up to date on known attacks directed at traditional wired IPSs and put countermeasures in place whenever necessary.

- **Use proprietary hardware and software**—Whenever possible, use proprietary wireless hardware and software. For every 100 people who have 802.11b hacking skills, there is less than one person who can hack non-802.11b wireless equipment.

- **Use unique network IDs**—Do not use the default network ID or extended service set ID (ESSID); use a unique ID. Recent surveys of wireless AP use show that about one half of all APs are using the default ID and are wide open to unauthorized users. Some newer operating systems, such as Windows XP, sniff the service set ID (SSID) or ESSID regardless of what you set it to. Even so, you should change your ESSID to something other than the default value.

- **Enable Wired Equivalent Privacy (WEP)**—Recently, published press reports have concentrated on the vulnerabilities of WEP; however, WEP capability does help improve security and should not be ignored. Surveys show only about 20 percent of APs have WEP enabled. If your APs have the capability to use WEP without a noticeable performance reduction, you should enable WEP.

- **Turn off beaconing**—If your network does not need to have beaconing enabled, turn it off. This prevents some network-scanning programs from sniffing the ESSID of the AP.

- **Use access control lists**—Use an access control list based on either MAC addresses or IP addresses. Sure, addresses can be spoofed, but remember: Each step that you take reduces the chances of hacking.

- **Implement 802.1x features**—Use these advanced security features whenever your AP or access controller supports them.

- **Enable all available security features**—Whether you are running an 802.11b network or a proprietary network, enable all the security features that your wireless equipment provides.

Advise those customers who need more security to run their own virtual private network, use firewalls with IPSec, or run a tunneling protocol.

Coexisting with Other Wireless Networks

In many cities, it is likely that there will be more than one WISP in town. The following sections provide some suggestions about working together with other WISPs so that everyone can benefit.

Cooperating with Competitors

You can cooperate with other WISPs in your area in many ways. Here are some ideas:

- **Split the market**—You provide service for the customers who you are most interested in, and you agree to let the other WISP provide service for the customers that it is most interested in.

- **Split the frequencies**—If your WISP and the other WISP both want to compete for the same customers, agree to use equipment that operates on different channels or on different bands. For example, the other WISP might operate on 2.4 GHz while you operate on 5.8 GHz.

- **Roaming agreements**—If your WISP and the other WISP are using similar equipment, you both might agree to allow your customers to roam between the two networks. This benefits your customers by widening the area where they can obtain service.

Interference from Other WISPs

If you discover an interference problem between your WISP and a competing WISP, it would be best if the two of you could meet and solve the problem between yourselves. You could agree to modify your frequencies, hopping patterns, or your coverage areas to minimize or eliminate the interference.

If you find that you have a WISP competitor who refuses to cooperate, your best course of action is probably to document the frequencies, power levels, and locations of the other WISP equipment and then make changes to your network to minimize the interference.

TIP   If possible, see if you can switch to the opposite antenna polarization, such as from vertical to horizontal. It might be inconvenient to change the polarization of your customer's antennas, but this is the simplest, lowest-cost way to minimize interference.

If you believe that the other WISP is operating with illegally high power, you can use a spectrum analyzer to determine the actual effective radiated power level. Then, try to schedule a meeting and diplomatically suggest that if he reduces his power down to the legal level, neither he nor you will have to waste time discussing the matter with the FCC.

If you believe that another WISP is intentionally interfering with you, you need to document that operation (again, with a spectrum analyzer) and then contact your lawyer to discuss the possibility of filing a civil lawsuit against the other WISP.

Interference with Amateur Radio Operations

The FCC licenses amateur radio operators; therefore, their operation has priority over license-free operation. Legally, you must not cause interference with amateur radio operation. Also, you must accept interference from amateur radio operation. In actual practice, it is pretty unusual to experience interference to or from amateurs because not many active amateurs operate on the 2.4-GHz and the 5-GHz bands. If an interference problem does occur, consider changing frequencies or reconfiguring your antenna system to eliminate the problem.

NOTE   You might want to consider getting an amateur radio license. It is a great way to experiment and learn a lot about wireless technology. It is also a good way to serve the public in times of emergency.

Living with the FCC

In the United States, the FCC is the government body that regulates all wireless communications, both license free and licensed. The next sections provide information that helps you to accomplish the following:

- Operate legally within the law
- Understand the FCC equipment certification process
- Respond to FCC inquiries
- Lobby the FCC

Observing FCC Power Limits

FCC regulations set maximum radiated power limits for license-free systems in the ISM and U-NII bands in the United States. These power limits are designed to minimize interference and maximize the number of people who can use the bands simultaneously.

There are thousands of times more users of license-free equipment than there are FCC personnel available to enforce the rules and regulations. It does not take many people running illegal high-power amplifiers to raise the interference level and make the bands unusable for everyone. To keep interference levels under control, license-free equipment must be tested along with the antenna system and certified to be operating within the FCC-specified power limits.

Most WISPs comply with the FCC rules and regulations. Unfortunately, a few WISPs are either not aware of the FCC power limitations or choose to ignore the rules. It is important for you to learn what the legal power limits are and to obey these limits. The alternative is to have the FCC tighten up its regulations or even to prohibit license-free operation completely.

NOTE	Tables 6-1, 6-2, and 6-3 in Chapter 6 list the FCC power limits in the United States, and Table 7-1 in Chapter 7 provides several examples of equivalent isotropic radiated power (EIRP) calculations.

If you are located outside the United States, it should be clear to you that observing the rules and regulations of your country's licensing authority is a wise decision that helps you enhance the stability of your network and allows you to continue to operate your network. A few countries require user licensing in the 2.4-GHz band. If this is true in your country, you should certainly obtain governmental approval before you deploy your network.

FCC Equipment Certification

The FCC requires that all license-free transmitting equipment be FCC certified. Certification means that a testing lab has verified that the equipment, the amplifier (if used), and the antenna system have been tested together (as a complete system) and found to comply with the FCC power and spectral purity requirements.

Most WISPs are curious and creative, and enjoy experimenting with various equipment and antenna combinations to obtain the best equipment performance. To stay within both the spirit and the letter of the law, you, as a WISP, need to do one of the following:

- Use equipment and antenna combinations that have already been sent to a certification lab by the vendor of the equipment.

- Use antenna systems that stay within the FCC power limits and that you have built in limited quantities (less than six units) for your own use.

- Use equipment and antenna combinations that you have sent to a certification lab and that have been successfully certified. This usually requires obtaining transmitter specifications from the manufacturer of the equipment and forwarding these specifications to the lab along with your antenna system.

- Submit the specifications for your new antenna systems to your wireless equipment manufacturer and request that the manufacturer apply for a "permissive change" to its existing equipment certification. The permissive change allows WISPs to use the new antenna system in place of the antenna system that the manufacturer originally certified with the equipment.

In the past, many WISPs ignored the equipment-certification step and used equipment that met the spirit of the law but not the letter of the law. In other words, many WISPs used equipment combinations that did not exceed the FCC power limits but that were not lab-certified to be within the power limits. Recently, with the vastly increased use of the license-free bands, the FCC began making unannounced visits to a few WISPs to confirm that they were using only certified equipment and antenna combinations.

If you are operating with one or more non-lab-certified equipment and antenna combinations, you might want to spend the money and send samples of your equipment to a lab for certification. This step will probably feel burdensome and will cost you up to several thousand dollars per certification run, but it will also save you from legal embarrassment, costly equipment changeouts, and FCC fines.

NOTE   Do an Internet search on "FCC Part 15 Certification Lab" to locate a lab near you.

Responding to FCC Inquiries

Hopefully, you will never experience a personal visit from the FCC or receive a letter or other written correspondence from it. If you are ever visited, remember that the FCC has the right to inspect your equipment at any time, and you must allow it to perform this inspection. By operating a transmitter, even though it is license-free, you give the FCC the right to inspect your equipment and request (or order) you to make any changes necessary to comply with the communications law.

If you ever receive written correspondence from the FCC, you will be given a specific period of time to make an official reply. If you do not reply within the specified period of time, you might be fined and ordered to shut down your equipment. The wise WISP always replies appropriately and in a timely fashion to any and all FCC correspondence.

Lobbying the FCC

Although the FCC makes the communications rules, it is also open to considering new rules and modifying existing rules. Companies and individuals can petition, lobby, and comment on changes to the communications laws. These changes might be beneficial to the public as a whole, beneficial to some segment of the wireless industry, or perhaps beneficial to only one wireless company. The most successful lobbying efforts are ones that use the services of FCC-specialized, Washington-based (expensive) law firms. Small companies that want to petition or lobby for changes will probably be most successful by joining one of the existing wireless communications groups that has regular contact with FCC personnel. Appendix B lists several of these groups.

Anticipating Emerging Trends

You have probably heard it said that the only constant is change. Changes in the wireless industry occur practically every week. The sections that follow describe trends that can affect the ways you conduct your wireless business.

CPE Equipment Cost Reductions

More and more people are using wireless LAN equipment in their businesses and homes. As this market becomes larger, it continues to drive down the cost of 802.11b hardware. This hardware cost reduction, in turn, reduces the cost of 802.11b equipment that is usable by WISPs. You might want to keep up to date on this trend because soon CPE will be available in the under-$200 price range, including a built-in antenna and power-over-Ethernet (PoE) capability.

802.11 Creep

802.11b has been so successful that it has become the de facto broadband wireless standard, and 802.11b capabilities are appearing in a wider variety of devices. Soon, 802.11b (and follow-on 802.11a and 802.11g technology) will be as common as the remote control for your television set.

Multiband wireless chipsets will appear that allow 802.11b capabilities to be included in most consumer devices, such as personal computers, personal digital assistants (PDAs), printers, cell phones, video cameras, and so on. The pervasive presence of 802.11b, 802.11a, 802.11g, and Bluetooth technology will be a double-edged sword for WISPs— they will be both a blessing and a curse. On the one hand, you will have access to usable technology at lower prices that will allow you to deliver more creative wireless services to your customers. On the other hand, you will need to learn how to work around the higher levels of wireless noise, interference, and hacking that will be present.

802.11b and Cellular Service Integration

The rollout of broadband (3G) service by the cellular telephone carriers is proving to be extremely expensive, requiring the investment of billions of dollars. In comparison, the rollout of broadband 802.11b hotspot service is inexpensive.

The cellular telephone companies will, at the very least, seek to leverage this trend to lower their cost of providing broadband service. This will lead them to deploy new cell phone handsets that include 802.11b technology. When a caller is out of range of a 3G cell site, the phone will attempt to roam to an 802.11b hotspot.

Cellular carriers might also seek to dominate the hotspot market. Remember: Wired telephone service was a monopoly in the United States until recently. The monopoly-created incumbent local telephone companies today own and operate most of the cellular telephony companies in the United States. In the same way, it is not unreasonable for these same companies to attempt to gain control and dominate the wireless hotspot market.

Other Trends

This section mentions a few more emerging trends that you, as a progressive WISP, can keep your eye on.

Community Networks

More and more people, intrigued by the concepts of wireless networking and community service, are deploying community networks that provide free 802.11b wireless Internet access. You, as a WISP, must determine the role that you want to play in this emerging community networking movement.

Hot Spots

The hot spot concept of providing broadband wireless Internet access to the public in selected public locations (such as airports) and in selected business locations is growing rapidly. As a WISP, you might want to participate in some way in this business. Following are some ways in which you can participate:

- Provide backbone bandwidth wirelessly for the hotspots that are located within your wireless service area.

- Make agreements with local hotspot operators that allow your fixed wireless customers to connect at the hotspots when they are away from their fixed location.

- Place your own hotspots in high traffic locations. This allows you to provide additional connectivity for your current wireless customers and advertise your fixed wireless services to everyone who sees or uses your hotspots.

802.16 Standards

The Institute of Electrical and Electronics Engineers (IEEE) 802.16 Working Group on Broadband Wireless Access has developed standards that allow interoperability between wireless metropolitan-area network (MAN) equipment operating between 10 GHz and 66 GHz. Although this standard does not cover the current license-free bands, the 802.16a working group is currently working to expand the standard to the licensed and the license-free bands between 2 GHz and 11 GHz. In the next few years, this work might lead to greater interoperability between wireless WAN equipment.

Broadband Optical Equipment

Short-range broadband optical equipment is available now. Point-to-multipoint optical equipment is under development and beginning to become available. Instead of using microwave radio links, this optical equipment uses either lasers or light-emitting diodes (LEDs) to send and receive broadband information. In the future, this optical equipment might have a role to play as part of your wireless network.

Avoiding Black Holes

Black holes in the galaxy are invisible, collapsed star systems that have gravity levels so intense that they suck all nearby matter in. The broadband wireless world also has a few black holes. Wireless black holes are not quite as intense as black holes in the galaxy, but the principle is the same. You cannot see these black holes in advance, but they can suck all your money away. The following sections describe a few of these money traps to avoid.

NLOS Equipment Performance

Every wireless product is a non-line-of-sight (NLOS) product, yet no wireless product is a true NLOS product. If this statement sounds like a contradiction, please go back to Chapter 6 and read the section "Non Line-of-Sight Features."

Remember: The goal of this NLOS section is to prevent your money from being sucked into a black hole. There is still no magic bullet that can prevent a microwave signal from being attenuated (and diffracted and lost) when it strikes an obstacle. This attenuation means that the signal cannot travel far through a series of dense obstructions. Table 9-2 summarizes the conditions that affect link distances in an NLOS environment. Review this table and the paragraphs that follow it before you purchase NLOS equipment.

Table 9-2   *Factors That Affect NLOS Link Distances*

NLOS Factor	Best NLOS Condition
Effective radiated power (or equivalent isotropic radiated power)	The higher the effective radiated power (within FCC rules), the greater the NLOS distance.
Frequency	The lower the frequency, the greater the distance.
Multipath environment	The fewer the reflection points, the less the multipath and the greater the distance.
Modulation type	OFDM is believed by some to be better in a multipath environment.
Antenna directivity	The more directive the antenna, the greater the distance.
Throughput	The lower the throughput, the greater the distance.
Obstacle quantity	The fewer the obstacles, the greater the distance.
Obstacle spacing	The more space between obstacles, the greater the distance.
Link distances	The shorter the link distance, the greater the throughput.

Even when all the factors that combine to determine communications distance are optimized, the best NLOS system does not communicate far in a densely obstructed environment. For example, although an NLOS system might work when the LOS path is obstructed by a few trees, the system does not work when the signal has to pass through a densely wooded forest.

In conclusion, it is better to spend your time determining how you can obtain better LOS paths (higher CPE antennas, more APs covering shorter distances, and so on) than dreaming about all of those potential NLOS customers who are magically going to get reliable connectivity through miles and miles of dense trees.

Receiver Performance Near High-Power Transmitters

Another black hole to watch out for is poor receiver performance when an indoor LAN card is used outdoors on a site that has several nearby high-power transmitters. In this environment, without additional filtering, these cards are not likely to receive very far. Remember the following about low-cost wireless LAN cards: They are designed for use indoors with a built-in antenna in a low-power environment. They are not designed for use outdoors, with external antennas near multiple high-power transmitters.

If you plan to use low-cost LAN cards with outdoor antennas on AM, FM, or TV towers or on rooftops that have multiple cell phone and paging system transmitters, plan to use bandpass filters to attenuate the nearby high-power signals. Without external filtering to protect LAN cards from overload, you might never get them to receive properly on such sites.

Commercial Tower Companies

The behavior of large (nationwide) commercial tower companies can sometimes consume your money like a black hole. Occasionally, tower company management behaves in ways that require you to spend thousands of dollars in installation and maintenance fees that you never anticipated spending. For example, these companies can require that subsidiary installation companies (that they own) do all your tower work. These subsidiaries might charge you thousands of dollars to perform routine installation and maintenance work on your own tower-mounted antenna systems.

NOTE   The conversation might go something like this:

You: "I think my amplifier on the tower has failed. Can I go up and replace it?"

The subsidiaries: "Gosh, we're sorry to hear that your tower amplifier has failed, Mr. Brown. Only we can climb that tower safely, and we'll have to charge you $3000 to climb the tower and replace your amplifier. By the way, we're kind of busy right now, but we should be able to get back to you in about 20 days."

Beware of the black hole! Be sure that you will be allowed to use your own (properly trained, insured, and affordable) installation company before you sign a lease to place your equipment and antennas on a commercial tower site.

Changes to Government Licensing Regulations

A governmental agency or communications commission regulates the use of license-free frequencies in most countries. This commission has the power to either stimulate or inhibit the use of license-free wireless technology. If license-free wireless appears to be beneficial, it is likely that the government will encourage additional users. If license-free wireless appears to be detrimental, the government can reduce or even end the use of license-free equipment. Recently, in one country, the government prohibited new license-free use of the 2.4-GHz band. Many unlicensed users deployed illegal high-power amplifiers, and the interference levels became so high that the government finally stepped in and banned all new users. If you were a WISP in that country and suddenly you could not add new customers to your network, you would find yourself falling into a black hole.

Never abuse the license-free operating privileges that you currently enjoy. The best guarantee that you will continue to enjoy license-free operating privileges is to operate legally and ethically.

Review Questions

1 A WISP is an extension of a wired ISP. True or false?

2 WISPs have been around since about 1995. True or false?

3 The most profitable wireless markets are those where broadband DSL and cable Internet access are already available. True or false?

4 The mobile market where users stay connected while driving around is the easiest market to serve. True or false?

5 Customers pay you to deliver bandwidth, not throughput. True or false?

6 You can be successful in the wireless business even if you don't understand the meaning of decibels. True or false?

7 All 802.11b equipment brands work with all other 802.11b equipment brands with no problems. True or false?

8 Why do wireless collisions reduce throughput?

9 The higher the percentage of retransmitted packets, the lower the network throughput. True or false?

10 You should always sell all the throughput that your network is capable of delivering. True or false?

11 The best way to deal with a WISP competitor is to add an amplifier. True or false?

Wireless Standards Summary

This appendix provides a summary table of the 802.11 standards. It also includes related standards such as 802.1x and 802.16.

Table A-1   *Wireless Standards*

Standard	Description
802.1x	802.1x defines a new framework of authentication and encryption procedures that are designed to improve security. Some vendors have begun to incorporate proprietary adaptations of these features into their wireless equipment.
802.11	802.11 is the original wireless LAN standard. It specifies both direct sequence spread spectrum (DSSS) and frequency hopping spread spectrum (FHSS) modulation techniques. DSSS modulation is specified with raw data rates of 1 Mbps and 2 Mbps on 11 (in the U.S.) 22 MHz-wide channels at 2.4 GHz. FHSS modulation is specified with a raw data rate of 2 Mbps using any of 78 possible hopping sequences at 2.4 GHz.
802.11a	802.11a specifies orthogonal frequency division multiplexing (OFDM) in three 5 GHz subbands. These subbands are 5.150 MHz to 5.250 GHz (indoor use only), 5.250 to 5.350 GHz (indoor or outdoor use), and 5.725 to 5.825 (outdoor use). There are four 20-MHz channels per subband. 802.11a equipment must provide raw data rates of 6 Mbps, 12 Mbps, and 24 Mbps and might provide raw data rates of 9 Mbps, 18 Mbps, 36 Mbps, 48 Mbps, and 54 Mbps.
802.11b	802.11b adds a high-rate DSSS physical layer with both a 5 Mbps and an 11 Mbps raw data rate. 802.11b uses the same 11 channels as the original 802.11 standard.
802.11d	802.11d is an attempt to add features that allow 802.11 radios to operate legally in countries outside of North America and Europe.
802.11e	The proposed 802.11e standard adds quality of service (QoS) enhancements to 802.11a, 802.11b, and 802.11g.
802.11f	The proposed 801.11f standard is an attempt to specify an inter-access point protocol (IAPP) that would allow communication between access points made by different manufacturers.

continues

Table A-1   *Wireless Standards (Continued)*

Standard	Description
802.11g	802.11g is a standard that allows faster data rates (up to 54 Mbps) at 2.4 GHz. The 802.11g standard allows OFDM, packet binary convolution coding (PBCC) modulation, and 802.11b complementary code keying (CCK) modulation. The CCK modulation makes 802.11g backward-compatible with 802.11b.
802.11h	When adopted, the 802.11h standard will add dynamic frequency selection and transmitter power control to 802.11a. Dynamic frequency selection allows an access point to select the best frequency to use to minimize interference. Transmitter power control allows the transmit power to be adjusted to the minimum level needed to communicate with the most distant user.
802.11i	802.11i is an ongoing effort to define a new set of wireless security features that provide improved authentication and encryption. 802.11i will incorporate security features from the 802.1x standard.
802.15.1	802.15.1 is a wireless personal area networks (WPAN) standard that operates at 2.4 GHz and is based on the Bluetooth v1.1 specification. Bluetooth is designed for short-range personal communications between notebook computers, cell phones, and other handheld devices.
802.16	The 802.16 standard is designed to allow metropolitan-area network (MAN) equipment from different vendors to interoperate in the frequency range of 11 to 66 GHz.
802.16a	Work is progressing on 802.16a extensions to 802.16 that would cover both licensed and license-free equipment operating in the 2 to 10 GHz bands. This includes the current 2.4 GHz and 5 GHz license-free bands.

Wireless Hardware, Software, and Service Provider Organizations

This appendix contains a listing of organizations that provide wireless hardware, software, services, test equipment, books, training, peripherals, and industry information.

Wireless Hardware

The companies listed in Table B-1 design and manufacture wireless hardware that is designed for broadband wide-area networking. In addition to these, many smaller companies exist that either manufacture equipment or resell equipment that is manufactured by larger companies. These smaller companies are too numerous to list in this section.

Table B-1   *Wireless Hardware Companies*

Company	Website	Hardware Offered
Alvarion	www.alvarion.com	2.4-GHz and 5-GHz frequency-hopping spread spectrum (FHSS) and direct-sequence spread spectrum (FHSS) equipment.
Aperto	www.apertonetworks.com	5-GHz license-free (and 2.5-GHz and 3.5-GHz licensed) point-to-multipoint system.
Cirronet	www.cirronet.com	2.4-GHz and 5-GHz WISP equipment.
Cisco	www.cisco.com	Aironet 2.4-GHz access point and bridge hardware; upgradeable to 5 GHz.
Lucent/ Avaya/Agere	www.wavelan.com; www.orinocowireless.com	2.4-GHz access point hardware; upgradeable to 5 GHz. Proxim purchased this entire line of equipment in 2002.
Motorola	www.motorola.com/canopy/	5-GHz point-to-point and point-to-multipoint equipment.
Netnimble	www.netnimble.net	2.4-GHz products and peripherals
Nokia	www.nokia.com	Rooftop 2.4-GHz mesh network.

continues

Table B-1 *Wireless Hardware Companies (Continued)*

Company	Website	Hardware Offered
Proxim	www.proxim.com	Wide range of wireless LAN and WAN equipment.
Raylink	www.raylink.com	FHSS bridges and access points.
Redline	www.redlinecommunications.com	5-GHz bridge.
Smartbridges	www.smartbridges.com	2.4-GHz LAN and WAN products
Solectek	www.solectek.com	2.4-GHz point-to-point and point-to-multipoint equipment.
Teletronics	www.teletronics.com	Bridges, access points, and accessories.
Trango	www.trangobroadband.com	5-GHz point-to-point and point-to-multipoint equipment.
Waverider	www.waverider.com	See website for details.
Western Multiplex	www.proxim.com	5-GHz equipment. Proxim purchased Western Multiplex in 2001.
Wi-Lan	www.wilan.com	See website for details.
YDI	www.ydi.com	2.4-GHz and 5-GHz equipment and accessories.

Low-Cost 802.11b Access Point Hardware

This section lists a few of the many companies that manufacture low-cost 802.11b wireless LAN access points. These access points are designed for use in indoor wireless LANs; however, wireless Internet service providers (WISPs) often add external antennas and deploy these access points in outdoor WANs. These low-cost access points do not have the full software functionality that more expensive equipment (designed for WISP use) has. Operators of free public-access community networks frequently use these low-cost access points:

- D-Link (www.dlink.com)
- Linksys (www.linksys.com)
- Netgear (netgear.com)
- SMC (www.smc.com)

Wireless Hotspot Hardware

The following companies provide hardware, software, or services for use by wireless hotspot providers:

- Airpathwireless (www.airpathwireless.com)
- Bluesocket (www.bluesocket.com)

- Boingo (www.boingo.com)
- Café.com (www.café.com)
- Colubris Networks (www.colubris.com)
- Funk Software (funk.com)
- Hotspotzz (www.hotspotzz.com)
- iPass (www.ipass.com)
- Joltage (www.joltage.com)
- NetNearU (www.netnearu.com)
- NoCat (www.nocat.net)
- Nomadix (www.nomadix.com)
- Sputnik (www.sputnik.com)
- Reefedge (www.reefedge.com)
- Wayport (www.wayport.com)

Free Space Optical Hardware

The following companies develop or supply free space optical networking equipment that might be useful to WISPs:

- Fsona (www.fsona.com)
- Omnilux (www.omnilux.net)
- Plaintree (www.plaintree.com)

Security Hardware and Software

Table B-2 lists a few of the many companies that supply equipment designed to make networks, both wired and wireless, more secure.

Table B-2   *Security Hardware and Software Companies*

Company	Website	Product
Global Technology Associates	www.gta.com	Wired firewall and VPN products
Multitech	www.multitech.com	Access point plus security products
Securepoint Technologies	www.securepoint.com	Wired firewall and VPN products
Smoothwall	www.smoothwall.org/community/home	Open source firewall
Sonicwall	www.sonicwall.com	Wired firewall and VPN products

Antenna Systems

The following companies manufacture antenna systems that are useful for outdoor wireless WANs:

- Cushcraft (www.cushcraft.com)
- Gabriel (www.gabrielnet.com)
- Maxrad (www.maxrad.com)
- Mobile Mark (www.mobilemark.com)
- Pac Wireless (www.pacwireless.com)
- Radio Waves (www.radiowavesinc.com)
- Superpass (superpass.com)
- Tiltek (tiltek.com)

Coaxial Cable

Table B-3 lists some companies that manufacture low-loss coax cable often used by WISPs.

Table B-3   *Coax Cable Manufacturers for WISP Use*

Company	Website	Product
Andrew	www.andrew.com	Extensive selection of antennas, coax cable, and antenna system products
Belden	www.belden.com	Coax cable
Times Microwave	www.timesmicrowave.com	Coax cable and coax connector products that are popular among WISPs

Towers and Antenna Mounting Hardware

Table B-4 lists some companies that manufacture towers and accessories that are suitable for WISP use.

Table B-4   *Tower or Accessory Manufacturers for WISP Use*

Company	Website	Product
Heights Tower	www.HeightsTowers.com	Aluminum towers
Rohn	www.rohnnet.com	An extensive line of steel towers and antenna-mounting products
Trylon	trylon.com	Aluminum towers

Lightning-Protection Equipment

The following companies manufacture lighting-protection equipment designed to protect outdoor antenna systems:

- Citel (www.citelprotection.com)
- Hyperlink (www.hyperlinktech.com)
- Polyphaser (www.polyphaser.com)

Grounding Equipment

The following companies manufacture grounding hardware designed for low-impedance lightning-protection systems:

- Erico (www.erico.com)
- Polyphaser (www.polyphaser.com)

Test Equipment

A wide range of test hardware and software is available to WISPs. The majority of this equipment is designed for indoor wireless LAN use; however, some units might prove useful in the outdoor WAN environment. Table B-5 lists some of the major testing hardware and software for WISPs.

Table B-5   *WISP Testing Hardware or Software Companies*

Company	Website	Product
Airmagnet	www.airmagnet.com	Laptop and handheld-based wireless LAN analysis tools
AiroPeek	www.wildpackets.com	AiroPeek Wireless LAN analyzer
Avcom of Virginia	www.avcomofvirginia.com	Spectrum analyzers
Berkeley Varitronics	bvsystems.com	A wide range of wireless LAN analysis tools
Ethereal	www.ethereal.com	A protocol analyzer that runs on Windows or UNIX
Kismet	www.kismetwireless.net	A software tool that locates access points
LP Technologies	www.lptechnologies.com	Spectrum analyzers
Netstumbler	www.netstumbler.com	A software tool that locates access points
Sniffer Technologies	www.sniffer.com	Wireless LAN analyzer

Peripheral Equipment Distributors

WISPs typically use a variety of peripheral equipment, such as cable, connectors, tools, and weather-sealing products. The following companies distribute a wide range of these products:

- Electro-Comm (www.electro-comm.com)
- Electro-Comm West (www.ecwest.com)
- Talley (www.talleycommunications.com)
- Tessco (www.tessco.com)

Wireless Software

The software listed by type in the following sections is useful for WISPs.

Access Point Software

Table B-6 lists some of the more commonly available software for wireless access points.

Table B-6   *Access Point Software*

Company	Website	Product
KarlNet	www.karlnet.com	Software that runs on access points and wireless clients that adds polling, bandwidth management, routing, packet aggregation, and other WISP features.
Mikrotik	www.mikrotik.com	Access point and router software with many features that are useful to wireless network operators.
Valemount Networks	www.station-server.com	StarOS access point and client software provides many WISP features.

Bandwidth Management Software

Managing wireless bandwidth is crucial for WISPs. The following companies provide bandwidth-management software. Several of these companies also supply optional hardware to run the software:

- Emerging Technologies (www.etinc.com)
- Packeteer (www.packeteer.com)
- Allot Communications (www.allot.com)

Wireless Link Planning Software

The following companies provide mapping software that helps you determine whether you have a line-of-sight path between two or more physical locations:

- EDX (www.edx.com)
- Microdem (www.usna.edu/Users/oceano/pguth/website/microdem.htm)
- Micropath (www.micropath.com)
- Pathloss (www.pathloss.com)
- Radio Mobile (www.cplus.org/rmw/english1.html)
- Topo (http://maps.nationalgeographic.com/topo)

Utility Software

Table B-7 lists some useful utilities for wireless networks.

Table B-7   *Wireless Utility Software*

Company	Website	Product
MRTG	http://people.ee.ethz.ch/~oetiker/webtools/mrtg/	Multi-router Traffic Grapher offers open source software that monitors network traffic levels.
Nagios	www.nagios.com	Nagios offers open source network monitoring software.
Qcheck	www.netiq.com/qcheck/howqcheckworks.asp	Qcheck offers software that performs throughput testing.

Site Survey Software

In the absence of a spectrum analyzer, the site survey utilities listed in Table B-8 are helpful to determine whether interference is present in a specific area. In addition to the following, most primary wireless LAN vendors provide free site survey software that operates with their hardware.

Table B-8   *Site Survey Software*

Company	Website	Product
Teletronics	www.teletronics.com	DSSS site survey utility that runs with the Teletronics 2 Mbps card and possibly the 11 Mbps card
Proxim	www.proxim.com	FHSS Site survey utility that runs with RangeLAN II cards

Services

The following organizations provide consulting and training services that are specifically designed for wireless security, wireless WANs, and WISPs.

Consulting

- The Final Mile (www.thefinalmile.net)
- Wireless InfoNet, Inc. (www.ask-wi.com)
- Wireless-Nets (www.wireless-nets.com)

Training

Table B-9   *Wireless Network Training Companies*

Company	Website	Type of Training Offered
Comtrain	comtrainusa.com	Tower-climbing training
Planet3 Wireless	www.cwne.com	Vendor-neutral wireless LAN training
Wireless InfoNet, Inc.	www.ask-wi.com	Vendor-neutral wireless ISP training
Wireless-Nets	www.wireless-nets.com	Wireless LAN training

Suggested Books for Further Reading

The following books provide information that is especially useful to designers of wireless WANs and WISPs:

- The *ARRL Handbook for Radio Amateurs* (published by the American Radio Relay League [www.arrl.org]). This book is a standard reference book in the wireless industry with more than 1000 pages of information.

- *ARRL UHF/Microwave Experimenter's Manual* (published by the American Radio Relay League [ARRL]). This book is a good microwave theory textbook.

- *802.11 Wireless Networks—The Definitive Guide* by Matthew Gast (published by O'Reilly and Associates). This is probably the all-around best 802.11 book in terms of providing practical 802.11 knowledge. It primarily covers indoor deployments, but some outdoor information is also included.

- *Microwave Radio Transmission Design Guide* by Trevor Manning (published by Artech House). This is an excellent microwave design book that explains microwave theory at the engineering level.

- *IEEE 802.11 Handbook—A Designer's Companion* by Bob O'Hara and Al Petrick (published by IEEE Press). This book provides a good engineering-level view of 802.11.

- *Broadband Fixed Wireless Networks* by Neil Reid (published by McGraw-Hill/ Osborne). This is a good reference book on many of the aspects of deploying wireless WANs, including licensed WANs.

- *Microwave Handbook* (published by the Radio Society of Great Britain [RSGB]). This is a three-volume set primarily intended for use by radio amateurs. The high quality of the theoretical information and the hands-on construction information make these books useful for anyone wanting to gain an in-depth understanding of microwave science and art.

- *Building Wireless Community Networks* by Rob Flickenger (published by O'Reilly and Associates). This book addresses many of the points that need to be considered by anyone who wants to deploy a community network based on 802.11b technology.

- *Lightning Protection and Grounding Solutions for Communication Sites* (published by PolyPhaser Corp.). This is an excellent book for anyone who wants to have an in-depth understanding of how to protect an outdoor wireless system from lightning.

- *Wireless LANs*, 2nd Edition by Jim Geier (published by Sams). The first edition of this book was one of the first wireless LAN books available. It provides a good description of 802.11 PHY and MAC-level operation as well as practical techniques that help you to deploy indoor wireless LANs.

Online Magazines

These are three of the online wireless news sources that publish articles of interest to outdoor broadband wireless and wireless hotspot service providers:

- Broadband Wireless Exchange (www.bbwexchange.com)

- Broadband Wireless Business (www.shorecliffcommunications.com/magazine/ index.asp)

- 802.11-Planet (www.802.11-planet.com)

WISP Industry Organizations

The following organizations address the particular needs of WISPs:

- Part-15.org (www.part-15.org)

- Wireless Communications Association International (WCAI) (www.wcai.com)

- Wireless Internet Service Providers Association (WISPA) (www.wispa.org)

E-Mail Lists

The following e-mail lists frequently contain information that is especially relevant to wireless service providers:

- Wireless ISP list (isp-wireless@isp-wireless.com)
- Usenet Wireless Internet Newsgroup (alt.internet.wireless)
- Wireless ISP equipment list (www.wisp-equipment.net)
- Wireless LANs discussion group (wirelesslans@yahoogroups.com)
- Broadband Wireless discussion group (broadbandwireless@yahoogroups.com)

FCC Rules and Regulations

You can find information about the FCC rules and regulations on the FCC website (www.fcc.gov).

Wireless Standards

You can obtain information on the various wireless standards from the following organizations:

- Bluetooth (www.bluetooth.com)
- IEEE (www.ieee.org)
- Wi-Fi (www.wi-fi.net)
- 802.16 (http://grouper.ieee.org/groups/802/16/)

Locating a WISP

You can locate a WISP at www.bbwexchange.com/wisps.

Community Networks and Wireless User Groups

For information about community networks and wireless user groups, use the following links:

- Los Angeles, CA (www.socalwug.org)
- New York City, NY (www.nycwireless.org)
- Portland, OR (www.personaltelco.net)

- San Francisco, CA (www.bawug.org)
- Seattle, WA (www.seattlewireless.net)
- Sebastopol, CA (www.nocat.net)
- St. Louis, MO (stlwireless.net)

The following two links take you to lists of community networks:

- www.toaster.net/wireless/community.html
- www.personaltelco.net/index.cgi/WirelessCommunities

Answers to Chapter Review Questions

Answers to Chapter 1 Review Questions

1 This book defines a broadband wireless connection as any wireless connection with a bandwidth of _____.

   Answer: In this book, a broadband wireless connection is defined as a wireless connection with a bandwidth of 128 kbps or faster.

2 What year did the U.S. Government first require licenses for all transmitters?

   Answer: The U.S. Government first required licenses for all transmitters in 1921.

3 What year did the FCC first allow broadband wireless equipment to be used without applying for a license?

   Answer: The FCC first allowed broadband wireless equipment to be used without a license in 1985.

4 What does the process of modulation do?

   Answer: Modulation is the process of adding information or "intelligence" to a wireless signal.

5 Name one way that a license-free broadband wireless WAN saves money.

   Answer: Deploying a broadband wireless WAN saves money because no monthly bill must be paid to an outside communications carrier, such as the telephone company.

6 Why is the real world different for every wireless link?

   Answer: The real world is different for every wireless link because terrain, interference, noise, and weather are different for every wireless link at any moment in time.

7 During antenna system installation, what safety practice helps protect workers on the ground from being injured by falling objects?

   Answer: Injuries to workers on the ground from falling objects can be minimized if the workers wear a protective hard hat.

8   A fall from 18 inches can cripple a person for life. True or false?

Answer: True. A fall from as little as 18 inches can cripple a person for life.

9   If you need to work in front of a wireless antenna, what should you do first?

Answer: If you need to work in front of a wireless antenna, you should first turn off any wireless equipment that is connected to that antenna.

10 Every outdoor wireless antenna system should include a lightning arrestor. True or false?

Answer: True. Every outdoor wireless antenna system should include a lighting arrestor.

Answers to Chapter 2 Review Questions

1   How does the wavelength of a wireless signal change as the frequency of the signal increases?

Answer: As the frequency of a wireless signal increases, the wavelength of the signal becomes shorter.

2   When a 2.4-GHz signal encounters an obstruction, what happens?

Answer: When a 2.4-GHz signal encounters an obstruction, some of the signal is attenuated, some of the signal is reflected, and some of the signal diffracts around the obstruction.

3   Does ionospheric reflection occur at microwave frequencies?

Answer: Ionospheric reflection generally does not occur at microwave frequencies.

4   How is wireless power measured?

Answer: Wireless power is measured using decibel (dB) ratios compared to a recognized reference level, typically 1 mW (dBm).

5   In the abbreviation dBm, what does the "m" stand for?

Answer: In dBm, the "m" stands for 1 milliwatt, or one-thousandth of one watt.

6   If 1Watt equals +30 dBm, then 2W equals how many dBm?

Answer: 2W equals +33 dBm.

7 The main lobe of a non-isotropic antenna radiates power in which direction?

A. In one horizontal direction

B. In two horizontal directions

C. Equally in all horizontal directions

D. Both A and C

Answer: D. The main lobe of a directional antenna radiates power in only one horizontal direction. The main lobe of an omnidirectional antenna radiates power in all horizontal directions.

8 If you can stand at one antenna and see the antenna at the other end of a wireless link, do you have a line-of-sight wireless path?

Answer: If you can see the other antenna *and* if you have a clear Fresnel zone, you have a line-of-sight wireless path. If you can see the other antenna but more than 60 percent of the Fresnel zone is obstructed, you do *not* have a clear wireless line-of-sight path, even though you might have an unobstructed optical LOS path. The obstructed Fresnel zone adds additional attenuation and the wireless performance is reduced.

9 Tripling the distance on an unobstructed wireless link requires increasing the power how many times?

Answer: Tripling the distance on an unobstructed wireless link requires a power increase of three squared, or nine times, assuming LOS paths.

Answers to Chapter 3 Review Questions

1 If you have one pair of backbone locations that need to be connected, which network architecture is the most appropriate?

Answer: Point-to-point architecture.

2 What type of antenna[md]omnidirectional or directional[md]does a point-to-point network normally use?

Answer: A point-to-point network normally uses a directional antenna.

3 When a microwave signal strikes an obstruction, what *always* happens to it?

Answer: The signal is always attenuated.

4 When a point-to-point network is expanded, what architecture is usually chosen? Why?

Answer: When a point-to-point network is expanded, normally point-to-multipoint architecture is used because it is cost effective for many users and it is easily expanded.

5 Why is SNR important in a wireless network?

Answer: SNR (signal-to-noise) ratio is important because high signal strength is not enough to ensure good receiver performance. The incoming signal must be stronger than any noise or interference that is present. For example, it is possible to have high signal strength and still have poor wireless performance if there is strong interference or a high noise level.

6 What network architectures use sectors?

Answer: Point-to-multipoint architecture and cellular architecture use sectors.

7 What are the consequences of selecting the wrong access point antenna system for a point-to-multipoint network?

Answer: Selecting the wrong antenna system in a point-to-multipoint network can result in poor network performance and the need for an antenna system redesign. An incorrect antenna selection can result in low signal levels or high noise levels. Either consequence requires that the antenna system be redesigned.

8 What architecture is used to allow frequency re-use while connecting several point-to-multipoint networks?

Answer: Cellular architecture is used to allow frequency re-use while connecting several point-to-multipoint networks.

9 What is the primary disadvantage of cellular architecture?

Answer: The primary disadvantage of cellular architecture is the careful frequency planning needed to minimize interference between sectors that use the same frequency.

10 What type of network architecture can be used if end users are located close together and have partially obstructed (non-LOS) paths between each other?

Answer: If end users are located close together and have partially obstructed paths, mesh architecture can sometimes be used.

11 What type of routing does a mesh network perform?

Answer: A mesh network performs dynamic routing.

Answers to Chapter 4 Review Questions

1 A physical site survey includes determining how to route cable from the wireless equipment to the antenna. True or false?

Answer: True.

2 Before you perform a physical site survey, you should know how high above the ground your antennas need to be mounted. True or false?

Answer: True.

3 If there is already wireless equipment operating on a building, you will first discover it during your RF site survey. True or false?

Answer: False. If there is already wireless equipment operating, you should discover it by asking about it during your initial meeting with building management.

4 Minimizing the distance between your wireless equipment and your antenna system is important. Why?

Answer: Minimizing the distance between your equipment and the antenna system is important when using coax cable because the longer the coax, the higher the signal loss and the smaller the wireless coverage range.

5 If power lines run near a roof edge, is it okay to mount your antenna near that roof edge? Why or why not?

Answer: If power lines run near a roof edge, it is not okay to mount an antenna system nearby. Antenna systems must be mounted far enough away so that it is impossible for them to fall or be blown into contact with power lines.

6 What is the biggest consequence from installing a wireless system in an area with a high noise level?

Answer: The biggest consequence of installing a system in a high noise level area is a reduction in network throughput.

7 If you have a wireless protocol analyzer, then you do not need a wireless spectrum analyzer. True or false?

Answer: False. A wireless protocol analyzer can supplement but not replace a spectrum analyzer. A spectrum analyzer is still needed to observe out-of-band and non-802.11b signals.

8 If the operation of license-free equipment causes interference to the operation of licensed amateur radio equipment, the operator of the license-free equipment is responsible for correcting the interference problem. True or false?

Answer: True.

9 The length of the spectrum analyzer sampling interval doesn't tell you anything about the level of RF interference in a particular area. True or false?

Answer: False. The more quickly that interfering signals are picked up, the higher the level of RF interference in a particular area.

10   In general, the higher the signal-to-noise ratio on a wireless link, the higher the wireless throughput. True or false?

Answer: True.

11   What part of a point-to-multipoint wireless network is the most vulnerable to a high noise level? Why?

Answer: The hub site access point receiver of a point-to-multipoint network is the most vulnerable to a high noise level. Noise reduces the signal-to-noise ratio, which reduces the size of the coverage area and the throughput of the network.

Answers to Chapter 5 Review Questions

1   When comparing light energy to wireless energy, a light bulb can be compared to what antenna element?

Answer: A light bulb can be prepared to the driven element of an antenna.

2   The orientation of an antenna's E-field determines what characteristic of the antenna's operation?

Answer: The orientation of an antenna's E-field determines the polarization of the antenna.

3   Relative to each other, the E-field of a vertically polarized antenna and the E-field of a horizontally polarized antenna are what?

Answer: The E-fields of a vertically polarized antenna and a horizontally polarized antenna are cross-polarized (at right angles) with respect to one another.

4   Omnidirectional antennas are available with either vertical or horizontal polarization. True or false?

Answer: True.

5   A diversity receiving system can automatically select the best signal from one of two antennas. True or false?

Answer: True.

6   When using a diversity system, the two antennas must always be the same type and point in the same direction. True or false?

Answer: True.

7   Anyone who deploys an outdoor license-free wireless system can provide reliable wireless service. True or false?

Answer: False. Only those people who learn wireless principles and apply those principles correctly can provide reliable wireless service.

8 A strong signal arriving at your receiver from another wireless network increases your network throughput. True or false?

Answer: False. A strong signal from another network reduces the throughput on your network.

9 How much is the typical cross-polarization isolation between a horizontally polarized and a vertically polarized antenna?

Answer: The typical cross-polarization isolation between a vertically polarized and a horizontally polarized antenna is 20 dB.

10 A sectorized antenna system does not allow you to serve more end users. True or false?

Answer: False. A sectorized antenna system does allow you to serve more end users.

11 In a sectorized antenna system, all the sector antennas should be identical. True or false?

Answer: False. In a sectorized antenna system, the sector antennas do not have to be identical. The horizontal beamwidth, vertical beamwidth, gain, and polarization of each sector antenna should be chosen to best meet the needs of that sector.

12 Sector antennas in a sectorized antenna system should always be mounted perfectly vertical. True or false?

Answer: False. Sector antennas should be mounted with a downtilt angle that maximizes sector coverage and reduces interference from outside the sector.

Answers to Chapter 6 Review Questions

1 Why is it important to visit an actual deployment site before you purchase wireless equipment?

Answer: It is important to visit actual deployment sites to learn about unpublished equipment interactions and unknown operational characteristics.

2 The electromagnetic waves that we call wireless exist at what layer of the seven-layer OSI reference model?

Answer: Electromagnetic waves exist at Layer 1, the physical layer.

3 How is a packet like a hamburger sandwich?

Answer: A packet is like a hamburger sandwich because the meat (the data payload) is sandwiched in the bun (packet management and control information).

4 Why does a wireless network need a big MAC?

Answer: A wireless network needs a big MAC layer because the MAC must deal successfully with management of all the invisible and unpredictable wireless-related issues.

5 Wireless bandwidth and wireless throughput are the same thing. True or false?

Answer: False. Wireless bandwidth and wireless throughput are not the same. Wireless throughput is always less than the specified wireless bandwidth.

6 The communications range under NLOS conditions is about the same as the communications range under LOS conditions. True or false?

Answer: False. The communications range under NLOS conditions is always less than the communications range under LOS conditions.

7 DSSS equipment hops from frequency to frequency. True or false?

Answer: False. DSSS equipment does not change frequency. FHSS equipment changes frequency.

8 Other things being equal, the higher the data rate, the shorter the communications distance. True or false?

Answer: True

9 If you start receiving interference from another network, the best thing to do is to get an amplifier. True or false?

Answer: False. When interference is high, an amplifier usually makes conditions worse. The best response is either to coordinate frequencies or to redesign your antenna system to minimize the effects of the interference.

10 Any 802.11b equipment works with any other 802.11b equipment. True or false?

Answer: False. Most 802.11b equipment works together; however, you can experience a number of incompatibilities if you fail to test thoroughly.

Answers to Chapter 7 Review Questions

1 A site survey is normally performed immediately after a wireless installation is completed. True or false?

Answer: False. A site survey is normally performed before installation.

2 Anyone can install wireless antennas on radio towers as long as they are not afraid of heights. True or false?

Answer: False. No one should install antennas on radio towers unless he has been properly and professionally trained to work on towers. The installer also needs to be equipped with the proper tools and be covered by the proper insurance.

3 At microwave frequencies, the signal loss in coax cable is relatively high. True or false?

Answer: True.

4 A typical lightning strike produces a peak current of approximately how many amps?

Answer: A typical lightning strike produces a peak current of approximately 18,000 amps.

5 Fading is normal for microwave signals. What term is used to describe the extra signal power that every microwave link needs to overcome this fading?

Answer: The term that describes the extra signal needed to overcome microwave fading is the fade margin.

6 What should you do immediately after you test the throughput on a newly installed wireless link?

Answer: After testing the throughput of a new wireless link, you should document the results.

7 Name one advantage of standardizing on only a few customer premise equipment packages.

Answer: Standardizing on only a few CPE packages lowers your inventory costs. In addition, it lowers your support costs.

8 If your job responsibilities require you to work regularly in high-RF environments, you should use what piece of personal protective equipment?

Answer: If your job responsibilities require you to work regularly in high-RF environments, you should use a personal RF monitor that provides an audible warning when RF levels exceed safety thresholds.

Answers to Chapter 8 Review Questions

1 For reliable network operation, signal strength is more important than SNR. True or false?

Answer: False. SNR is more important than signal strength.

2 A reliable wireless link needs a line-of-sight path and an unobstructed Fresnel zone. True or false?

Answer: True.

3 Will the noise level always be low in a rural area?

Answer: Not necessarily. Noise in a rural area might be low or it might be high.

4 How many nonoverlapping 2.4 GHz channels are available for use in the United States?

Answer: There are three nonoverlapping channels.

5 The consequence of a low SNR is reduced network throughput. True or false?

Answer: True.

6 Reusing a DSSS frequency at the same AP location requires how many decibels of antenna isolation?

Answer: Reusing the same frequency in the same location requires approximately 121 dB of antenna isolation.

7 To avoid interference, collocated FHSS sectors should use different hopping sequences and different hopping sets. True or false?

Answer: False. Collocated FHSS sectors should use different hopping sequences within the same hopping set.

8 When is the SNR highest at an AP?

Answer: The SNR is the highest just after the AP has been installed. As time passes, the noise level increases and the SNR goes down.

9 When the percentage of retransmitted packets reaches 20 percent, you should start looking for the cause of the network slowdown. True or false?

Answer: False. The network performance starts to slow down when the retransmit percentage goes above 10 percent. Start looking for the cause when the retransmit percentage goes above 10 percent.

10 Explain why it is necessary to write down the results of your noise-reduction efforts.

Answer: It is necessary to write down the results of your noise-reduction efforts so that you don't waste time repeating the same tests the next time a noise problem occurs.

Answers to Chapter 9 Review Questions

1 A WISP is an extension of a wired ISP. True or false?

True.

2 WISPs have been around since about 1995. True or false?

True.

3 The most profitable wireless markets are those where broadband DSL and cable Internet access are already available. True or false?

False. The most profitable wireless markets are those where DSL and cable Internet access are not available.

4 The mobile market where users stay connected while driving around is the easiest market to serve. True or false?

False. The mobile market is the hardest to serve.

5 Customers pay you to deliver bandwidth, not throughput. True or false?

False. Customers pay you to deliver throughput.

6 You can be successful in the wireless business even if you don't understand the meaning of decibels. True or false?

False. To be successful in the wireless business, you must understand how to work with decibels.

7 All 802.11b equipment brands work with all other 802.11b equipment brands with no problems. True or false?

False. Often, software incompatibilities result in equipment that does not work well together.

8 Why do wireless collisions reduce throughput?

Collisions reduce throughput because each collision wastes a time slot that could have carried useful traffic.

9 The higher the percentage of retransmitted packets, the lower the network throughput. True or false?

True.

10 You should always sell all the throughput that your network is capable of delivering. True or false?

False. You should leave some throughput unsold to be sure that your network does not crash if heavy interference suddenly develops.

11 The best way to deal with a WISP competitor is to add an amplifier. True or false?

False. The best way to deal with a WISP competitor is to meet with him and propose that you both cooperate and coordinate.

INDEX

Numerics

C

cable, 225
  coaxial cable
      manufacturers, 296
      runs, 172
  interfaces, 187
  jumpers, 172
  pigtails, 172
  power-handling capabilities, 171
  routing, physical site surveys, 98-99
  running, rooftop-mounted antennas, 239
  types, 171
  upper frequency limits, 171
calculations
  dBm power reference level, 36
  EIRP (Equivalent Isotropic Radiated Power), 228
  fade margin calculations, 52-53
  Fresnel zone clearances, antennas, 94
  wireless link budget calculations, 49-53
cellular architecture, 71-75
  access points, connectivity, 85
  advantages, 72-73
  disadvantages, 74-75
  evaluating, 84-86
  geographical coverage, 73
  limited spectrum, re-using, 74
  low interference, verification, 74
  network capacity, 73
  redundant end user coverage, 73
  roaming, 73
  testing, 75
  usage, 75
certification, FCC equipment certification, 281-282
circularly polarized antennas, 143-144, 148, 199
coaxial arrestors, 241
coaxial cable
  loss, feed systems, 170
  manufacturers, 296
  runs, 172
collaboration, installation, 226
commercial tower companies, cost considerations, 286
Communications Act of 1934, 7
community networks, 284
  resources, 302
compasses
  headings, measuring, 88
  using, 260
configurable power control, transmitters, 201
connections, waterproofing, 235-236
connectivity, access points, cellular architecture, 85
controlled equipment environments, locating, controlled equipment environments, 97
converters, Ethernet, 204
corner reflector antennas, 152
cost
  hardware
      point-to-multipoint architecture, 70
      point-to-point architecture, 61
  license-free wireless networks, advantages of, 9

point-to-multipoint architecture
      facilities, 70
      installation, 71
  point-to-point architecture
      costs, 62
      facilities, 61
coverage, testing, 127
coverings, antennas, 173
CPE (customer premises equipment), 66, 225, 274
  cost reductions, 283
criteria evaluations, RF site surveys, 124-126
cross polarization, antennas, 144-145
  isolation, 164
current (electron flow), 20-21
customer premises equipment (CPE). *See* CPE (customer premises equipment)
cycles per second, 20

D

Data Encryption Standard (DES), 207
data link layer
  bridging features, 203-204
  functions, 185
  MAC sublayer features, 205
  protocols, 185
  security features, 205-207
data rates
  12-Mbps to 60-Mbps, 197
  1-Mbps to 11-Mbps data rates, 197
  distances, compared, 196
  sub-1 Mbps data rates, 197
  throughput, compared, 195-196
dBm power reference level, 35-36
dBs (decibels), 272-273
dedicated bandwidth, shared bandwidth, compared, 214
deployment speed, license-free wireless networks, advantages of, 10
DES (Data Encryption Standard), 207
desense, 258
DHCP (Dynamic Host Configuration Protocol) servers, 208, 265
dialup telco interfaces, 187
diffraction, signals, 28
Direct Sequence Spread Spectrum (DSSS). *See* DSSS
directing antennas, physical site surveys, 38-39, 99
directional antennas, 259
direction-finding techniques, noise, 259-261
directors, antennas, 138-139
dish antennas. *See* parabolic reflector antennas
distance
  data rate, compared, 196
  hub sites, measuring, 88
  links, doubling, 53
distributers, peripheral devices, 298

S

Sample of Physical Site Survey Data Form

Surveyor Name		Phone/E-Mail	
Site Address		Site Owner	
Site Manager		Phone/E-Mail	
Facility Manager		Phone/E-Mail	
Existing Wireless Equipment		Existing Antenna Locations	
New Equipment Location		Power Source	
Path Length		Fresnel Zone Clearance	
Roof Height		Roof Access Location	
Antenna Location		Antenna Height Above Ground	
Antenna Mounting Hardware Needed		Antenna Heading/Tilt	
Nearby Obstructions		Distant Obstructions	
Cable Type and Length		Cable Entry Point	
Cable Route			
Grounding Locations (Mast and Building Entrance)		Ground Wire Route (Mast and Building Entrance)	
Lightning Protection Description		Lightning Protection Location	
Site Evaluation	Good	Acceptable	Not Acceptable
Comments and Recommendations			
Follow-Up Issues			
Drawings Attached			

IF YOU'RE USING

CISCO PRODUCTS,

YOU'RE QUALIFIED

TO RECEIVE A

FREE SUBSCRIPTION

TO CISCO'S

PREMIER PUBLICATION,

PACKET™ MAGAZINE.

Packet delivers complete coverage of cutting-edge networking trends and innovations, as well as current product updates. A magazine for technical, hands-on Cisco users, it delivers valuable information for enterprises, service providers, and small and midsized businesses.

Packet is a quarterly publication. To start your free subscription, click on the URL and follow the prompts:

www.cisco.com/go/packet/subscribe

☐ **YES!** I'm requesting a **free** subscription to *Packet*™ magazine.

☐ No. I'm not interested at this time.

☐ Mr.
☐ Ms.

First Name (Please Print) _____ Last Name _____

Title/Position (Required) _____

Company (Required) _____

Address _____

City _____ State/Province _____

Zip/Postal Code _____ Country _____

Telephone (Include country and area codes) _____ Fax _____

E-mail _____

Signature (Required) _____ Date _____

☐ I would like to receive additional information on Cisco's services and products by e-mail.

1. Do you or your company:
- A ☐ Use Cisco products   C ☐ Both
- B ☐ Resell Cisco products   D ☐ Neither

2. Your organization's relationship to Cisco Systems:
- A ☐ Customer/End User   E ☐ Integrator   J ☐ Consultant
- B ☐ Prospective Customer   F ☐ Non-Authorized Reseller K ☐ Other (specify):
- C ☐ Cisco Reseller   G ☐ Cisco Training Partner   _____
- D ☐ Cisco Distributor   I ☐ Cisco OEM

3. How many people does your entire company employ?
- A ☐ More than 10,000   D ☐ 500 to 999   G ☐ Fewer than 100
- B ☐ 5,000 to 9,999   E ☐ 250 to 499
- c ☐ 1,000 to 4,999   f ☐ 100 to 249

4. Is your company a Service Provider?
- A ☐ Yes   B ☐ No

5. Your involvement in network equipment purchases:
- A ☐ Recommend   B ☐ Approve   C ☐ Neither

6. Your personal involvement in networking:
- A ☐ Entire enterprise at all sites   F ☐ Public network
- B ☐ Departments or network segments at more than one site D ☐ No involvement
- C ☐ Single department or network segment   E ☐ Other (specify):
  _____

7. Your Industry:
- A ☐ Aerospace   G ☐ Education (K–12)   K ☐ Health Care
- B ☐ Agriculture/Mining/Construction U ☐ Education (College/Univ.) L ☐ Telecommunications
- C ☐ Banking/Finance   H ☐ Government—Federal   M ☐ Utilities/Transportation
- D ☐ Chemical/Pharmaceutical   I ☐ Government—State   N ☐ Other (specify):
- E ☐ Consultant   J ☐ Government—Local   _____
- F ☐ Computer/Systems/Electronics

CPRESS

PACKET

PACKET

Packet magazine serves as the premier publication linking customers to Cisco Systems, Inc. Delivering complete coverage of cutting-edge networking trends and innovations, *Packet* is a magazine for technical, hands-on users. It delivers industry-specific information for enterprise, service provider, and small and midsized business market segments. A toolchest for planners and decision makers, *Packet* contains a vast array of practical information, boasting sample configurations, real-life customer examples, and tips on getting the most from your Cisco Systems' investments. Simply put, *Packet* magazine is straight talk straight from the worldwide leader in networking for the Internet, Cisco Systems, Inc.

We hope you'll take advantage of this useful resource. I look forward to hearing from you!

Cecelia Glover
Packet Circulation Manager
packet@external.cisco.com
www.cisco.com/go/packet